About the author

John Eaton is a practising solicitor of twenty-five
years' experience, specializing in financial planning
and investment work. He is a regular contributor to
various legal and financial journals, and was the
author of scripts for 'Law Line', a popular telephone
advisory service on legal topics. For five years he was
Radio Pennine's 'legal eagle'. He works in Leeds, and
this is his first book.

John Eaton

Midland

Guide to

Inheritance

First published 1992, by Bloomsbury Publishing Limited, 2 Soho Square, London W1V 5DE

Copyright © 1992 by Bloomsbury Publishing Limited

A CIP record for this book is available from the British Library

ISBN 0 7475 1086 5

10 9 8 7 6 5 4 3 2 1

Designed by Geoff Green
Typeset by Hewer Text Composition Services, Edinburgh
Printed by Clays Ltd, St Ives Plc

John Eaton

Midland

Guide to

Inheritance

BLOOMSBURY

Author's acknowledgements

I am particularly indebted to the following people:

Diana Mackay of Professional & Business Information PLC for volunteering my services in the first place;

Kathy Rooney of Bloomsbury Publishing for her calm and regular reassurances and support;

Julie and **Jane** for their infinite patience and good humour in typing, re-typing, and re-re-typing during those muggy summer days;

Richard du Pré of Equitable Life for helpfully providing so many of the actual figures and rates quoted in the illustrations, especially in Chapter 16;

Midland Bank PLC for their sponsorship of the book, and helpful suggestions on some of the more technical aspects;

Margaret, **Gretchen** and **Yorke** for so cheerfully remaining a one-parent family for three months.

Contents

Introduction

PART ONE: PREPARATION

1 Making a Will   3
Why make a Will?   3
What happens without a Will?   4
Choosing your executors   6
Appointing guardians   8
Who should inherit what?   9
Claims by dependants   12
Rewriting the Will and Deeds of Variation   13
The formalities of executing a Will   14
The cost of making a Will   15
How to make a Will   16
A specimen Will   17

2 Lifetime Financial Planning   20
Inheritance Tax (IHT) planning   21
Lifetime gifts   22
Transfers on death   25
A dozen practical points   28

PART TWO: WHAT TO DO WHEN SOMEONE DIES

3 The Practicalities   35
Steps to take when someone dies   35

4 Winding up an Estate   38
Preliminary steps   38
Establishing assets and liabilities   40
Obtaining the Grant of Representation   43
The family home   45
Payment of liabilities (including Inheritance Tax)   49
What if there is no Will?   51
Claims by dependants   52
Rewriting the Will: Deeds of Variation   52
Dealing with a future inheritance   53
The time and cost of a winding up an estate   54
Do it yourself?   56
Sample estate accounts   59

PART THREE: INVESTING INHERITED MONEYS

5 Investment Policy   65
Establishing your requirements   65
The importance of budgeting   66
Paying off debts   68
The threat of inflation   69
The risk/reward ratio   72
Capital, income and overall return   73

6 Taxation
Income Tax   76
Capital Gains Tax (CGT)   82
Tax-effective investments   89
Tax-saving tips   92

7 Types of Investment   96
Investment principles   96
Deposit and cash-based investments   99
    Bank and building society accounts   99
    National Savings Bank Ordinary & Investment accounts   100
    TESSAs (Tax-Exempt Special Savings Accounts)   100
    Cash Unit Trusts   101
    Foreign currency accounts   102
    Offshore sterling accounts   102
Fixed-interest and guaranteed investments   103
    Gilts   103

Guaranteed Bonds   104
National Savings Certificates (NSC)   105
Other National Savings products   106
Annuities   107
Equity-based investments   109
Ordinary Shares   112
Convertible Unsecured Loan Stocks, Preference Shares
    and Capital Bonds   114
Unit Trusts   115
Investment Trusts   118
Personal Equity Plans (PEPs)   120
Business Expansion Schemes (BES)   122
Property   124
Enterprise Zones   125
Alternative investments not producing income   126
Collectibles   127
Futures and options   129
Woodlands and agricultural property   130
Insurance-based investments   131
Single Premium Bonds   132
Broker Bonds   134
Regular Premium Insurance Policies and Qualifying
    Policies   135
Second-hand Policies   136
Friendly Society Bonds   137
Annuities   138
Pensions   139
Lump sum investments and regular payment investments 140
Becoming a 'Name' at Lloyds   143

8 Investing in Property   147
Direct and indirect investment in UK property   147
Foreign property   149
Other syndicated property investments   151

9 Insurance   153
Life insurance: protection or investment?   153
Different types of life policy   155
Other risks to consider insuring against   157

10 Financial Packages Unravelled   161
School fees plans   161
Capital conversion plans   164
'Back-to-back' policies and other fancy packages   165

11 Going Offshore   167
Why invest abroad?   167
Offshore sterling funds   168
Currency funds   168
Offshore trusts   169

12 Planning Your Retirement   170
Retirement considerations   170
Pensions   171
Other ways of providing post-retirement income   175
Home income plans   175

13 Helping Others   178
Giving to charity   178
Gifts to individuals   183
Interest-free loans   189
Investments for children   189

14 Trusts   194
Trustees   194
Advantages of using trusts   195
Types of trust   196
Tax treatment   198
The cost of trusts   200

15 Obtaining Professional Advice   202
Going it alone   202
Investor protection and the Financial Services Act (FSA)   205
Types of adviser   206
Choosing the right adviser   208
Who pays? Commissions explained   211
How to complain   213
Compensation for loss   215

16 Possible Investment Portfolios   217
Children   218
Single people   223

Married couple without children   226
Married couple with young children   229
Married couple with older children   232
The fabulous fifties – pre-retirement   235
Grandparents   243
Post-retirement   247

17 Conclusion   254
The European factor   254
The political factor   254
The technical factor   256

Glossary   259

Further Reading   263

Useful Addresses   265

Index   270

Introduction

Three factors have contributed to the publication of this book:

- The continued increase in the amounts inherited each year – currently estimated to be over £10 billion p.a.
- The publicity surrounding the activity of several rogue operators in the area of financial services, and the recent collapse of Barlow Clowes and several other firms, involving the loss of millions of pounds of investors' money.
- The passing of the Financial Services Act, with its dual objectives of providing higher standards of protection for the investor and promoting and regulating activities in the financial sector.

Although there are a number of publications about Wills and winding up estates, plus many books and magazines dealing with investment topics, there was an evident need for one comprehensive, practical guide summarizing the practical and financial issues connected with inheritances generally. The intention of this book is therefore to fill that gap and provide practical guidance and advice on most aspects of inheritance, with particular reference to the investment of inherited assets.

How to use this book

The Midland Guide to Inheritance is not the type of book which you would normally wish to read through at one go. It is intended as a practical guide which can be dipped into for reference purposes, giving readers some background knowledge and helping to point them in the right direction.

The book is divided into three main sections: the first looks at inheritance from the point of view of someone who has assets and wants to know how to make a Will. This also includes advice on pre-death financial planning.

The second and third sections consider inheritance from the family's point of view, after the testator's death. The reader is taken through the practical aspects of winding up an estate, and given numerous ideas about what might be done with inherited money. Indeed, the selection of case studies in Chapter 16 aims to cover almost every inheritance eventuality.

Inevitably, the subject of Wills, inheritance and taxation involves technical terms and legal jargon. For ease of reference these words have been collected together in a glossary at the end of the book. This means that definitions can quickly be located and that sections can be read independently of each other.

Finally, a word of caution. This book is intended to be a general guide and to provide practical suggestions over a wide range of topics; it is not a detailed or comprehensive summary which would enable readers to dispense with professional advice and do everything by themselves. While there is no reason why readers who have the time, interest and ability should not draw their own Wills, wind up a parent's estate or manage their own investment portfolios, it is generally sensible to enlist the services of someone who is professionally qualified in the relevant area. The cost of doing this should be more than offset by the saving in time, effort and worry. However, it is a sad fact that many people apparently prefer to pay more for a cure later on than for prevention at the start.

Part One
Preparation

1 Making a Will

Why make a Will?

It is surprising how many people seem to think that either they are immortal or that making a Will is equivalent to signing a death warrant. In fact, making a Will is a painless process which can save a great deal of future difficulty and distress. To prove the point, there are at least eight good reasons for making a Will, and no good reasons for not making one.

1. Making a Will is the best way of trying to ensure that what you want to happen after your death, *does* happen. Without a Will, the laws of intestacy could well result in the very opposite of your wishes coming about and cause unnecessary distress and expense to your family.

2. By appointing your own executors you will be able to choose the people who will administer your estate so that it can be wound up as quickly and smoothly as possible.

3. Where young children are involved, you can provide for the appointment of legal guardians. The problem of looking after the children could be an extremely painful and distressing one if no clear arrangement has been made.

4. You can give your executors wider powers of investment and administration than they would otherwise have. (This can be a distinct advantage where, for example, young children are to benefit.)

5. With a Will things are not left to chance. You can arrange a particular financial plan to provide for the people you care about. If your estate will be a large one – for example, if you are heavily insured – you can avoid the problem of young beneficiaries receiving 'too much too soon'; it might be advisable for them not to inherit everything when they are 18, but to postpone their inheritance until a more mature age.

6.   Making a Will enables you to arrange your affairs so that Inheritance Tax and other liabilities are kept to a minimum.

7.   A straightforward Will costs less than £100 and can actually save money because it makes the adminstration of the estate quicker and cheaper, and unnecessary difficulties and obstacles can be avoided.

8.   Non-financial considerations, such as your desired funeral arrangements, can be included in a Will and thus avoid poss- ible misunderstandings.

You may think that you do not need to make a Will because the assets are in joint names, or in the sole name of your spouse. This may be so, but suppose you survive your spouse and inherit his or her estate? Or suppose that you both die together in an accident? In these cases it is obviously sensible for each spouse to have a Will and keep it up to date, and especially so if there are children. The cost involved is very small for the resulting peace of mind.

What happens without a Will?

Where someone dies intestate (without leaving a Will) there is no method of ascertaining the deceased's wishes. The law therefore sets out certain rules which will decide the distribution of the estate in an attempt to achieve a fair balance between the surviving family members. The actual distribution depends on the size of the estate and on which family members survive the deceased.

As seen in the chart opposite, problems can easily arise where there is no immediate family, or where the estate is over £75,000. For example, if a husband (with a wife and young child) dies intestate, leaving only a house worth £150,000, his widow would be entitled to the personal possessions, the first £75,000 of the estate (plus interest) and the income for life from half the remainder. The child would be absolutely entitled to the other half on attaining 18. As the assets in the estate consist only of the house, it might have to be sold to enable the distribution to be completed (unless the child was over 18 and agreed otherwise).

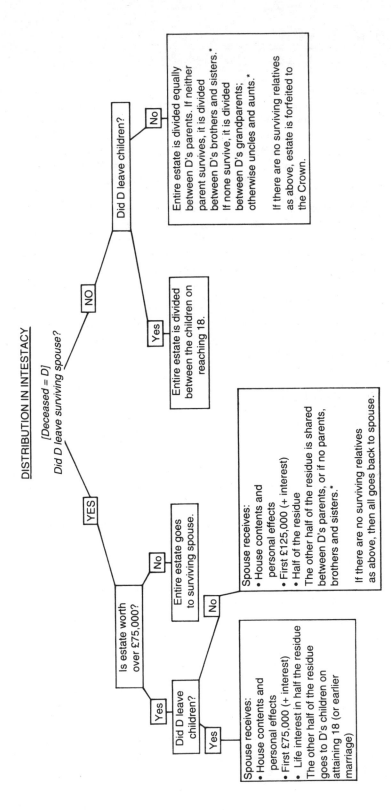

DISTRIBUTION IN INTESTACY

[Deceased = D]
Did D leave surviving spouse?

Is estate worth over £75,000?

YES

Did D leave children?

Yes

Spouse receives:
- House contents and personal effects
- First £75,000 (+ interest)
- Life interest in half the residue

The other half of the residue goes to D's children on attaining 18 (or earlier marriage)

No

Entire estate goes to surviving spouse.

No

Spouse receives:
- House contents and personal effects
- First £125,000 (+ interest)
- Half of the residue

The other half of the residue is shared between D's parents, or if no parents, brothers and sisters.*

If there are no surviving relatives as above, then all goes back to spouse.

NO

Did D leave children?

Yes

Entire estate is divided between the children on reaching 18.

No

Entire estate is divided equally between D's parents. If neither parent survives, it is divided between D's brothers and sisters.* If none survive, it is divided between D's grandparents; otherwise uncles and aunts.*

If there are no surviving relatives as above, estate is forfeited to the Crown.

* In these cases, if a potential beneficiary has died, leaving a child or children, these children take the share which their parent would have received.

Figure 1

Case History

For the last 15 years of her life, Mabel (aged 86) had been looked after by her nephew George, whom she treated like a son. Mabel had tried to make her own Will, leaving everything to George, but she had obtained only one witness instead of two, so the Will was technically invalid and she therefore died intestate. Mabel had been a spinster with no children, but had nine brothers and sisters, all of whom had died in Mabel's lifetime, leaving a total of 27 children (of which George was one) scattered liberally around the globe.

Under the laws of intestacy, all those nephews and nieces were legally entitled to share Mabel's estate in the original nine proportions. After a year, they had all been traced and the solicitors wrote to inform them of their entitlement to share Mabel's estate (which consisted of £800 in a local Co-op). The solicitors suggested that, in the circumstances, they might ignore the technical defect in the Will and allow the estate to be transferred to George in recognition of his moral entitlement. Twenty-five of the beneficiaries agreed but one confirmed that 'after due consideration, I should have the share to which I am legally entitled'. An explanation of this development to the other beneficiaries resulted in five of them saying, 'If she is having hers, we are having ours.' At this point the local Co-op went into liquidation, so it was two years before the funds became available.

The 'happy ending' in this particular case arose when the solicitors charged £791 for winding up the estate, divided the remaining £9 equally between the 27 beneficiaries, but then rebated all their costs to George, so that eventually justice was done.

Choosing your executors

It is the responsibility of the executor to 'execute' the terms of your Will, which means that he or she is responsible for dealing with all your affairs – implementing the funeral arrangements, collecting and listing the assets of the estate, paying all the liabilities (debts, taxes, legacies and adminstration costs) and then distributing the estate in accordance with the terms of the Will. If there are ongoing trusts for the benefit of young children, for example, the executor often changes hats and becomes a trustee when he (or she) has completed the administration of the estate. A trustee is basically a kind of caretaker or manager, who is responsible for looking after the assets contained in the trust, the terms of which can be set out in a lifetime trust (see Chapter 14) or in the Will itself.

It is sensible to have at least two (but not more than four) executors/ trustees. An executor is allowed to receive a benefit under a Will, so there is no reason why a spouse or adult child should not be an executor. Effectively the choice is between one or more of the following categories:

A relative (spouse or child)

Advantages

- Inexpensive, local, already involved and on the spot.
- The relative will presumably be entitled to receive most or all of the estate and should therefore be involved in the distribution.

Disadvantages

- A wife or child may feel overwhelmed at undertaking extra responsibilities at a time when they have enough to cope with.
- Lack of expertise on technical aspects (particularly if there are minor children and ongoing trusts, when the technical requirements would make it advisable to have a professional trustee).
- Possible conflict of interest between duties as an executor, and requirements as a beneficiary.
- May have predeceased, be ill or unable to act.

A friend

Advantages

- Inexpensive (although it would be a nice gesture to leave a legacy as a thank you), local, trustworthy and on the spot.
- The friend will be familiar with the affairs and requirements of the family.

Disadvantages

- A friend may lack the technical expertise which may be required in some cases, or may be unable or unwilling to act.

A professional trustee (e.g. solicitor or accountant)

Advantages

- Professional and technical knowledge which can be advantageous, particularly where there are young children and/or ongoing trusts.

- Knowledge of the family circumstances and requirements.
- Familiarity with most of the procedural difficulties and problems, and the ability to take an unbiased overview when required.

Disadvantages

- Expense; a professional trustee will usually charge on the basis of the time involved (see Chapter 4, The time and cost of winding up an estate).
- Mortality; trustees may predecease the testator, or die before the administration has been completed.

A Bank

Advantages

- Technical expertise and competence.
- Permanence; one disadvantage of individual executors/trustees is that they might die before the testator, who would then have to find someone else.
- Security of a large financial institution.

Disadvantages

- Expense; the banks operate a scale fee which should be checked out and compared with fees charged by other advisors.
- The approach may seem less personal; bank personnel are also mortal, or may simply be moved to another branch.

It is possible to combine executors from any of the above categories. In fact, a common solution is to appoint a family member as the sole executor but substitute a friend and a professional executor (either a solicitor, accountant or bank) if the family member should not survive. Whichever you choose, it is courteous (and common sense) to ask first.

Appointing guardians

This important part of a Will (when the testator has young children) is often overlooked, sometimes with grave consequences, as the following case history illustrates.

C

Case History

Martin and his wife Angela were killed in a car crash. Their Wills (which they had drawn up themselves) had simply dealt with the distribution of their assets; they had not provided for the appointment of guardians to their four young children (aged between four and ten) who were left in the large family home. Both sets of grandparents, although in their seventies, wanted to look after the grandchildren. The grandparents with the larger house wanted the executor to sell the family home; the other grandparents wanted to move into the family home to look after the grandchildren.

The dispute between the grandparents became increasingly bitter and the grandchildren ended up as pawns in what had then developed into a long-standing feud. Even court proceedings could not resolve the situation. The cost to all the family members at the end of the day — both in terms of legal expenses and emotional 'wear and tear' — was enormous. All that bitterness and cost could have been avoided if only Martin and Angela had appointed guardians in their Wills when they drew them up.

On the death of one parent, the surviving parent will be responsible for the children, but on the death of that survivor (or in the event of joint deaths in an accident) it is sensible to appoint a guardian to 'stand in the shoes' of the parents and look after the upbringing, education and welfare of the children.

The choice of guardians will obviously depend on the children's requirements rather than on professional or legal knowledge. Indeed, it is better if the same persons do not act as executors and guardians so that the two functions can be kept separate; the guardians will require funds to spend on the children, and those funds will be controlled by the executors. Dividing the responsibility will remove the risk of any suggestion that the guardians may have used the estate's money to feather their own nests or that they have spent funds unnecessarily.

Who should inherit what?

Remember that only assets which are in your own name will pass under your Will; your Will will have no effect on the distribution of property which passes outside your estate. For example, your half-share in a house which is held as joint tenants will pass automatically by survivorship to the other joint owner, the death benefit under a pension scheme will usually be paid by the trustees to the family member(s) whom you will already have nominated; assets passing under a trust which you have established in your lifetime (e.g. a life insurance policy) will also be paid automatically to the beneficiary, as will trust funds in which you had a right to the income for life. You should therefore take the following steps:

- Write down a list of all the assets which belong to you in your own name, and note their approximate values.
- Calculate what the family financial position would be if you were to die tomorrow (this may also highlight the need for more financial advice or further life insurance cover, for example).
- Prepare a list of all the possible beneficiaries (spouse, children, grandchildren, parents, godchildren, sons-in-law, daughters-in-law, other relatives, friends, charities).
- Decide whether you wish to leave any specific items to any of these beneficiaries (e.g. jewellery to a daughter, golf clubs to a business partner, or wine collection to a gourmet friend).
- Be aware of the danger of beneficiaries inheriting 'too much too soon'. You may not agree with the maxim that 'the best inheritance is the habits of industry', but many a life has been made more difficult rather than easier by a child inheriting a substantial sum on attaining 18. Generally speaking, if you want to leave a substantial legacy to a young child, it would be sensible for the child to receive the capital on attaining an older age, say 25. That way the child would be less vulnerable and less likely to spend the legacy unwisely, the funds would probably still be available for a specific purchase, for example, towards the cost of a house, and if the money *were* required before the older age (say the child wished to get married at 21), the trustees can be given power to accelerate the payment of the legacy.

  In the case of a smaller legacy (say up to £1,000) there is no reason why it should not be left to a child direct, but in the case of very young children the legacy should either be conditional on attaining 18, or the executors should be empowered to pay the legacy to the child's parent or guardian.
- Put the needs of the family – and especially those of a surviving spouse – ahead of pure tax saving. A spouse's comfort and security are more important than depriving the Inland Revenue of a few pounds. However, it is important to consider whether you would wish your spouse (or any other main beneficiary) to receive your assets absolutely with no strings attached, or whether you might prefer the assets to be held in trust for them. For example, if you think it likely that your spouse might remarry in the event of your death, you might prefer to leave him or her a legacy of a fixed sum, but leave the bulk of the assets in

trust for the spouse to draw the income during his or her life. Again, the trustees could be given power to make capital available to the spouse if required, but the existence of a trust would ensure that on your spouse's eventual death (or perhaps remarriage) the assets could then pass to your children, rather than perhaps going outside the family.

- If your estate will be substantial, such that your spouse would be unlikely to require all the assets or all the income, consider leaving an immediate legacy to your children, or even putting all your estate into a mini trust. This will leave your executors with the flexibility of distributing the estate within two years of your death, as seems most appropriate (and tax-effective) at that time (see Chapter 2, Inheritance Tax planning)

- In the case of each beneficiary, ask yourself the question: 'What would I wish to happen if that person were to die before me?' Then decide on the appropriate alternative provision.

- Having decided on the legacies, you must then decide on the distribution of the residue – the remainder of the estate after the legacies and all debts and liabilities have been paid. You may wish the residue to pass to a surviving spouse, to be divided between children or other beneficiaries, or to be held in trust for a spouse or other beneficiaries. In that event you must also decide on the ultimate distribution of the residue when the trust comes to an end (such as on the death of the trust beneficiary).

- It is also as well to include a 'sweeper up' clause specifiying who should benefit if the residuary beneficiary (the person entitled to the residue) should fail to inherit. If no family members survive, would you wish the residue to go to other distant relatives, or to be divided between certain friends? It is at this stage that many testators provide for the residue to go to a deserving charity, rather than to a distant relative who may be sufficiently well off in any case. There is no shortage of deserving charities, but a convenient solution for someone who has no particular preference is to leave the funds to the Charities Aid Foundation, which will then distribute the funds between selected individual charities either at its own discretion or in accordance with your or your family's wishes.

Claims by dependants

Unlike some European countries, the UK allows testators to enjoy 'freedom of testamentary disposition'. This means that in principle you are free to dispose of your property as you wish. However, an Act of Parliament in 1975 stipulated that where an application is made to the court by a dependant – and where the court is of the opinion that the distribution of your estate (either by your Will or under the rules of intestacy) does not make 'reasonable provision' for that dependant – the court can order the appropriate financial provison to be made for the dependant out of your estate (overriding the terms of the Will or intestacy). The provision can include periodical payments, a lump sum, or a transfer of property.

Who are dependants?

- A surviving spouse
- A former spouse who has not remarried
- Any child of the deceased (including illegitimate children, step-children, or even someone simply treated as a 'child of the family')
- Any other person who was being maintained by the deceased

The court will take into account the size and nature of the estate and the financial resources and needs of both the applicant and the beneficiaries under the estate. In the case of a spouse and former spouse the court will also take into account the applicant's age, duration of the marriage and the applicant's contribution to the family welfare.

When making a Will, therefore, you should consider whether you have any dependants (within the wide meaning of the word set out above) for whom you should make 'reasonable provision'. If you wish to disinherit any possible beneficiary, you should take care (and professional advice), particularly if that beneficiary falls within the above definition of 'dependant'.

The Act also contains 'anti-avoidance measures' to prevent a testator from trying to avoid a claim against his or her estate under the Act. The court could, for example, undo or reverse lifetime gifts by the deceased if they were made specifically to avoid a claim by a dependant. However, the best precaution for a testator is to ensure that reasonable provision is made for his dependants and/or to include in the Will a full explanation of why any particular dependant has not been provided for (or treated more generously).

Rewriting the Will and Deeds of Variation

Many people are still surprised to learn that it is often possible for the beneficiaries to 'rewrite' the Will of a deceased person, or even (in certain cases) to amend the distribution on an intestacy. This is done by signing a Deed of Variation within two years of the date of death. This can be a very useful tool, rectifying any unfair situation which might arise, or saving tax (see below).

C

Using a Deed of Variation

Correcting Unfairness

David died intestate. The house (in his name) was worth £175,000, contents £10,000 and investments £20,000. David left a widow, Wendy, and two children over 18. Under the rules of intestacy, Wendy is entitled to the house contents, £75,000-worth of assets and a life interest in £60,000 (i.e. half the residue). The children share the remaining £60,000.

To avoid having to sell the house, the children and Wendy enter into a Deed of Variation, effectively 'writing a Will' for David, whereby Wendy receives the house and contents outright (avoiding the necessity for a sale) and the children take the £20,000 investments.

Saving Tax

Donald's Will leaves everything to his widow, Wanda. At the date of Donald's death his estate comprises shares in the family business valued at £200,000, plus investments worth £100,000. Wanda has inherited Donald's half-share in the house by survivorship, and receives a lump sum and a pension from Donald's former employers. Although no Inheritance Tax is payable on Donald's death, inheriting his entire estate would increase Wanda's own estate on her death.

Wanda and the children therefore enter into a Deed of Variation, whereby Wanda renounces the shares in the business in favour of the children. Owing to a special reduction of 50 per cent for business property, the shares are valued for tax purposes at £100,000, so there is no Inheritance Tax on this transfer. On Wanda's subsequent death, her estate does not include the shares (which in the meantime have increased in value to £400,000). The result? A saving in Inheritance Tax on Wanda's death of over £80,000.

As these examples illustrate, a Deed of Variation is an extremely valuable tool in the tax-planner's armoury and should always be considered following a death. However, there are pitfalls and formalities which make it desirable to obtain professional advice:

- Although the deed is retrospective to the date of death for the purposes of Capital Gains Tax and Inheritance Tax, it is not retrospective for Income Tax purposes which means that, for example, a parent might fall into the Income Tax trap (see p.183).
- The deed is only effective if a proper form of election is sent to the Inland Revenue.
- It may not always be possible to have a Deed of Variation where some of the beneficiaries are children under 18 (unless the variation can only increase, rather than reduce, their original entitlement).

The formalities of executing a Will

Not least because of the scope for fraud or 'undue influence', the rules prescribe many formalities in connection with the execution of a Will, for example, the appearance of the document, the place where the testator and witnesses must sign, and the method of witnessing. Any defect in these formalities (say, both witnesses are not present when the testator signs) will mean that the Will is invalid and the testator will therefore be intestate. The formalities include:

- The necessity to revoke any earlier Wills.
- (Preferably) the date on which the Will is executed.
- Two witnesses, both of whom should be physically present when the testator signs the Will. (Note: the witnesses can be related to each other, but neither of them should be beneficiaries under the Will, or they will forfeit their benefit.)
- The Will should contain a proper 'attestation clause'; this simply confirms that the Will has been correctly signed and witnessed.
- Where the Will is more than one page, the testator and both witnesses should also sign at the foot of each page.

There is nothing to stop you from drawing up your own Will, any more than extracting your own teeth. Although the latter may be more painful, the former could well be more expensive. In the first place, it is essential that the wording of the Will is totally unambiguous. For example, does a bequest of 'all my money to my wife' include Premium Bonds? A coin collection? Shares? Suppose the Will provided for 'my entire estate to be divided between my husband and my two children'. Clear enough at first sight, but does it mean that the husband would receive one half and the two children, a quarter each, or would each of the three family members receive a third? And what would happen if the testatrix had remarried after making her Will, so that the husband at the date of death was different from the one at the time when she made the Will? And what if one of the children had died in her lifetime . . .?

As it is vital for a Will to be worded properly and the formalities concerning its execution to be observed, it is best to have it drawn up by a professional. Several commercial firms are now advertising a Will-making service, but it is probably safer (and probably no more expensive) to follow the traditional route and consult a solicitor or your bank – especially if there are any complications which may require other taxation, legal or financial advice.

The cost of making a Will

This is a classic case of 'How long is a piece of string?' Every testator has different requirements and no two Wills are the same. Some commercial Will-making firms quote a flat fee for a Will; Midland Bank, for example, charges £50 plus VAT. This may be adequate in many cases, but generally it is a case of 'you get what you pay for'. A Will is such an important document – a transfer of all your assets and the provision for your family's future – that each Will should be tailor-made and drawn up by a professionally qualified person. Although solicitors' charges are generally based on the time taken, this is not usually so with Wills. In fact, most solicitors charge less than the actual cost of the time, since they wish to encourage people to make Wills rather than deter them. In the case of a complicated estate or a time-consuming Will, a charge of £150 or even £200 would not be excessive. However, for a relatively straightforward Will a solicitor's average charge would be nearer £50 (or perhaps even less), generally with a special rate for 'double Wills', where spouses each make their Wills in similar terms. An average charge for a double Will would be between £50 and £100; Midland Bank charges £85 plus VAT. In view of the importance of the document (and the consequences of getting it wrong), this should be regarded as money well spent.

How to make a Will

If you follow the advice in this book, you will decide to consult a solicitor or your bank rather than draw up your own Will. Even so, it will still save time (and therefore money) if you undertake the following preparatory work:

- Make a list of the family assets (who owns what) and their values.
- Decide on the executors (see Chapter 1, Choosing your executors), then decide on 'reserve' executors in case the original executors should not survive you.
- If you have children under 18, decide whom you would wish to appoint as guardians (see Chapter 1, Appointing guardians).
- Decide on any specific legacies, i.e. gifts of particular items such as jewellery, musical instruments, photographic equipment, etc.
- Decide on any cash legacies which you would wish to give, even if your spouse or family survive you (e.g. legacies to godchildren, grandchildren, friends or charities).
- If you have shares in a business, decide on the destination of those shares. Perhaps your family would prefer to have the monetary value of the shares rather than the shares themselves.
- Decide where you wish to leave the residue and whether it should be left outright or in trust (see Chapter 1, Who should inherit what?).
- In each case where you have selected beneficiaries, ask yourself what you would wish to happen to their benefit (whether a legacy or a share in the residue) if they do not survive you. Should their share pass to their spouse or to their children (and if so, at what age?), or should it increase the amount available to the other beneficiaries?
- With regard to the residue, be sure to include a 'sweeper-up' – a 'long-stop' beneficiary (perhaps a charity) who would inherit the residue if your main beneficiaries did not survive (or, in the case of young children, survived but failed to reach the qualifying age at which they would inherit).
- Obtain advice as to the special powers and administrative provisions which might be required for the executors and trustees, e.g. full powers of investment, a power to 'appropriate' specific assets to a beneficiary as part of his or her share, and a power to accelerate the payment of capital (if it is required before the beneficiary reaches the age when he or she would be strictly entitled to receive it).

- Decide on any particular provisions with regard to the immediate arrangements, e.g. donation of any organs for transplant or research purposes, any special funeral arrangements (cremation or burial?).
- Having made your Will, ensure that it is kept up to date, particularly if there are events which might cause you to change your mind (e.g. death of a beneficiary), or might automatically change the Will (e.g. your own remarriage or divorce, or change in your financial circumstances).
- If any small amendments or additions are required (e.g. to cancel, or increase a legacy), ask your solicitor or bank to draw up a short codicil for you.

Making a Will and keeping it up to date is a good example of prevention being better than cure. For the relatively small expense involved, you surely owe it to your family to ensure that you minimize the distress and trouble which would be caused by your death. In addition, making a Will allows you to save tax and gives you peace of mind that your family's financial future is secure.

Keep your Will in a safe place at home, or (preferably) leave it with your bank or solicitor. If you leave your Will in the safekeeping of others, leave a note at home saying where it is, and also inform your executors.

A specimen Will

THIS IS THE LAST WILL AND TESTAMENT

of me

ALGERNON WATSON of 22b Baker Street London N1 General Practitioner —————————————————————————

1. *I HEREBY REVOKE* all former Wills made by me —————

2. *I APPOINT* my Wife *EUGENIA WATSON* to be the sole Executrix and Trustee of this my Will but if she shall die in my lifetime then *I APPOINT* my friend *SHERLOCK HOLMES* of 22b Baker Street London aforesaid and my Solicitor *BASIL MORIARTY* of 16 High Street Camden Town London N11 to be the Executors and Trustees of this my Will and *I BEQUEATH* (duty free) the sum of £100 to each of my Trustees in acknowledgement of his services in proving my Will ——————————————————————

3. *I GIVE AND BEQUEATH* (duty free) the sum of £500 to my friend Annette Charmante of 14 Avenue Foch Paris ——————————

4. *I GIVE AND BEQUEATH* the sum of £100 each to such of my Grandchildren as shall be living at the date of my death and *I DECLARE* that the receipt of the Parent or Guardian of any minor Grandchild shall be sufficient discharge to my Trustees for the payment of such legacy ——————————————————————

5. *I GIVE AND BEQUEATH* (duty free) all my jewellery and other articles of personal adornment to my Daughter Isobel Fountain absolutely ——————————————————————

6. *I GIVE AND BEQUEATH* (duty free) all my remaining Personal Chattels *UNTO* my Trustees with the wish that they shall distribute the said Personal Chattels in accordance with the wishes which I have expressed to them during my lifetime* ——————————

7. *SUBJECT THERETO* and if my Wife the said Eugenia Watson shall survive me for thirty days then *I GIVE DEVISE AND BEQUEATH* all my estate both real and personal and whatsoever and wheresoever (subject to payment of all my debts and funeral expenses) *UNTO* my said Wife absolutely ——————————

8. *IN CASE* my said Wife does not so survive me or if Clause 7 fails for any other reason then *I GIVE DEVISE AND BEQUEATH* all my said estate *UNTO* my Trustees upon trust to sell and convert the same into money (with power to postpone the sale and conversion for so long as they shall decide) and to stand possessed of the proceeds of such sale and conversion (hereinafter referred to as 'my Residuary Estate') *UPON TRUST* in equal shares for such of my children as shall be living at the date of my death and shall attain the age of 21 years *PROVIDED ALWAYS* that if any child of mine shall die before attaining a vested interest and shall leave a child or children living at his or her death then any such child or children (meaning a grandchild or grandchildren of mine) as shall survive me and attain the age of 21 years shall take (equally if more than one) the share of my Residuary Estate which my original child would have taken had he or she survived me ——————————

9. *IN CASE* the trusts concerning my Residuary Estate shall wholly fail then my Trustees shall stand possessed of my Residuary Estate *UPON TRUST* for such Charities as my Trustees shall (in their discretion) apoint within two years of the date of my death and in default of appointment upon trust for the Charities Aid Foundation of 48 Pembury Road Tonbridge Kent TN9 2JD for the general purposes of such Foudation *AND I EMPOWER* my Trustees to accept the receipt of the Treasurer or Secretary in respect of all moneys bequeathed hereunder ——————————

10. *I EMPOWER* my Trustees:–
(a) To invest transpose and retain trust moneys in assets of whatsoever nature whether or not income-producing with the

same absolute freedom in their choice of investments as if they were the beneficial owners absolutely entitled ————————

(b) To advance the whole or any part of the expectant or contingent share in my Residuary Estate to any beneficiary under this my Will to or apply the same for the maintenance or general benefit of such beneficiary ————————————————

11. *I FURTHER EMPOWER* any professional Trustee of this my Will to charge and be paid in all usual professional and other charges for work done by him or his firm in connection with the proving of this my Will and the execution of the trusts hereof ———

12. *I EXPRESS* it to be my wish that on my death my kidneys (or any other organs which may be appropriate) may be made available for the purposes of transplantation ————————————

13. *I EXPRESS* it to be my wish that on my death my body shall be cremated and my ashes scattered ————————————

IN WITNESS whereof I have hereunto set my hand to this and the preceding sheet of paper this   day of   One thousand nine hundred and ninety-two

Witness's Name . . . .
Address . . . .
. . . .
. . . .
Occupation . . . .   (Testator's signature)

Witness's Name . . . .
Address . . . .
. . . .
. . . .
Occupation . . . .

* These wishes will usually be contained in a 'side letter' kept with the Will.

2 Lifetime Financial Planning

One sensible principle of financial planning is, 'Do not let the tax tail wag the family dog'. However, tax is only one of many aspects to be taken into account; peace of mind, financial security, simplicity and administration costs are all equally important. Unfortunately, some keen financial planners tend to overlook these items when putting forward marvellous tax-saving schemes.

Having said that, it is of course desirable and sensible not to pay any more tax than necessary, and to minimize the tax bill where possible. Financial planning really boils down to ordering your affairs so that (a) while you're alive your income and capital are sufficient to give you peace of mind and enable you to pursue the lifestyle and activities which you choose, and (b) after your death, your family and chosen beneficiaries should continue to enjoy similar benefits as far as possible.

Of course, there may be special situations, such as providing for a handicapped relative with particular needs, or paying school fees for children or grandchildren. Saving tax is therefore often an incidental rather than a primary function of financial planning, which should really start with three deceptively simple questions:

1. Where are you now?
2. Where are you going?
3. Where would you like to be? (i.e. Exactly what do you want?)

Financial planning should help you from 1. to 3., saving as much tax as possible along the way.

Forward-planning checklist

- All your present assets (property, investments, cash, insurance policies, business interests, etc.)
- Your present income (earnings, investment income, pension)
- Your regular liabilities and outgoings

- Any changes which you anticipate to the above
- Your general requirements and future plans

When you have produced a broad plan, it should then be possible to implement it as tax-effectively as possible. In the context of tax planning generally, there are three main taxes to consider: Income Tax, Capital Gains Tax (CGT) and Inheritance Tax (IHT). Income Tax and CGT are dealt with in Chapter 6; this chapter concentrates on IHT.

Inheritance Tax (IHT) planning

IHT is a tax payable on disposals of capital (assets or cash) unless the disposal is covered by one of the exemptions or special rules (see below). Disposals include both lifetime gifts and transfers on death (death is simply the 'final disposal').

The first point to make about IHT is that it only applies where the disposal exceeds the Nil Rate Band (i.e. the threshold), which is currently £140,000. So if your total assets do not exceed £140,000 in value, or if you die leaving an estate worth under £140,000, then (unless you have made any substantial gifts within the previous seven years, or are the income beneficary of a trust fund for life) you don't need to worry about Inheritance Tax at all, and you need not bother reading the rest of this chapter.

IHT variables (affecting the amount of any IHT payable)

- The *type* of disposal – lifetime gifts, for example, may be 'fully exempt', 'potentially exempt' or 'fully chargeable'. Death is always a chargeable disposal.
- The *value* of the property disposed of. The value is the open market value at the date of disposal, but calculated as the amount by which the value of the donor's estate is reduced. This is not always the same as the value of what is given away (see below). In addition, certain types of property, such as agricultural property, woodlands and certain business property, enjoy special treatment, reducing their value for IHT purposes.
- Any exemptions available (see list below).

The rate of IHT is currently 40 per cent for disposals on death, and 20 per cent for chargeable lifetime disposals.

C

Gift reducing donor's estate

Jim owned 60 per cent of the shares in ABC Limited. The company is valued at £500,000 (so 60 per cent would be £300,000). Jim gives a third of his holding, i.e. 20 per cent of the shares, to his son. The value of the disposal for IHT purposes is not £100,000 (20 per cent of the value of the company), but probably over £200,000. This is because Jim has given away control of the company, as Jim's own holding is now down to 40 per cent. The value of the gift for IHT purposes is the value by which Jim's own holding has reduced.

Lifetime gifts

Exempt gifts

Individually, the exemptions from IHT on lifetime gifts may seem small, but cumulatively, taking advantage of the exemptions on a regular basis, can produce a substantial saving in Inheritance Tax.

Exemptions

- Gifts up to £3,000 per annum per donor. (Both a husband and wife could therefore give away £3,000 in each tax year with no IHT problems); this exemption can be carried forward for a maximum of one year.
- 'Small' gifts (up to £250 p.a. per donee). (Grandparents with ten grandchildren could therefore each give away £2,500 per year, in addition to the £3,000 each mentioned above).
- Gifts between husband and wife (assuming the recipient is domiciled in the UK).
- Normal expenditure which is made out of income (not capital), is regular and does not reduce the donor's normal standard of living. (This can be very useful to cover payment of premiums into a life policy held in trust for the family, for example.)
- Gifts on the occasion of a marriage – up to £5,000 from each parent, £2,500 from each grandparent, or £1,000 from any other individual.
- Expenditure for family maintenance (e.g. to maintain a separated spouse or dependent child).
- Gifts to charities or political parties (without any maximum limit).

Potentially exempt transfers (PETs)

In addition to the exempt gifts mentioned above, there are also potentially exempt transfers, which are gifts made by one individual to another, or into certain types of trust. The gift is called 'potentially exempt' because it will escape IHT altogether if the donor survives for seven years after making the gift. In other words, IHT will be payable on a gift of, say, £200,000, only if the donor dies within seven years. Between three and seven years after the death, there is 'taper relief', i.e. a sliding scale of the rate of tax payable. There is therefore no need to notify the Inland Revenue at the time of making a PET, but it would be sensible to tell your accountant or financial adviser, and to keep good records yourself.

Chargeable transfers

Any other gifts (i.e. those which are not exempt and are not PETs), such as a gift into a Discretionary Trust, will be chargeable transfers. These are charged on a cumulative basis but still have two advantages: if the donor survives the gift by seven years, the amount of the gift 'drops out' of the IHT calculations; and the rate of tax on chargeable lifetime transfers is nil up to the threshold of £140,000, and only 20 per cent over that threshold. A chargeable transfer of assets worth £150,000 would therefore entail IHT of only £2,000 (20% × £10,000), and after seven years the full £140,000 nil rate band would be available again.

Only when the cumulative total of *chargeable* transfers exceeds the Nil Rate Band (currently £140,000) is any tax payable. So a first-time gift into a Discretionary Trust (a chargeable transfer) of £100,000 would still not trigger the payment of any tax, as it would be within the Nil Rate Band.

Most lifetime gifts are either exempt, or are PETs, so very rarely is IHT payable at the time of the gift. IHT would be payable subsequently only if the donor fails to survive the PET by seven years *and* if the total of the PET plus the value of the donor's estate exceeds the Nil Rate Band.

Many people ask, 'Can I give away more than £3,000 a year without paying tax?' Of course you can. You can give away £100,000 in one go without paying tax (if you can afford it). A straightforward gift is *not* a chargeable transfer, unless you die within seven years of making it. Only then would the £100,000 be added to your estate to see whether the cumulative total then exceeds the Nil Rate Band. If it does, IHT would be payable on the excess.

Exempt and Chargeable Transfers

Date	Event	IHT position
January 1990	Husband (H) gives wife (W) assets worth £200,000	No IHT because exempt (transfer to UK-domiciled spouse)
January 1991	H dies leaving estate worth £150,000 to W	No IHT because exempt (transfer to UK-domiciled spouse)
December 1991	W gives £100,000 to son	£3,000 exempt, £97,000 is a PET. No tax payable at this stage but £97,000 remains 'on the IHT clock'
June 1992	W (having spent most of her inheritance) dies leaving estate (then worth £40,000) to son	£97,000 is brought back and added to £40,000 (chargeable transfers on death). Cumulative total is now £137,000; this does not exceed the Nil Rate Band, so no IHT is payable
July 1992	Son gives £120,000 to a Discretionary Trust for the family	This is a chargeable transfer, but no IHT payable as it falls within the Nil Rate Band (£140,000)
July 1999	Seven years expire from previous transfer	July 1992 transfer drops out altogether; full Nil Rate Band available again
November 1999	Son dies leaving estate worth £200,000 to widow	Chargeable transfer, but no IHT payable because transfer to spouse is exempt
December 1999	Widow dies leaving a total estate (worth £240,000) in trust for children	Chargeable transfer; the total exceeds the Nil Rate Band by £100,000 so IHT of £40,000 (40% × £100,000) is payable out of estate

Gifts with a reservation of benefit (GROBs)

The final point in connection with gifts is a warning note about 'having the toffee and the ha'penny'. There are detailed rules concerning Gifts with a Reservation of Benefit. If you make a gift but 'reserve a benefit' (e.g. giving away your house but continuing to live in it), the GROB rules treat the subject matter of the gift as if it was still in your estate at the date of death. In other words, the seven-year period starts to run only *after* you have completely excluded yourself from any benefit or direct enjoyment from the gifted property. There are certain technical devices to reduce the impact of the GROB rules, for which professional advice is essential.

Finally, on the question of gifts, you might wish to read about trusts, which are covered in Chapter 14. Trusts often represent 'delayed gifts' and can serve as very flexible 'holding' vehicles; you can unload assets from your own estate and leave them in the hands of trustees, who will then look after the assets on behalf of the beneficiaries. This caretaker arrangement can continue for many years until the assets are eventually distributed either to the original beneficiaries, or to their children or grandchildren. Although trusts can play a very useful role in financial planning, it is worth taking professional advice on whether to make gifts outright, or via a trust.

Transfers on death

As mentioned earlier, death is regarded as the final transfer of the whole estate. The actual IHT payable depends on the value of the estate (which will also be affected both by the value of any lifetime transfers within the previous seven years and by the value of any trust in which the deceased had a life interest. The value of such lifetime transfers is added to the value of the assets in the estate at the date of death. There are several complicated valuation rules, including rules which allow a reduced value (for IHT purposes) for certain types of property. For example, the value of a controlling interest in a business (where certain conditions are satisfied) can be reduced by 50 per cent. Similarly, there is a special relief for agricultural property and for woodlands.

When the IHT liability has been calculated, it should be paid (by the personal representatives, or by the beneficiary of the property, depending on the terms of the Will) within 12 months of the date of death. The IHT on certain property can be paid by annual instalments.

C

Calculating Inheritance Tax

In 1990 Sylvia, a widow, made a gift of £20,000 to her only son. In 1993 Sylvia dies, leaving:

Asset	Value £
House	90,000
Contents	10,000
Building society & investments	35,000
Value of estate	£135,000
Add back 1990 gift of £20,000 (less annual exemption of £3,000)	17,000
Value of estate for IHT	£152,000
Less Nil Rate Band	£140,000
Amount chargeable to IHT	£12,000
IHT at 40%	4,800

Another example may help to illustrate how some basic financial planning can save a substantial amount of Inheritance Tax for the benefit of the family.

C

Saving Inheritance Tax

Take the case of Harold (aged 70) married to Mary (aged 65) with two children and four grandchildren. At the moment, their estates are as follows:

Asset	Total value	Harold	Mary
House (in joint name)	150,000	75,000	75,000
Contents (in joint names)	20,000	10,000	10,000
Insurance policies	30,000	30,000	–
Cash in bank & building society	25,000	20,000	5,000
Stock Exchange investments	40,000	30,000	10,000
Villa in Spain (joint)	50,000	25,000	25,000
Second house (let to tenants)	85,000	85,000	–
	£400,000	£275,000	£125,000

Pension scheme death benefits
(payable to Mary on Harold's death)   £40,000

By his Will, Harold has left all his estate to Mary. If they take no further action, on Harold's death his estate will be valued at £275,000, as above but there would be no IHT because it all passes to an 'exempt' beneficiary (his surviving spouse).

On Mary's subsequent death, however, the IHT position would be as follows:

Assets as above (i.e. Mary's and those inherited from Harold)	400,000
Add pension death benefits (paid to Mary on Harold's death)	40,000
	£440,000
Less Nil Rate Band	140,000
Amount chargeable to IHT	£300,000
Inheritance Tax payable (40% x £300,00)	£120,000
The family would therefore inherit a net total of £320,000, i.e:	
Total estate as above	440,000
Less IHT payable as above	120,000
	£320,000

Suppose that Harold and Mary were to take the following steps:

- Harold and Mary give the villa in Spain to their children. (This would be a PET, so no IHT would be payable unless they die within seven years.)
- Harold makes regular gifts of £3,000 per annum to the children, plus £250 to each grandchild (i.e. a total of £4,000 free of IHT each year).
- Harold alters his Will and leaves the tenanted property direct to his children, plus a legacy of £1,000 to each grandchild and the rest to Mary.

Harold expires (conveniently) seven years and one day later. The position would then be as follows:

1. Harold's death

Harold's estate has been reduced by £53,000 (the total given away, half the villa and seven years' gifts at £4000 p.a.)

	£	
Harold's estate now worth	222,000	
Chargeable assets left to chidren and grandchildren (second house & legacies)	89,000	(covered by £140,000 Nil Rate Band)
Residue to Mary	133,000	(exempt; surviving spouse)

2. On Mary's death

Mary's original estate		125,000
Less given away villa in Spain		25,000
		100,000
Add pension death benefit	40,000	
Inherited residue of Harold's estate	133,000	173,000
Total estate on Mary's death		273,000
Nil Rate Band		140,000
Chargeable		133,000
IHT at 40%		53,200

(as opposed to £120,000 on earlier calculation – a saving of £66,800)

Net estate for family [£273,000-£53,200 IHT] =   £219,800

3. Family receives

Spanish villa	50,000
Total of seven years' lifetime gifts	28,000
Mary's estate	219,800
Harold's estate (tenanted house and legacies)	89,000
Total	386,800
as compared with	320,000

if no action were taken –

a saving of over	£66,800

A dozen practical points

To get as much space between the water and the bridge as possible, you can either lower the water or raise the bridge. Similarly, to increase the amount available for your surviving family, you can reduce the tax, or generate extra funds 'outside' your estate. Reducing the tax will generally entail one of three approaches:

- **Reducing your assets**, e.g. by giving them away, thereby reducing the taxable size of the estate.
- **Converting your assets** into assets of a different type (e.g.

woodlands) to obtain the benefit of a reduced value for IHT purposes.

- **Freezing your assets** so that any future increase in value occurs 'outside' your estate (e.g. making an interest-free loan to other family members, who can then obtain the benefit from the money which they have borrowed).

Producing funds outside the estate generally means using insurance policies and or trusts, which are dealt with in Chapters 9 and 14 respectively.

In summary, therefore, if your estate is likely to be subject to Inheritance Tax, consider taking the following steps:

1. Transfer assets to your spouse so as to balance your estates. This will have four advantages:
   - Possible Income Tax benefits (see Chapter 6).
   - The order in which deaths occur will not matter as much.
   - The survivor will be provided for.
   - On the first death you can make use of the Nil Rate Band by bypassing the spouse and leaving assets direct to the children.
2. Give away assets which you can afford to do without. In particular, give away assets which will increase in value (so that the appreciation will be outside your estate), and if children are involved, consider trusts (see Chapter 14).
3. Utilize the annual exemptions: £3,000 per donor, £250 per donee, regular gifts out of income, and gifts on the occasion of a marriage.
4. Keep proper records and a running total of any gifts made (over and above the exemptions mentioned above).
5. Reduce the size of your estate by other means:
   - Spending your money on yourself and your spouse – after all, you can't take it with you. Most people would prefer to be assured of comfort and enough funds to see them through all contingencies, even if this means paying some extra IHT on the survivor's death, rather than give too much away and then worry about how they will afford nursing home fees or end up being dependent on their children).
   - Reduce the capital in your estate and use it to create capital outside your estate, perhaps by purchasing an annuity (see below).
   - Create a debt against your estate, e.g. by a home income plan (see Chapter 12).

C

Purchasing an Annuity

Bill (age 75) and Janet (age 72) have two children. Their estates are as follows:

Asset	Total value	Bill	Janet
House (in joint names)	100,000	50,000	50,000
Cash & investments	100,000	70,000	30,000
Totals	£200,000	£120,000	£80,000

By their Wills Bill and Janet have each left their estates to each other, and on the survivor's death, to the children. On this basis, the survivor's estate will be worth £200,000, on which the IHT chargeable will be £24,000 (40 per cent of the excess over £140,000).

If Bill and Janet were to purchase a joint life annuity [see Chapter 9] with £60,000 from their liquid capital, they could use all or part of the monthly instalments to pay premiums into a 'joint life/last survivor' policy in trust for the children. The policy would then mature on the death of the survivor, producing a tax-free sum of, say, £50,000. In this example, Bill and Janet would have avoided IHT altogether; the survivor's estate would have been reduced to £140,000 (where it would be covered by the Nil Rate Band). On the survivor's death the children would inherit the estate (worth £140,000) plus the tax-free proceeds of the insurance policy.

Always seek professional advice when purchasing an annuity, as there are numerous technical pitfalls.

---

6. If sufficient funds are available, purchase assets which may qualify for special IHT reliefs, e.g. woodlands, Business Expansion Schemes, agricultural land. Obtain professional advice on this.

7. Use any spare cash to make interest-free loans to family members. The interest (and/or the growth) obtained from the money borrowed and reinvested will belong to them, not to you; only the original amount of the loan will be included in your estate for IHT purposes.

8. Generate assets outside your estate by using suitable life policies and/or trusts (see Chapters 9 and 14).

9. When IHT is payable on death, opt to pay by instalments on certain types of property, such as land.

10. Ensure that you have a valid Will. If your estate is large enough, use the Nil Rate Band to leave assets direct to children or grandchildren. Consider putting all your estate into a Mini Discretionary Trust (see Chapter 1, Who should inherit what?).

11. Consider giving a Power of Attorney to someone you can trust (e.g. a mature child, a close friend or relation, or your professional adviser), who will be called your attorney. As you get older and the risk of incapacity (either mental or physical) increases, it can save

considerable inconvenience and expense if you have a Power of Attorney in place. This would give your attorney full power to act on your behalf, should it be necessary. Signing a Power of Attorney now will not deprive you of the ability to manage your own affairs; it will simply serve as an insurance policy against the risk of your affairs grinding to a halt in the event of your incapacity in the future.

12. See a solicitor, your bank or other professional adviser specializing in financial planning as soon as possible. The sooner you start, the more scope there is for sound investment and a secure future.

Part Two
What to do When Someone Dies

3 The Practicalities

Steps to take when someone dies

If you know you are an executor of a deceased person's Will, or are appointed an administrator in an intestacy, the following steps should be taken to deal with the practical aspects.

Notification

- Inform the doctor immediately, unless the death occurred in hospital. (If the death was unexpected, the police should also be informed.)

Will

- If the deceased left a Will, check the terms (possibly with the solicitors) particularly to establish who the executors are and ascertain any special instructions, such as the funeral arrangements or donation of organs.

Registration of death

- The death must be registered within five days.

Coroner

- If death occurred suddenly or in any unusual circumstances, it should be reported to the Coroner. If the Coroner thinks the death needs further investigation, he or she will arrange for a post-mortem examination, which may in turn lead to an inquest.

The funeral cannot take place until after the outcome of the Coroner's investigations, but the Coroner can usually issue an interim death certificate.

- If the cause of death is natural, the Coroner will confirm this to the registrar so that you can proceed to register the death immediately.

Registering the death

- To register the death you should take the doctor's medical certificate stating the cause of death to the local registrar of births and deaths, who will then issue a disposal certificate, authorizing burial or cremation, and a death certificate (cost around £2). It is useful to obtain three or four copies of the death certificate.

Undertaker

- You can then make the funeral arrangements. Give the disposal certificate to the undertaker, who will make the necessary arrangements for the burial or cremation.
- The undertaker will also assist with the appropriate incidental arrangements (disposal of ashes, place of grave, notices for the local press, etc., in addition to the transport arrangements).

Funeral service

- If a funeral service is required, you will need to make the necessary arrangements with the local minister, and agree where the service is to be held.

Cost of the funeral

- If the undertaker's belong to the National Association of Funeral Directors, they will abide by an agreed code, and will provide a written estimate of the cost. The cost will depend mainly on the type of coffin chosen but generally speaking an average funeral costs between £500 and £1,000.

Sometimes the deceased will have provided for the cost of the funeral in one of three ways:

1.   A separate savings account. (However, there may not be sufficient in the account, and often it will be frozen until the Grant of Probate has been obtained.)
2.   An insurance policy. (Although the insurance moneys will generally be payable immediately, there may not be sufficient to cover the cost of the funeral.)
3.   A 'prepaid' scheme in which costs have been agreed and paid in advance.

In most cases, however, the deceased will not have made any special arrangements, so the cost will have to be paid out of the estate. In this event, unless there are funds immediately available in the estate or some of the family are prepared to lend the required amount to the executors, it may be some time before the executors are able to pay for the funeral. In this case it is a courtesy to explain the situation to the funeral directors at the time.

This chapter is intended as a basic reminder of the practical steps. All the procedures are explained in much further detail in the Consumers' Association's excellent book, *What to Do when Someone Dies* (see Further Reading, p.263).

4 Winding up an Estate

Preliminary steps

Having dealt in Chapter 3 with the practicalities of registering the death and completing the funeral arrangements, this chapter is concerned with the legal formalities involved in winding up an estate. (It assumes that you are a Personal Representative (PR) of the deceased – either an executor of a Will, or an administrator (usually the next of kin) if he or she died intestate. There are, of course, a few other practical aspects which you may also need to attend to, such as arranging for a memorial service and the inscription on a headstone, if required, arranging for the Post Office to redirect any mail addressed to the deceased, and the unenviable task of sorting out all the deceased's effects and belongings – throwing out rubbish, but collecting any unpaid bills, uncashed cheques and business papers.

An executor's authority

- The legal authority of an executor under a Will dates back to the date of death, once probate has been granted. If there is no Will, however, the next of kin do not have any legal authority to deal with the deceased's assets until a Grant of Representation has been obtained. It is therefore safer (particularly where there is no Will) if you delay the disposal of any assets until the Grant of Representation has been obtained.
- If for some reason an executor appointed by the Will does not wish, or is not able, to act as executor, he or she can renounce the right to apply for probate by signing a Form of Renunciation (obtained from any law stationer). Where there is no Will, the administrator will usually be the next of kin; in the unlikely event of any conflict, the 'batting order' follows the order of entitlement on an intestacy (see Chapter 1, Figure 1). Thus, if a

surviving spouse did not wish to become the administrator, any children over 18 could apply, then the parents of the deceased, and so on. If there are no family members able or willing to apply for the Grant, a creditor of the estate can do so.

- Alternatively, a person named as executor who is unable or unwilling to act can appoint a substitute (an 'attorney') either to obtain the Grant of Probate or to complete the administration of the estate. This can be useful where the executor is abroad, but if the appointment is for any other reason (e.g. incapacity), you should obtain professional advice as the rules are very technical.

Duties of Personal Representatives (PRs)

- To ensure that the deceased is buried (or cremated).
- To establish what debts the deceased owed at the date of death.
- To identify and collect in all the deceased's assets so that all the debts and liabilities can be paid.
- To pay any Inheritance Tax which may be due on the estate (see Points to Watch p.41).
- To distribute the remaining net estate in accordance with the terms of the deceased's Will (or the rules of intestacy) and to submit a final account to the beneficiaries, including the information which they may need for tax purposes.

In most cases, the PRs will need to obtain the appropriate authority from the Probate Registry (part of the High Court). This authority is contained in the Grant of Probate (where there is a Will) or Letters of Administration (where the deceased died intestate). Both these Grants are included in the term 'Grant of Representation', and to obtain the appropriate authority the PRs must undertake the steps set out on p.43.

In two cases it is possible to wind up the estate without obtaining a Grant of Representation, which will obviously save a substantial amount of time, difficulty and expense.

Where the estate is very small, with a total value of under £15,000 and not more than £5,000 in any one account, the PRs may be able to collect the assets without being required to produce a Grant of Representation. Other assets, such as a car, or the deceased's personal effects, can also be transferred by physical delivery without the PRs having to obtain or produce a Grant of Representation. However, where there is a Will in existence, it should be retained for future reference if necessary.

Where the property is in joint names, ownership passes automatically by survivorship to the remaining joint owner, who simply needs to produce the death certificate for the assets to be transferred into his or her sole name. Where the size of a couple's joint estate is not very large (so that they would wish the survivor to inherit everything), it is often sensible for them to hold *all* the assets (including the house) in their joint names so that on the first death all the assets will pass automatically to the survivor without any need for a Grant of Representation. This saves time and money, and makes things much simpler for the survivor. However, if the value of the deceased's half-share in the assets exceeds £125,000, the executors still need to complete an Inland Revenue account. And if the amount of the half-share exceeds £140,000, Inheritance Tax must still be paid (unless the survivor is a spouse, when the surviving spouse exemption will apply and no IHT is payable).

If the deceased's estate includes land, or if any of the investment institutions insist on seeing a Grant of Representation before they will release the funds, then the PRs have no choice but to apply for a Grant of Probate or Letters of Administration. They will first need to establish the net value of the estate for IHT purposes. If the net value of the estate (including any chargeable gifts made in the seven years before the date of death) is less than the Nil Rate Threshold (£140,000), or if the estate, irrespective of its size, is left to an exempt beneficiary (a spouse, charity or political party), no IHT is payable, but the PRs will still need to carry out the remaining steps described in this chapter.

Establishing assets and liabilities

The PRs need to list all the assets belonging to the deceased and the values at the date of death. Anything with a saleable value should be included – from the deceased's house, to clothing and jewellery. To do this the following steps must be taken:

- Obtain possession of all insurance policies, bank books, passbooks, share certificates, etc.
- Write to the banks, building societies and Director of Savings, obtaining details of the exact values at the date of death.
- Value any stocks and shares (preferably by obtaining an official probate valuation from a stockbroker, the charge for which can often be covered by the commission on any eventual sale of the investments).
- Write to the deceased's employer/pension provider to establish whether there are any arrears of wages or pension due.
- Write to the Inspector of Taxes to establish whether there is any

outstanding tax liability or (as is often the case) repayment of tax due to the estate.

- Value the deceased's personal effects and share of the house contents. If the estate is dutiable, it would be sensible to obtain a professional valuation of the contents and effects. It is also sensible to agree the value of the deceased's interest in the house and any land with the local district valuer, to whom you should write with your suggested values.

Having listed and valued the assets, the PRs then prepare a similar list of debts and liabilities outstanding at the date of death. To establish these the PRs will:

- Check whether all the usual household bills (gas, electricity, water, telephone, community charge, etc.) have been paid.
- Write to the Inspector of Taxes to establish whether there is any outstanding tax liability (Income Tax or Capital Gains Tax) to the date of death.
- Write to the bank to establish the amount of any overdraft.
- Unless absolutely confident that there are no other liabilities, advertise (in a local paper and the *London Gazette*) for creditors or claims against the estate.

Points to watch

Assets outside the estate
The PRs do not need to include in the probate forms (or the IHT calculations) the value of assets which pass outside the estate, such as death benefits payable under a pension fund, or the proceeds of insurance policies which are held in trust.

Interest under a trust
If the deceased had an interest under a trust (e.g. a widow who had a life interest under her late husband's Will) there are complicated rules which may result in the value of the trust being added to the value of the deceased's estate for IHT purposes. In such cases professional advice is essential.

Assets passing to exempt beneficiaries
For IHT purposes, the executors can deduct from the net estate the value of assets which pass to exempt beneficiaries, such as a surviving spouse

or a charity. (Again, professional advice would be required where the asset passing to an exempt beneficiary is expressed as a proportion of the estate, such as 'half the residue'.)

Assets subject to the special valuation rules

Certain assets, such as an interest in woodlands, agricultural land, or business interests (e.g. shares in the family business), may qualify for a special reduction in value for the purposes of calculating the IHT.

Assets in joint names

Only the value of the deceased's proportionate share in the asset (usually 50 per cent) should be included in the probate forms. Often a 'joint interest' also qualifies for a discount to reflect the fact that, for example, a half-share in a house is not really a marketable commodity.

Who pays the IHT?

Generally, the IHT bill is paid by the PRs out of the residuary estate. However, there are occasions when some of the IHT may be payable by a beneficiary. These include where there have been chargeable lifetime gifts within the previous seven years, where the dutiable assets include a share in joint property which passes to the other joint owner, or where the Will directs that the IHT on a particular asset should be payable by the recipient of that asset.

As all these points suggest, unless the estate is fairly straightforward, it would be sensible for the PRs to obtain professional advice in connection with the probate formalities, particularly if Inheritance Tax is payable.

Calculating Assets & Liabilities

John, a self-employed shopkeeper and a widower, died on 1 January 1992, leaving a daughter who owned the house jointly with him. In addition to his estate, he had an insurance policy in trust for his daughter, to whom he had also made a gift of £10,000 on the death of his wife in 1989.

Assets	Value at death
Half-share in house worth £125,000 (with discount for 'unmarketability')	£60,000
Personal effects and share of house contents (estimated value)	4,500
Premium bonds	5,000
Bank account (including accrued interest)	240

	£	£
Building society account (including accrued interest)		4,010
Stocks, shares and unit trusts		65,250
Value of retail business (including goodwill and stock, £20,000, less special relief of 50 per cent attributable to business property)		10,000
		149,000

Liabilities		
	£	£
Accountant's fees	115.00	
Outstanding electricity bill	75.00	
Income Tax owing to date of death	150.00	
Half of outstanding mortgage debt on house	10,000.00	
Funeral account	660.00	11,000
Net estate		138,000
Add back PET (gift) made in 1989 (£10,000 less £3,000 annual exemption)		7,000
		145,000
Nil Rate Threshold		140,000
Amount chargeable to IHT		5,000
IHT at 40% on £5,000		2,000

Obtaining the Grant of Representation

As mentioned previously, unless the estate is quite straightforward and you are a devotee of paperwork, the expense of obtaining professional advice in connection with the grant is probably worth the saving in time, inconvenience and technicalities. However, if only to give an idea of the actual paperwork involved in applying for a grant, the following is a brief summary of the necessary steps. (There are slightly different forms for 'personal' applications for probate, but all the relevant forms can be obtained from the local Probate Registry.)

Inland Revenue account

If the total gross value of the estate exceeds £125,000, if the deceased had made a chargeable transfer or a gift with a reservation of benefit within the previous seven years, or if the deceased had an interest under a trust, then a formal Inland Revenue account (listing all the assets and liabilities in detail) will be required. In all cases where the estate is under £125,000, there is no need for the PRs to complete an Inland Revenue account.

Paying any Inheritance Tax

Where the estate is dutiable (i.e. where the total exceeds £140,000, including any chargeable lifetime gifts) the relevant account should be lodged with the Capital Taxes Office, together with a cheque for the amount of the Inheritance Tax (see p. 49, Payment of Liabilities (including IHT)).

Oath for executors/administrators

The PRs need to complete and swear the relevant form of Oath. This combines an account of the deceased's death and Will, with a formal application to the court for the Grant of Probate (or Letters of Administration) and a commitment by the PRs to complete all the formalities of the administration in the correct way. The executors swear the Oath before a solicitor.

Lodging the papers at the Probate Registry

The executors then take or post the Oath (together with the original Will) to the local Probate Registry, enclosing a cheque for the registry fees charged, which are based on a sliding scale, dependent on the value of the estate. (For example, on an estate worth between £70,000 and £100,000, the fee is £215; over £100,000 the fee is £250 plus £50 for every additional £100,000 of value.)

Issue of the Grant

When any Inheritance Tax has been paid, the Probate Registry will issue the Grant of Probate (or Letters of Administration), which effectively provides the legal authority to enable the PRs to encash, collect and dispose of all the assets belonging to the deceased and to proceed with the winding up of the estate (see p.58).

For those not using a solicitor it is perfectly possible to make a personal application for the Grant of Probate, although, as stated above, this should not be undertaken lightly. However, on request the Probate Registry will provide a pack containing an explanation of how to make a personal application and all the relevant forms.

To save time and inconvenience it is a good idea to obtain extra copies of the Grant of Representation – one per asset in the estate. Copies are only 25p each, and the cost is simply added to the fees payable to the Probate Registry.

Many relatives are understandably concerned about details of a family member's Will being published in the newspaper. Unfortunately, as the Will is a document of public record, there is little you can do to prevent publicity; however, the chances of a local reporter picking up the details are slightly reduced if the application is made, not through a local Probate Registry, but through a registry in another area. For example, the executors of a Yorkshire-based testator might reduce the chance of local publicity if their application is made to the Bristol Probate Registry.

The family home

Valuation aspects

Usually the family will have a fair idea of the value of the home. If the estate is not dutiable, the family's valuation will often suffice for probate purposes. However, if the value of the estate is near the IHT threshold, or if the estate is dutiable anyway, it is sensible to agree the value of the house with the district valuer, especially if the house is to be retained. (If the house is to be sold, the intended selling price can be inserted in the probate papers and any adjustment can be made later.)

Valuation is also affected by any outstanding mortgage debt (or the deceased's share), which should be deducted from the value of the property (or the deceased's share). If the deceased's Will does not mention the mortgage, it will have to be paid by the person who inherits the house. However, the mortgage debt will often be covered by an insurance policy on the deceased's life, or the Will may direct the mortgage debt to be paid out of the residuary estate so that the beneficiary receives the house free of mortgage liability.

If the house was in joint names, remember the possiblity of claiming a discount to take account of the lack of marketability of a half-share (see p.40, Establishing assets and liabilities). If the other joint owner is a surviving spouse, the value is irrelevant for IHT purposes because of the surviving spouse exemption.

An important point to be aware of is that there are two forms of joint ownership:

joint tenants,
which is the more common and where there are automatic rights of survivorship on the death of either owner, and

tenants in common,
where the value of the deceased's share does not pass automatically by survivorship to the other joint owner but passes under the deceased's Will.

The significance of the distinction is beyond the range of this book, but could be of relevance, especially in larger estates or where there is a possibility of remarriage by a surviving spouse. Professional advice should be obtained if this situation arises.

What happens to the house?

Whether the house is sold or retained depends on the requirements of the family, whether the deceased left a Will, and if so, the terms of the Will. It may be appropriate to explain that all trustees have a Power of Appropriation, which enables them to appropriate an asset (such as a house) instead of cash to satisfy the entitlement of any beneficiary. For example, if a husband left half of his estate to his wife without mentioning the house, the trustees could appropriate (transfer in its existing form) the house to the widow, as long as the value of the house did not exceed the value of the half of the estate bequeathed to her.

If the house was in joint names,

the deceased's share will generally pass automatically by survivorship to the other joint owner, who then has complete control over the property. No document of transfer is necessary; a death certificate should simply be placed with the deeds, or if the property is registered at the Land Registry, the death certificate should be produced there, so that the ownership certificate can be amended into the sole name of the survivor.

Where the property is in the sole name of the deceased,

problems can arise, at least if family members are likely to need to continue occupying the property.

If the property has been left to a beneficiary outright, the PRs simply transfer the ownership of the property (by a document called an Assent) to the beneficiary, who then becomes outright owner of the property.

If the property is not required for occupation by a family member, it will be sold by the PRs. If the net proceeds exceed the value at the date of death by more than £5,500, Capital Gains Tax may be payable on the surplus profit. The net cash then becomes part of the residuary estate.

If the property is required for occupation, say by a widow and/or children, the deceased should have provided for this in his Will. If the Will does not mention the property specifically, the PRs may be able to exercise their Power of Appropriation and transfer the house to a surviving widow or the surviving children, provided that the value of the house is within the value of their inheritance. (They could of course pay the difference to the PRs, to avoid the house being sold.)

However, if the deceased died intestate and was survived by a spouse and children, further difficulties can arise. In this situation the spouse would be entitled to the first £75,000 and a life interest in half the remainder of the estate. If the house was worth more than £75,000, it would have to be sold, unless the children were all over 18 and agreed otherwise (see Figure 1, p.5).

Practical suggestions

- Ensure that you make a Will to avoid the many problems which can arise in connection with the family home.
- If there are family members who would need to remain in the house, provide in the Will for them to have the right to reside in the house and make provision for the relevant costs and expenses of doing so.
- If the house is still subject to a mortgage, make arrangements for the mortgage to be repaid, either from a life policy or out of the residuary estate.
- Where the total estate is not large and the marriage is stable, husband and wife should generally own the property as joint tenants. In other cases, obtain professional advice as to whether it might be worth holding the property as 'tenants in common'.
- Following the death of the house-owner, watch for the 'CGT trap' if the house is valued on the low side for probate purposes. If Inheritance Tax is not payable (so the Revenue is unlikely to query the value of the property), it can make sense to place a high value on the house for probate purposes. This value then becomes the 'acquisition cost' of the beneficiaries for Capital Gains Tax purposes. If the house is then sold at a profit over the probate value, Capital Gains Tax may be payable on that profit. The lower the value for IHT purposes therefore, the higher the potential profit for Capital Gains Tax purposes. If the estate is dutiable, the position may be reversed, since it may be cheaper to pay Capital Gains Tax at 25 per cent than IHT at 40 per cent.
- Remember the 'longstop' device of a Deed of Variation, which can be used to amend the terms of a Will (or of a intestacy) if that would benefit the family. To use this all the beneficiaries must be over 18 and agree to the variation (see p.13).

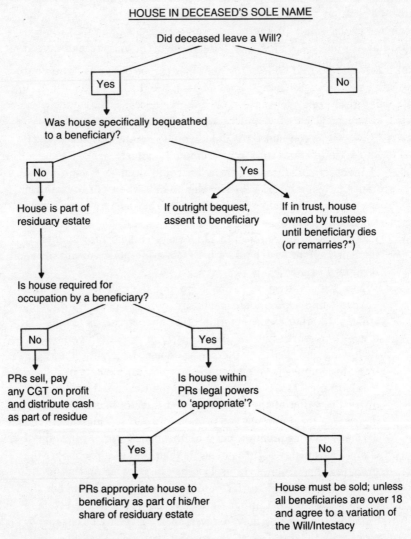

HOUSE IN DECEASED'S SOLE NAME

Did deceased leave a Will?

Yes

No

Was house specifically bequeathed
to a beneficiary?

No

Yes

House is part of
residuary estate

If outright bequest,
assent to beneficiary

If in trust, house
owned by trustees
until beneficiary dies
(or remarries?*)

Is house required for
occupation by a beneficiary?

No

Yes

PRs sell, pay
any CGT on profit
and distribute cash
as part of residue

Is house within
PRs legal powers
to 'appropriate'?

Yes

No

PRs appropriate house to
beneficiary as part of his/her
share of residuary estate

House must be sold; unless
all beneficiaries are over 18
and agree to a variation of
the Will/Intestacy

* The testator may have provided for his or her spouse's right of occupation to cease in
the event of remarriage.

Figure 2

Payment of liabilities (including Inheritance Tax)

You will remember that one of the duties of the PRs is to discharge all the liabilities of the estate. These include any debts owing prior to the date of death, and any liabilities arising on and after the death.

It is self-evident that none of the liabilities can be paid unless and until the PRs have sufficient cash. If there is insufficient cash in the estate, the PRs will have to sell some assets, such as the deceased's shares. In that event, although they are not under a legal duty to do so, it is customary to consult the residuary beneficiaries as to which assets they would prefer to be sold.

Common post-death liabilities

- Legacies.
- Income Tax on any untaxed interest received by the PRs.
- Capital Gains Tax on any chargeable gains made by the PRs. (By concession they are allowed the full 'individual' exemption, currently £5,500, for the year of death and two years after.)
- Inheritance Tax and probate court fees.
- Trustees out-of-pocket expenses. (Note: Professional trustees cannot make a charge for their services unless the Will expressly authorizes this.)
- Legal fees on the distribution of the estate.

In the case of legacies the PRs should obtain a receipt from each legatee. In the other cases, the PRs should only pay against invoices submitted to them, except in the case of Inheritance Tax and probate court fees. As explained in Preliminary steps, these must be paid before the grant can be issued, but generally, the PRs have to produce the grant before the funds in the estate are available to them. The solution to this vicious circle is usually one of the following:

- Obtaining cash from the estate in advance of producing the Grant of Representation. Funds in any National Savings Account will usually be released for this purpose, and often a bank or building society will also agree to allow the PRs to withdraw from the deceased's account, provided that the cheque is to be used only to pay the IHT (and court fees) and is drawn in favour of the Inland Revenue (and the Probate Registry).
- By obtaining a private loan, perhaps from one of the beneficiaries who may have sufficient funds available (for

example, from an insurance policy maturing on the death), or from a surviving holder of a joint account with the deceased who will then be immediately able to operate the joint account.

- By obtaining a bridging loan from a bank (usually, but not necessarily, the deceased's bank). In this connection, it may be convenient for the executors to open an 'executors' account' at the same bank to act as the central source for all the funds which they will subsequently need.

Once the Grant of Representaton has been obtained and the PRs have collected or sold sufficient assets, they will then repay the loan, plus the interest and charges.

Paying Inheritance Tax

- IHT is generally payable within 12 months. If it is paid late, interest will be charged.
- The IHT applicable to certain types of property (e.g. the house, land, a family business, certain unquoted shares) can be paid by instalments over 10 years, unless the property is sold during that time, when the balance of the IHT is immediately payable.
- Certain types of property (e.g. shares in a family business) also qualify for a reduction of up to 50 per cent in the valuation for IHT purposes.
- During the administration, it sometimes becomes apparent that the values submitted to the Capital Taxes Office were incorrect, perhaps because an asset was wrongly valued, or further assets may have come to light, or the deceased did not own some of the assets originally listed in the estate. In those cases, the PRs notify the CTO, which will issue an amended assessment showing the correct amount of IHT. The PRs must then pay the additional tax, or the CTO will refund any overpayment.
- If assets in the estate (usually shares) are sold within two years of the date of death, and the proceeds amount to less than the original probate value, then (subject to certain conditions) the PRs can substitute the amount of the proceeds for the original figure and claim a repayment of the IHT.
- Where the deceased had made a chargeable transfer in the seven years before death, or where he or she was a beneficiary of a trust, the total IHT bill is divided between the PRs (who pay the deceased's proportion) and the donee of the gift (or the trustees of the trust). However, professional advice should be obtained in

these cases.

● When the PRs are satisfied that all the assets and liabilities are finally correct, they should apply to the CTO for a Clearance Certificate, which operates as the Inland Revenue's final receipt, and confirmation of the values of the various assets. (It may also be of significance for Capital Gains Tax purposes, see Chapter 6.)

Inheritance Tax Case History $\boxed{C}$

Jack dies, leaving the shares in his business (worth £300,000 gross) to his son, and the residue of his estate to his widow. On Jack's death the residue is exempt and the shares qualify for a 50 per cent reduction in value under the special relief for business property. Jack's chargeable estate is therefore valued at £150,000, of which £140,000 is covered by the Nil Rate Band. The chargeable estate is therefore £10,000, on which the IHT payable (by Jack's son) is £4,000. Jack's son can either arrange to pay the IHT in one go, or he can choose to pay it by instalments over the next 10 years. If Jack's son sells the business during that period, however, any outstanding IHT would have to be paid immediately.

What if there is no Will?

When someone dies intestate (without a Will), the PR is called an administrator rather than executor. The choice of administrator is determined by the intestacy rules, which state that the next of kin (in a fixed order of priority) are entitled to apply for the Grant of Representation (see Figure 1, p.5). There are three practical differences between winding up an intestate's estate and winding up an estate with a Will:

---

1. The authority of an executor relates back to the date of death whereas the authority of an administrator starts only with the Grant of Representation. It can therefore be unwise for the family to dispose of any of the deceased's assets before the grant is obtained, especially where there is no Will.

2. The powers of an administrator, which derive from a 1925 Act of Parliament, are usually more limited than the powers of an executor, who enjoys all the benefits of the 1925 Act, plus any additional powers given by the Will. For example, an executor will usually be given much wider powers to advance money to a beneficiary, and to invest any money in a wider range of investments.

3. As mentioned in Chapter 1, where there is no Will the law sets out the terms which will decide the distribution of the

deceased's estate on the basis of what it assumes the average testator would wish (see Figure 1, p.5). These rules are very rigid and often produce a result which the deceased would not have wished, particularly where the estate is over £75,000, when a trust will be automatically created if the deceased is survived by a spouse and children. It is in that sort of case where a Deed of Variation can sometimes be useful, but this may not be possible if the children are under 18. In such circumstances the PRs may have to sell the house in order to comply with the intestacy rules – another overwhelming reason why everyone should make a Will in the first place.

Claims by dependants

It sometimes happens that the deceased may have disinherited a family member by striking him or her out of the Will, or they may simply have forgotten to provide for someone such as a former spouse (see Chapter 1, Who are dependants?). In that event, under a 1975 Act of Parliament, a dependant has the right to apply to the court for 'reasonable provision' to be made from the estate. The application must be made within six months from the date of the Grant of Representation, so the PRs should not complete the distribution within the first six months, at least until they are quite certain that there is no possibility of a claim being made against the estate. If a claim is made, the PRs will need to consult solicitors in order to negotiate a settlement; if the claim is not settled, the cost of going to court could well use up a large proportion of the money in the estate.

Rewriting the Will: Deeds of Variation

These have been mentioned in Chapter 1 in connection with the preparation of a Will. Although there has been talk of amending the law, at the time of writing it is still possible for the beneficiaries to 'rewrite' the Will of a deceased person, or to amend the distribution of an estate where the deceased died intestate.

Deed of Variation advantages

- To correct unfairness (see p.13).
- To save IHT on the death of the deceased (e.g. a 'chargeable' beneficiary might renounce some or all of his benefit in favour of

the deceased's widow, as assets which pass to a surviving spouse are exempt from IHT).

- As part of longer term financial planning (e.g. a son with sufficient assets of his own might redirect his inheritance to his own child, or into trust, thereby reducing the son's estate and his own future IHT liability).

Safeguarding the surviving spouse

Jack dies intestate, leaving a house worth £160,000 and £15,000 in the bank. He is survived by his widow Gill, and son George aged 20. Under the rules of intestacy, Gill is entitled to the first £75,000, leaving a remainder of £100,000. Gill is also entitled to the income from half this amount; the other half goes to George. However, as there is only £15,000 cash in the estate, the only way George can be paid is for the house to be sold. In this case, George executes a Deed of Variation under which he agrees that the house should be transferred to his mother (or that Gill should at least be entitled to live in the house for as long as she wishes during her lifetime).

C

Deed of Variation formalities

- It must be in writing. (It is sensible to have the deed prepared by a solicitor.)
- It must be signed within two years of the date of death.
- If the deed is to be effective for IHT and CGT purposes, a special Form of Election must be signed by the beneficiaries and sent to the Inland Revenue within six months of the deed.

Dealing with a future inheritance

There is one somewhat technical, but not uncommon, situation, which gives rise to a unique IHT-saving opportunity. This concerns the ability of a reversioner (see Glossary, p.259) to give away an asset (his or her eventual inheritance) free of IHT because it is regarded as having no value at the time.

Usually, a lifetime gift of assets entails a disposal for IHT purposes, so there may be a potential IHT liability for the next seven years. In the case of a trust, the life tenant (i.e. the person entitled to receive the income) is deemed to be the owner of the trust assets for IHT purposes. The death of the life tenant is therefore treated as a disposal of the trust assets. The value of these is added to the value of the life tenant's own personal assets, and if the total exceeds the threshold (£140,000), IHT is payable.

However, in the case of a Reversion (an inheritance that passes on to someone else when the original recipient of the income dies), the tax laws say that the Reversion has no value at all (on the basis that the value of the capital is regarded as belonging to the life tenant for IHT purposes, so there is no value left in the Reversion).

This provides a unique opportunity for the reversioner to give away his reversion during the lifetime of the life tenant (often his parent). This means that when the life tenant dies, the funds will bypass the reversioner (so that they will never be included in the reversioner's estate) and pass straight to the recipient chosen by the reversioner.

Avoiding IHT by using a Reversion

By his Will, Sam provided for his estate to be held by his trustees to pay the income to his widow Janet during her lifetime. After Janet's death, Sam's estate is to pass to his two children, Kevin and Kate. Janet is the life tenant. Kevin and Kate own the Reversion, which will 'fall in' (become payable) on Janet's death. During their Mother's lifetime, Kevin and Kate sign a deed disposing of their Reversion into a new trust for their own children or grandchildren. When Sam's estate becomes distributable (on Janet's death), the assets will go straight into the trust for Kevin and Kate's children and grandchildren, without any further risk of Inheritance Tax on the death of Kevin or Kate.

C

This scheme is of particular value where there is an existing Will trust, an elderly life tenant (often a widow) and reversioners who may be, say, in their fifties and reasonably well placed, so that they do not need the assets which they would otherwise inherit on the life tenant's death.

The time and cost of winding up an estate

Although time and cost are infinitely variable, it should be possible for the PRs to obtain an estimate of both, particularly if the administration is to be handled by solicitors or bank trustees.

Time

You may hear a reference to 'the executor's year'. This is not a legal time limit; it is simply an indication of what should be sufficient time to enable a normal estate to be wound up. If a Grant of Representation is not necessary (because the estate is very small or all the assets are in joint names, for example), the winding up formalities can be completed in a matter of weeks, if not days; bringing the tax affairs up-to-date is likely to be the only delaying factor. Where a grant is necessary, however, the

time involved will depend on the nature of the assets and the complexity
of the estate. If the assets can be relatively easily valued and no
Inheritance Tax is payable, the PRs should be able to complete the
winding up in 3–6 months. However, if the estate includes land or shares
in a family business, where the values have to be negotiated and agreed
with the Inland Revenue, it may take several months (or even years)
before the values are finally agreed. In these cases, there are two short
cuts which can often prove useful.

First, if a Grant of Representation is required quickly, the PRs can
always include estimated values in the original account; the figures can
then be amended and the IHT position adjusted at a later date, when the
final values have been settled.

Second, as the PRs are often able to collect and sell most of the assets
quite quickly and consequently have a large amount of cash in the
executors' account, there is no reason why they should not make a
'payment on account' to the beneficiaries. As long as sufficient funds are
maintained to settle any items, such as an outstanding claim by a
dependant, payments on account should not pose a problem. However, to
save complications, any payments should be made proportionately
between the beneficiaries, or compensating interest should be allowed on
the final distribution.

Cost

Banks, being trust corporations, usually charge on a percentage basis,
although the charges often include a fixed fee element. While the main
banks have slightly different scales, the National Westminster Bank
charges are not untypical:

5% on the first £50,000

3% on the next £50,000

2% on the balance over £100,000

Thus, the bank's charge for winding up an estate of £250,000 would be
in the region of £7,000.

Solicitors' charges are governed by the Solicitors' Remuneration Order,
which means that they must make a 'fair charge' based on a number of
factors. Time constitutes the largest part of the bill, but the cost also
reflects the importance, size, complexity or urgency of the matter, and the
value of the estate. What generally happens is that the solicitors
calculate charges on the basis of time incurred, plus a percentage of the
value, usually between $\frac{1}{2}$ and $1\frac{1}{2}$ per cent. A rule of thumb would be $\frac{1}{2}$ per
cent on the value of the house, 1 per cent on the remainder, and an
additional $\frac{1}{2}$ per cent if the solicitor has also acted personally as a trustee.

On a straightforward estate of £250,000 therefore, the solicitor's charges would probably be between £2,000 and £3,000.

By the same token, for a straightforward estate of, say, £100,000, consisting of a house and two or three bank and building society accounts, the scale charged by a bank trustee would be between £3,000 and £4,000; a solicitor's costs would be unlikely to exceed £1,000. If no Grant of Representation were required, the costs could even be under £100 in a very straightforward case.

Practical points

- If the PRs intend to instruct solicitors, or if there is a bank trustee, present them with as many details of the estate as possible at the beginning. Also, be sure to ask for a *projected timetable*, and agree on a *schedule of progress reports*. If these have been confirmed in writing in advance, it will be a reassurance to the PRs and also a useful discipline on the solicitors or the bank.
- Ask at the outset for an estimate of costs. A bank trustee will quote its scale fee. The solicitors will quote a variable charge because they do not know exactly how much work will be involved, but this will usually still be quite a bit less than the bank's scale fee.
- If you require absolute certainty, it is possible to agree a fixed fee with the solicitors, but this may work out at more than they would have charged on the normal basis, as they will need to build in a contingency element to allow for extra time or difficulties which may arise.

Do it yourself?

As this chapter illustrates, obtaining a Grant of Probate or Letters of Administration, and winding up an estate are usually fairly complicated tasks with several pitfalls and areas where specialist knowledge is required. All but the most straightforward of estates require some knowledge of the laws of succession and intestacy, tax laws (Income Tax, CGT and IHT), and the ability to deal with a substantial amount of paperwork and formalities.

If it is not necessary to obtain a Grant of Representation because the estate is small or because all the assets are in joint names, the relatively straightforward nature of the administration means that it would be worth considering doing it yourself. However, the straightforward nature of the work would also be reflected in an equally low fee if you used a solicitor.

In all other cases, particularly if a Grant of Representation is required, most people would consider that the cost involved (which is borne by the estate in any event) is well worth the saving in time and effort, quite apart from the peace of mind in knowing that the administration will be completed in a proper and professional manner. Vested interest aside, the author would genuinely advise readers to consult a solicitor in all cases (except perhaps the most straightforward ones, where everything is in joint names).

For those intrepid souls who would like to wind up an estate on their own, Chart 1 (p.58) may serve as a useful reminder. For the more cautious ones who do obtain professional advice, the chart may help to shed some light on the steps which your solicitor (or the bank) will be pursuing on your behalf.

Attend to the funeral arrangements.

Establish assets and liabilities.

Was the deceased entitled to an interest under a trust*?

— Yes → Grant of representation will be necessary if the estate will be dutiable; negotiate the value with district valuer.

— No → Does the estate include a house or land?

— Yes

— No → Grant of representation may not be necessary (depending on value of other assets).

Did the deceased leave a will?

— Yes

— No → Letters of administration?

Do you need a Grant of Probate?   or   Letters of administration?

Yes   No   Yes   No

Complete the Oath and Inland Revenue Account (Note: Account not required if estate under £125,000).

Is IHT payable?

— Yes → Complete Inland Revenue Account and arrange loan for payment of IHT. Pay direct to CTO

— No → Send Oath, forms (and Will, if applicable) to Probate Registry with court fee for the Grant and copies.

Receive Grant of Probate/Letters of Administration.

Advertise for claims against the estate.

Any claims* received?

Register the Grant and copies in respect of all the assets and investments.

Collect in all the assets and cash; effect any necessary sales.

Open executor's/administrator's bank account to act as a central 'collecting pot', and pay all money into this.

Consider whether a Deed of Variation might be of benefit.

Pay all debts due at date of death. (Note: Remember any tax liabilities.)

If shares sold at a profit over value at death, calculate and reserve for CGT.

Repay any loan obtained for Inheritance Tax (obtain certificate showing interest charged).

Pay cash legacies and obtain receipt from legatees.

Pay legatees of other assets: transfer car, personal chattels, shares, etc.

Arrange for transfer of house by 'assent'.

Inform Inland Revenue of any alterations in the estate (additional assets or debts, alteration in the suggested value of land or shares), and pay (or reclaim) any additional (or overpaid) IHT.

Does the Will/Intestacy create any trusts*?

Have there been any claims against the estate, either in response to advertisements, or by a dependant claiming reasonable provision*?

Pay any further expenses incurred in the administration.*

Obtain and complete the PRs tax return for the period of administration.

Obtain tax 'clearances'.

If required, or if delay anticipated, make a payment on account to residuary beneficiaries.

Where IHT has been paid, obtain official clearance certificate from the Capital Taxes Office.

When all legacies, debts and liabilities paid, calculate residue available for distribution.

Prepare tax certificates for the beneficiaries.*

Prepare estate distribution accounts; obtain beneficiaries' approval of the accounts and their release of the PRs.*

Distribute the residue. (If there are on-going trusts, e.g. for minor children, set up new trust file*, transfer assets into names of trustees, notify HM Inspector of Taxes and take advice on investment policy.)

* Professional advice is required where these apply.

Chart 1

Sample Estate Accounts

Fred died intestate in January 1991, leaving a widow, Ann, and two children, Jason (19) and Charlotte (14). His estate consisted of a house in joint names, an insurance policy (which paid off the mortgage on the house), and several bank and building society accounts, all in joint names.

On Fred's death, as all the assets (except for the insurance policy, which paid off the mortgage) are in joint names, there is no IHT (surviving spouse exemption) and there is no need for a Grant of Representation. The accounts can therefore effectively comprise a list of the assets in which Fred's half-shares pass to Ann.

If Ann dies shortly afterwards (whether one week or two years later), the position is different, since a Grant of Representation will now be necessary, and IHT will be payable if the value of Ann's estate exceeds the Nil Rate Threshold (£140,000). Suppose that Ann has had the foresight to make a Will in which she has appointed her son Jason, together with the family solicitor, David Hewitt, as executors and trustees. Say she had also appointed some family friends as guardians for Charlotte, and has authorized the PRs to retain the house for the children to live in until Charlotte is 21. On the distribution of Ann's estate, the estate accounts might be prepared as follows:

MRS A. SMITH Deceased

ESTATE ACCOUNTS

Date of death:	30 September 1991
Net value of estate:	£149,800
Executors:	Jason Smith and David Hewitt
Probate granted:	1 March 1992 out of Bristol District Probate Registry
Distribution terms:	Estate divisible, half between son Jason, and half in trust for daughter Charlotte on attaining 21 (24.6.96)

CAPITAL ACCOUNT

Assets

House 'The Larches', Beckfield Drive (as valued for probate)	120,000
Premium bonds	1,000

Income Tax repayment to date of death	180	
Income Tax repayment during administration	20	
Huddersfax Building Society –		
(two accounts; capital amount at death)	<u>28,000</u>	150,000

Liabilities
Debts owing to date of death

Electricity account	150	
Funeral account	<u>650</u>	
	800	

Administration expenses

Probate Court fees	100	
Inheritance Tax (40% x £149,800 – 140,000)	3,680	
Hewitt & Co; solicitors' costs winding up		
estate (including VAT)	<u>998</u>	5,578

Balance, carried to Distribution Account: | | <u><u>144,422</u></u>

INCOME ACCOUNT

Receipts	Gross	Tax	Net
Huddersfax Building Society interest			
Half year ended 31.12.91	1,300	325	975
To closure (31.3.92)	720	180	540
National Midloyds Bank;			
Interest on Executors' Account	<u>100</u>	<u>25</u>	<u>75</u>
	<u>2,120</u>	<u>530</u>	<u>1,590</u>

Payments
National Midloyds Bank:
Charges and interest on bridging
loan to pay IHT   140

Balance transferred to Distribution Account: <u>1,450</u>

DISTRIBUTION ACCOUNT

Balance transfered from Capital Account		144,422
Balance transferred from Income Account		1,450
		145,872

Distribution as follows:

One half to Jason:

Half-share in 'The Larches'	60,000	
Cash to balance	12,936	72,936

One half due to Charlotte at 21
Retained by trustees to hold
on the trusts of the Will:

Half-share in 'The Larches'	60,000	
Cash to balance	12,936	72,936
		145,872

We approve the above accounts, and acknowledge receipt of all amounts
due to us

. . . .

(Jason Smith)   (David Hewitt)

Part 3
Investing Inherited Moneys

5 Investment Policy

So far this book has looked at the position from the testator's point of view to see what is involved in making a Will, and has then considered the position from a family point of view, describing how to wind up the estate and so forth. The remainder of the book now considers the financial consequences on the rest of the family of inheriting the testator's funds, and examines the practical points and choices facing someone who has capital to invest.

As each chapter in this book could justify a separate book on its own, it must be stressed that the remaining chapters are intended merely to provide a practical outline of the factors and choices to take into account when dealing with inherited moneys. Readers who do require further detail should consult Further Reading (see p. 263) and/or talk to their own professional financial adviser. (If you do not have or know a financial adviser, see Chapter 15, Choosing the right adviser.)

Assuming that you have inherited, or are about to inherit, some money, you are now seeking ideas as to how best to deal with it. To do this you must establish three vital points:

- Your own requirements.
- The amount of surplus funds.
- The risk/reward ratio and your own attitude to risk.

Establishing your requirements

The first step is to take complete stock of your present situation. Are you happy with it? If not, in what respects (not just financial) would you seek to improve it? What sort of lifestyle do you want to enjoy? Are you looking just for more money? If not, what else do you want? A new challenge? More free time? To change the world? To emigrate? To provide security for old age? To help the younger family members establish themselves? To pursue a particular crusade or project? How will the death of a parent or grandparent affect you (not just financially)? These, and perhaps other questions must be asked and answered before you consider, let alone implement, any long-term investment strategy.

Although it may sound unlikely, the problems, worries, stress, possible complications and responsibilities that result from acquiring substantial assets can often exceed the material benefits to be gained from the extra cash. (The two unhappiest people in the author's personal acquaintance are both millionaires.) In the context of inheritance, it has to be mentioned that many young lives have deteriorated rather than improved by inheriting too much, too soon. (This is a point for testators to bear in mind when deciding the age at which they would want their children or grandchildren to inherit.)

The importance of budgeting

Assuming that you are clear in your own mind as to what you want for yourself and your family, you are now ready to consider the investment of your inheritance. This leads to the question of 'surplus', which must now be quantified. The best way of doing this – and a sensible step in any event – is to draw up a personal budget, that is a summary of your anticipated income and expenditure on an annual basis over the next few years. (A sample budget is illustrated below.) Also, it can often be a salutary exercise to prepare an additional statement showing what the position of the family finances would be if you (or the main breadwinner) were to die.

Completing a budget spreadsheet should at least enable you to assess your approximate expenditure on a monthly or yearly basis. Precision is not necessary, but it is vital to have some idea of what you will need to spend each year and how much income you will need to cover it.

If additional capital has been received through an inheritance, remember to build into your model an allowance for any proposed changes in lifestyle, such as moving to a more expensive house. Your anticipated annual expenditure can be measured against the projected after-tax income of the family (again allowing for interest on the extra money inherited). Whatever is left over is then 'surplus' income.

Similarly, any capital you have, such as savings, which is not likely to be required in the short term can be regarded as surplus capital. These will already be invested somewhere, even if only in a tin box under the bed. 'Investing' simply means placing an asset (usually cash) where it will produce the benefit you want. Investment does not just mean stocks and shares; in the context of inheriting capital you may now have a choice of taking early retirement, working part-time, changing jobs, taking more holidays, or whatever, so these requirements will determine where you actually 'invest' the inherited money.

Personal budget – Outgoings per month

I. *Unavoidable expenditure*

1. **Food**   £

2. **Housing**
   (i)   Mortgage/Rent   £
   (ii) Rates   £
   (iii) Wates Rates   £

3. **Heating**
   (i)   Electricity   £
   (ii) Gas   £
   (iii) Other fuel, etc.   £

4. **Insurance**
   (i)   Contents   £
   (ii) Building   £
   (iii) Life assurance   £
   (iv) Motor   £
   (v)   Mortgage protection   £
   (vi) Other   £

5. **Travel/motor**
   (i)   Season ticket   £
   (ii) Car tax   £
   (iii) Petrol   £
   (iv) Other fares   £
   (v)   Garage/car repairs   £

6. **Other**
   (i)   Maintenance payments   £
   (ii) School fees/clothes   £
   (iii) Telephone   £
   (iv) Medical/Dental   £
   (v)   H.P./loan repayments   £
   (vi) Miscellaneous   £

                           TOTAL   £

II. *Household Costs*
   (i)   Kitchen equipment   £
   (ii)   Cleaning and toiletries   £
   (iii) Hairdressing   £
   (iv)   Decorating   £
   (v)   Birthday, Xmas presents   £
   (vi)   Evening classes   £
   (vii) Subscriptions/membership, fees £
   (viii) Pets (Food, Vet Fees, etc.)   £
   (ix)   TV rental & licence   £
   (x)   School trips   £
   (xi)   Pocket money/Allowance   £
   (xii) Holidays   £

                           TOTAL   £

III. *Flexible Costs*
   (i)   Clothes   £
   (ii)   Furnishing   £
   (iii) Magazines and newspapers   £
   (iv)   Cosmetics   £
   (v)   Postages and stationery   £
   (vi)   Garden & tools   £
   (vii) Laundry   £
   (viii) Xmas entertainment   £

                           TOTAL   £

IV. *Desirable costs*
   (i)   Charity Donations   £
   (ii)   Eating out   £
   (iii) Cinema and theatre   £
   (iv)   Alcohol and tobacco   £
   (v)   Hobbies/sport   £
   (vi)   Toys   £
   (vii) Books   £
   (viii) Records/tapes   £
   (ix)   Gambling   £

                           TOTAL   £

Investment possiblities

- Your own business.
- A business run by someone else, whether the Midland Bank, the Government, Marks and Spencer, or your entrepreneur neighbour.
- Assets such as a house, works of art, or other collectibles.
- An experience, such as an exotic holiday, a new car, or a training course.
- A loan to someone else.

Paying off debts

You can also 'invest' by reducing your outgoings, such as paying off your debts. This is generally a sensible move, especially if the interest on the debt is not allowable for tax. What about paying off your mortgage? It is difficult to give an unequivocal answer as there are arguments both ways.

Why pay off a mortgage?

- The psychological benefit of clearing off a liability hanging round your neck.
- The financial benefit of being relieved of the monthly repayments.

Why keep a mortgage?

- Once you have used up your capital in paying off the mortgage, it may be difficult to replace later.
- If you need to raise further funds in the future, the interest on any future loan may not qualify for tax relief.
- You will probably be entitled to mortgage interest relief on most, if not all, of your current interest payments, so the interest received from the money invested could nearly equal (or even exceed) the net cost of your borrowing.
- In that event, the monthly mortgage interest would be virtually covered – but you would still have the capital available for future use if required.

• 'It pays to be a borrower in times of inflation.' Generally speaking, a mortgage enables you to buy an *appreciating* asset (the house) with *depreciating* currency because inflation is reducing the *real* cost of the mortgage debt year by year. Depending on where you invest the surplus funds (which you could have used to pay off the mortgage), your savings could be *increasing* in real tems, while the amount you owe on the mortgage is reducing with inflation.

Case History

In 1950 David inherited £10,000, just as he was about to purchase a house for the same amount. He did not use his inheritance, but obtained a 100 per cent mortgage, and invested his savings in a portfolio of shares. When David died in 1980, he still owed the building society the full £10,000. In the meantime, the house was worth over £150,000 and his portfolio of shares was worth over £100,000. David was therefore £90,000 better off than he would have been if he had paid cash for the house in the first place.

C

The question of whether or not to pay off a mortgage boils down to a comparison between the monthly cost of the mortgage and the net return on the money invested. As a general principle, as long as tax relief at basic rate is available in respect of interest on loans up to £30,000, a higher-rate taxpayer with surplus funds should probably pay off the mortgage debt, while a borrower who owes more than £30,000 would probably be well advised either to repay the mortgage or at least to reduce the debt to £30,000.

The threat of inflation

Perhaps the biggest argument in favour of pursuing a wider investment policy than simply placing inherited funds in a bank or building society is the threat of inflation. Apart from leading to higher prices, inflation also reduces the purchasing power of the pound in your pocket. The 1970 pound, for example, is worth less than 15 pence today.

In other words, if you had £1,000 under the bed in 1971 and brought it out today, it would buy only a ninth of what you could have bought in 1971. Putting it the other way round, a 1971 investor would need approximately £1,000 in 1991 to buy what could have been bought for £100 in 1971.

THE VALUE OF THE POUND

| £1 in 1971 | worth 52p by 1976 | worth 28p by1981 | worth 21p by1986 | worth 14p by 1991 |

The average annual rate of inflation over the 20 years shown was 9.95%.

Figure 3

The effects of forecasting inflation

A useful rule of thumb to calculate how long it will take for inflation to halve the value of your savings is to divide the inflation rate into 72. For example, if inflation is currently 6 per cent, in 12 years (72 divided by 6) £1,000 will be worth £500. Putting it the other way round, in 12 years' time you will need £2,000 to buy what £1,000 buys today. If inflation averaged 12 per cent, then it would take only six years for the real value of your funds to halve.

As inflation eats into the real value of money, most people wish to protect both their capital and their income against inflation – that is to invest their capital so that it can grow in value (preferably at the rate of inflation or more), and invest it in such a way that the annual income may also increase over future years. Effectively this means investing in assets which are either 'guaranteed' to keep pace with inflation, or which may or may not keep pace with inflation.

Guaranteed investments include Index-Linked Gilts and some National Savings products (see Chapter 7). If you hold these investments to maturity, the repayment value should (after allowing for inflation) be at least equal to the original value in real terms.

Variable investment – less secure but potentially more rewarding investments – include 'equity-based' assets. The value of these is not guaranteed, and will vary with a number of factors, including interest rates, the laws of supply and demand, and political and economic developments.

Both types of investments are dealt with in more detail in Chapter 7. For present purposes, suffice it to say that as long as inflation continues, the only certainty in cash-based investments (such as banks and building society accounts) is that they will *decrease* in real value (i.e. purchasing power) by the rate of inflation each year. Given this, it is not unfair to describe such accounts as 'guaranteed depreciation accounts'.

If the prospect of inflation does concern you and you wish to preserve the real value of your assets (in terms of spending power), you should be prepared to invest at least part of your capital in equity-based assets which offer the prospect of at least keeping pace with the rate of inflation.

However, just as the prices of equity-based assets and the income from them can go up, so they can go down, especially in the short term. Over longer periods, say, five years or more, experience shows that the trend has been upwards, and that, by and large, equities have more than kept pace with inflation (see Figure 4, below).

Performance of Equities 31/12/65–30/8/91   *Source*: Johnson Fry Asset Managers PLC

Figure 4

Investing in equities (i.e. the equity capital, or ordinary shares in public companies) as part of a long-term plan can be a vital part of any investment strategy. Buying equities for short-term profit is speculation rather than investment, and is only for the experts, the brave, or the foolhardy.

Someone who invested £1,000 in the shares of Marks & Spencer in 1980 would in November 1991 have an investment worth £7,360. By contrast, someone who had invested £1,000 in the shares of Polly Peck in 1980 would have seen his or her investment worth over £1,500,000 in August 1990, but later that year the company went into receivership, and it is likely that this investment would have been worthless.

The risk/reward ratio

Generally speaking, the greater the potential reward, the greater the risk element; this is what is meant by the 'risk/reward ratio'. It does not mean that every investment is as risky as Polly Peck, or that it will show the same rewards as Marks & Spencer in the previous example. A key factor in any investment programme is the investor's own attitude to risk. This will depend on several factors, ranging from the investor's personality and previous experiences to the amount of surplus money available. Some people, if they are unable to see the value of their savings written in a passbook, cannot sleep at night. For that temperament, it would be utterly wrong to choose an investment with a high risk factor.

Case History

A client inherited £10,000 which he gave to his investment adviser with instructions to 'go all out' for maximum capital growth; the client confirmed he was prepared to accept the maximum level of risk, but wanted weekly progress reports. The following Monday morning the adviser telephoned the client to confirm the good news that his investment was now worth £20,000. When the client asked how he had managed to produce such an impressive reward over such a short period, the Adviser answered, 'In view of your requirements, I called in at the local casino on Saturday evening and placed it all on red' – a good example of the risk/reward principle.

In the context of discussing risk, it is appropriate to repeat an obvious but often unheeded warning against allowing yourself to be persuaded to invest in a surefire scheme which will 'double your money in three years'. Despite the publicity surrounding recent financial scandals, such as Barlowe Clowes, Levitt, and BCCI, it is amazing how many people allow their common sense to fly out of the window when they think they smell an extra profit. The final general warning, before passing on to more specific matters, must therefore be 'Beware of greed'.

There is no short cut to riches. If someone offers you a return of 12 per cent when 10 per cent is the maximum generally available, the investment can *only* be either a con or unduly risky. If a return of 12 per cent were really available, why would everyone else be investing at 10 per cent? The answer, of course, is that a 12 per cent return is not available without a much higher degree of risk, and such investments are generally not suitable for the private investor. Whether you see an advertisement or receive an unsolicited telephone call promoting any type of 'get rich quick' opportunity, or offering a profit above what is normally available, – do *not* part with money before taking proper professional advice.

This is where we revert to the concept of surplus. Clearly the larger the surplus available to you, the more you can afford to accept a degree of risk in order to obtain the higher potential rewards. The smaller your surplus, the more conservative your approach should be. (See the 'risk pyramid' on p. 98.)

Capital, income and overall return

The final section of this chapter consists of a brief explanation of three terms which are frequently used in investment and financial matters. It is important to appreciate the distinction between 'capital' and 'income', not least because of the tax consequences, but also in connection with trusts.

Put simply, capital could be described as the tree, and income as the fruit from it. In investment terms the capital is the amount invested and the income is the yield received from the investment. This could be in the form of interest paid on a bank or building society account, or the dividends paid on shares or unit trusts. In some cases the yield is not a 'separate fruit', but takes the form of an addition to the capital itself; for example, National Savings Certificates simply increase in value by a certain amount each year.

Generally speaking, only income is subject to Income Tax; the capital may be subject to Inheritance Tax (see Chapter 2) or Capital Gains Tax (see Chapter 6).

The distinction between capital and income helps to underline the importance of the third term – the overall return on an investment. This refers to the total amount you get back for an investment, after allowing for the tax for which you are personally liable. If an investment produces capital growth of 10 per cent in one year, plus income of 8 per cent before tax (which will be 6 per cent after tax), a basic-rate taxpayer would have enjoyed an overall net return of 16 per cent.

Capital Investment Comparisons

- Emma inherits £10,000, which she invests in a guaranteed bond which matures for £11,000 after one year. If Emma is a basic rate taxpayer, the profit of £1,000 would be tax-free, representing a return of 10 per cent.
- James invests £10,000 in a one-year building society account which offers 10 per cent interest at the end of the year. After deduction of tax from the interest, James receives £10,750, so his overall net return is $7\frac{1}{2}$ per cent. (If the interest had been paid every six months, James could have reinvested the first interest payment for the remaining six months to increase the overall return slightly.)
- Peter invests his £10,000 in the purchase of 5,000 shares in Marks & Spencer PLC. At a price of 200p each, they offer a yield of 4 per cent gross. Peter sells his shares a year later for £10,900, when the price is 218p, by which time he has received two dividends totalling £300 net of tax. Peter has therefore received a total of £11,200, which represents an overall net return of 12 per cent — 9 per cent in tax-free capital growth and 3 per cent in net income.

One final point in connection with calculating the return on an investment concerns the 'miracle' of compound interest. In particular, where the income is not paid out to the investor but added back to the capital, this means that you will now have the increased amount of capital working for you. In the case of a building society, the first interest added back will itself be earning further interest, and so on as each interest payment is added back. The effects of this 'compounding' can be quite dramatic in terms of capital growth. For example, at a stable interest rate of 10 per cent, an investment will double in value after approximately seven years, and will double again in a further seven years. An investment of £10,000 today, therefore, left to grow in an investment producing a 10 per cent return year in year out, would be worth approximately £80,000 in 20 years' time just through the 'miracle' of compound interest. It is helpful to bear that in mind, particularly when considering performance figures put forward by over-persuasive salesmen.

Compound Annual Return (CAR)

CAR confirms the actual return to the investor after taking account of the interest which has been earned during the year. For example, suppose that £10,000 is invested in an account offering 8 per cent net interest payable every six months. After six months, £400 would be added to the account, so £10,400 would then be earning interest for the rest of the year. When earning this interest on interest, the CAR would show the actual return to you after taking account of this compounding. The more often interest is added, the higher will be the CAR, as the interest is compounding more frequently. CAR therefore provides a useful way of comparing the true return between the various types of savings accounts.

In summary, there are three external factors which may affect the return which any particular investment offers you: inflation, interest rates, and taxation. The first two have been discussed in the context of investment policy generally. The next chapter contains a brief explanation and summary of everything you wanted to know about Income Tax and Capital Gains Tax but were afraid to ask.

6 **Taxation**

This book is not intended to be a tax manual (more comprehensive books on taxation for the interested reader are listed in Further Reading on p. 263). However, a basic knowledge of the three most relevant taxes in connection with investment and inheritance (i.e. Income Tax, Capital Gains Tax and Inheritance Tax) will be of assistance. Chapter 2 has already dealt with Inheritance Tax, so this chapter outlines the basic principles of the other two taxes insofar as they are relevant to the investment of inherited moneys.

Income Tax

Anyone who receives income in this country may be liable to pay Income Tax, irrespective of age or usual place of residence. Taxable income is defined in various Acts of Parliament and includes all income from your job and investments. The latter includes such things as interest from a bank or building society, dividends from shares and rent from a lodger or tenant. It does not include capital receipts such as gambling winnings, Premium Bond prizes, proceeds from sale of investments or (in most cases) maturity values of insurance policies.

Rates of Tax

At the time of writing there are two rates of Income Tax for individuals:

- Basic rate (25 per cent) which applies to taxable income up to the total of £23,700.
- Higher rate (40 per cent) which applies to taxable income over £23,700.

Taxable income

Your tax liability is determined by your taxable income, namely, the amount left after you have deducted any allowances and reliefs to which you are entitled.

Allowances (in order of importance)

Personal Allowance
Every man, woman and child is entitled to a Personal Allowance, i.e. a proportion of their income which they may receive free of tax. The Personal Allowance currently stands at £3,295 per annum.

Married Couples' Allowance
In addition to the Personal Allowance, a married man can claim a Married Couples' Allowance – currently £1,720. If his income is not sufficient to use this allowance in full, he can transfer it to his wife.

Age Allowance
Anyone over 65 whose income does not exceed a certain threshold (currently £13,500) receives a higher Personal Allowance (currently £4,020 for an individual between 65 and 74, or £4,180 for an individual over 75). If one spouse is over 65, the Married Couples' Allowance is similarly increased (see below).

	Husband (age 66)	Wife (age 62)
Personal Age Allowance	£4,020	£3,295
Married Couples' Age Allowance	2,355	–
Total allowances	£6,375	£3,295

C

In this case, the husband and wife can receive the figures indicated without being liable to Income Tax. However, if their income exceeds the threshold of £13,500, the Age Allowance is withdrawn at the rate of £1 for every £2 of income over £13,500. The effect of this is to produce a tax rate of $37\frac{1}{2}$ per cent on the excess over £13,500, which is known as the 'Age Allowance trap' (see example following).

	A	B
Single person aged 68 has income of	13,500	14,500
Age Allowance		
In case **A**, unrestricted	4,020	
In case **B**, restricted by half the excess (£1,000) over £13,500, i.e. £500 reduction		3,520
Taxable income	£ 9,480	£10,980
Tax at 25%	2,370	2,745

Additional tax payable on B's extra £1,000 = £375 (i.e. $37\frac{1}{2}$ per cent)

Other Allowances

Among these are allowances for single parents with a child, for blind people and a special Bereavement Allowance for a widow during the year after her husband's death.

Reliefs

These are payments which can be deducted from your total income in order to arrive at the taxable amount.

Loan interest for purchase of main residence

Broadly speaking, the interest payable on the first £30,000 of any loan obtained to purchase your main residence will be eligible for tax relief. This is usually given by allowing the taxpayer to deduct the tax relief from the interest payment, a scheme known as MIRAS (Mortgage Interest Relief At Source). A married couple can re-apportion the tax relief between them as they think best.

Interest on a loan to purchase rented property

This is subject to certain conditions, which should be discussed with your financial adviser.

Interest on a loan used in the business

Such relief may provide further working capital, be used to purchase a business asset, or to purchase shares in a family company.

Covenanted payments to charities

Provided the covenant is for more than three years, you can deduct tax at your full rate (40 per cent for a higher-rate payer) from the amount which you promise to pay the charity. The charity can then reclaim the tax deducted, making this a very tax-effective way of giving money to charity.

Gift aid

A one-off gift to charity of over £600 cash will also qualify for tax relief (at the higher rate as well as the basic rate), and the charity can similarly reclaim the tax deducted from the gift.

Private medical insurance premiums paid by persons over 60 years of age

This is subject to certain conditions, which should be discussed with your financial adviser.

Pension contributions

Up to the allowable limits (see Chapter 12) the amount of any qualifying contributions which you pay into a pension scheme will also obtain tax relief at your highest rate, i.e. you can deduct the amount of the premium from your total income in order to reduce the taxable amount of your income.

Deductible business expenses

Depending whether you are employed or self-employed, certain expenses incurred in connection with your job (e.g. 'pure' business travel and the cost of necessary clothing or equipment) can also qualify for tax relief.

The cost of certain investments

There are one or two other special types of investments which qualify for tax relief, e.g. an investment in an authorized Business Expansion Scheme (BES) or Enterprise Zone (see Chapter 7).

Married women and separate taxation

Now that tax laws have finally entered the twentieth century, married women are treated as taxpayers in their own right and their tax affairs are no longer treated as part of their husbands'. This new system of separate taxation has thrown up many opportunities for saving tax within a family, yet it has been estimated that a total of over £2.5 million excess tax was paid and not reclaimed by married women in 1991. The big difference is that *each* spouse now has his or her own Personal Tax Allowance in addition to the Married Couples' Allowance, which can be transferred from husband to wife if this will benefit the couple. If both partners pay tax at the basic rate and if their incomes exceed their allowances, no further action may need to be taken. However, if either spouse has no income (or if the income is below the Personal Allowance), there is an excellent opportunity to save tax by transferring income to that spouse. Income cannot be transferred as such, of course, but it will often be possible to transfer assets which produce taxed income, such as money in a building society account.

In the following case study, assume that Henry has £20,000 in a building society account and Amanda, who has a part-time job, has no assets. As the figures show, by transferring the money in the building society account into Amanda's name, the family's tax bill is reduced by £1,027.

Transferring money to reduce tax

	A		B	
	BEFORE TRANSFER of building society funds		AFTER TRANSFER of building society funds	
	Henry	Amanda	Henry	Amanda
Salary	£25,000	–	£25,000	–
Building society interest (before tax)	5,000	–	–	5,000
Total income before tax	30,000	–	25,000	5,000
Less Personal Allowance	3,295	3,295	3,295	3,295
	26,605	–	21,605	1,605
Less Married Couples' Allowance	1,720	–	1,720	–
	24,885	–	19,885	1,605
Tax payable	6,399*	–	4,971*	401*
Total tax bill	£6,399		£5,372	
Increase in net income (i.e. reduction in tax)			£1,027	

*£23,700 @ 25% = £5,925
*£ 1,185 @ 40% = £ 474

*£19,885 @ 25% = £4,971
*£ 1,605 @ 25% = £ 401

A similar benefit is available where one spouse pays at the basic rate of 25 per cent and the other pays at the higher rate of 40 per cent. In this case, assets which produce income could be transferred to the spouse paying the lower rate of tax; this would achieve a saving of 15 per cent (the difference between the two rates) on the income produced by the assets transferred.

Joint income

Income produced by property which is owned jointly will be treated as belonging to husband and wife in equal shares, unless they jointly elect to the contrary. The election is made on Form 17 (available from the Inland Revenue). Similarly, interest on a mortgage in joint names will also be split 50/50, but can be re-apportioned so that, for example, the spouse with the larger amount of income would receive all the mortgage interest relief.

Method of collection

In essence, the system is quite simple; you disclose your income to the Inspector of Taxes on the appropriate Tax Return Form. If further tax is due, the Collector of Taxes sends you an assessment, which must be paid within the appropriate time, or your PAYE code will be adjusted, so that the tax due will be collected by increased deductions from your monthly wages. If you have paid too much tax, you complete the relevant Repayment Claim Form which you send to your Inspector of Taxes, who will then repay the appropriate amount. Most taxpayers automatically receive a Tax Return Form from their Inspector of Taxes, which they are legally obliged to complete and return. If you have not received a form but you receive income which is taxable, you should notify the Inspector of Taxes, who will then send you the appropriate form. The penalities for tax evasion are high, and it is worth remembering that certain institutions such as banks and building societies are legally obliged to notify the Revenue if the interest earned on an individual's account in any year exceed certain limits (e.g. £500 for a bank account).

Repayment of tax and non-taxpayers

As mentioned earlier, if your income does not exceed your Personal Allowance, you will be entitled to reclaim any tax deducted from that income; the claim should be made on the official form available from your Inspector of Taxes.

Case Study

Gretchen is a 19-year-old student who inherits a £10,000 legacy from her grandfather. She intends to use this as a deposit on a house in a few years' time, but at the moment she would like some spendable income and access to the cash if necessary. She therefore invests the cash in a building society notice account, offering 10 per cent gross interest, subject to three months' notice. By completing the relevant form with the building society, Gretchen can arrange for the interest (which will amount to £1,000 p.a.) to be paid gross. Alternatively, if she forgets to do so (or if she has other income which has borne tax), she can wait until the end of the year and then reclaim all the tax deducted from her investment income (including the £250 deducted from the building society interest) provided her total gross income does not exceed her Personal Allowance of £3,295.

Tax and investments

Different investments have different tax treatments, and certain investments are therefore more appropriate for certain levels of taxpayer (see p.89, Tax-effective investments.) These include investments where:

- Income is paid *net* of basic rate tax; (a non-taxpayer would need to reclaim the tax deducted).
- Income is paid *gross* (but is subject to tax if the investor is a taxpayer).
- The income is entirely tax-free (these would be particularly attractive to higher-rate taxpayers).
- The income is not paid out but is accumulated within the investment so that the return is in the shape of capital growth.

Capital Gains Tax (CGT)

As the name suggests, Capital Gains Tax is simply a tax on 'gains', that is the profit made from the disposal of a chargeable asset. Disposals include gifts as well as sales, but they do not include gambling gains, wins on the pools, or Premium Bonds.

Chargeable assets

These include all assets, unless they are specifically excepted. The main exemptions comprise:

- Personal effects under £6,000 in value.

- Cars.
- Cash.
- National Savings products.
- Gilts (i.e. Government securities).
- Assets of national, historic or scientific interest.
- Life assurance policies (if they have not been purchased from someone else).
- 'Wasting assets' (e.g. leases with a life of less than 50 years).
- Investments in a Business Expansion Scheme (BES).
- Investments in a Personal Equity Plan (PEP).
- Your principal private residence (including half a hectare of adjoining land, or a larger amount if it is appropriate to the size of the building).

A profit made on the disposal (including a gift) of any of the above items will not be liable to CGT, but a profit made on the sale of shares, unit trusts, or a second house, for example, would be liable to CGT.

Rate of tax

For an individual the net gain is now added to their income and CGT is applied at the appropriate Income Tax rate; this would be 25 per cent if the total of actual income plus the net gain does not exceed £23,700, or 40 per cent if the net gain takes the total over the basic rate threshold of £23,700. Most trusts will pay at 25 per cent, but Discretionary Trusts and Accumulation and Maintenance Trusts (see Chapter 14) pay at 35 per cent.

Who is liable?

The brief answer to this is any taxpayer resident in the UK. A taxpayer who emigrates and becomes a non-resident is not liable to UK tax. Indeed, if the figures are large enough, the prospect of saving CGT can often be a factor in deciding whether or not to emigrate.

There is also good news for married couples in that, to some extent, they have the best of both worlds. As spouses are now treated separately for tax purposes, including Capital Gains Tax, each spouse has his or her own annual exemption (see p.86, Other exemptions). In addition, transfers *between* spouses are exempt from Capital Gains Tax; a gift from husband to wife will not produce a liability because the wife is treated as having acquired the asset at the husband's original acquisition cost.

Where assets in joint names are sold at a profit, the gain is apportioned in the ratio of their ownership interests (often, but not necessarily, 50/50).

Calculation of the gain

The rule is that you deduct from the net proceeds of sale the original cost of acquiring the asset as increased by any capital expenditure on improvement, and the 'indexation allowance' (which takes into account the effect of inflation while you have owned the asset).

There are special rules where the asset was owned before 31 March 1982 (see below).

Losses

Gains and losses incurred in the same tax year are 'netted off' against each other, so a profit of £8,000 on the sale of one asset and a loss of £3,000 on the sale of another would produce a net profit of £5,000. This sum would be covered by the Annual Exemption (see p.86), so no CGT would be payable. An overall loss can be carried forward (without time limit) to reduce gains made in any future years. Losses can arise not only when an asset is actually sold at a loss, but if, for example, a company goes into liquidation and the asset becomes worthless. However, a loss by one spouse cannot be set against gains made by the other spouse.

The importance of 31 March 1982

Where you owned an asset on 31 March 1982, the 'base cost' of that asset can be taken as its value on 31 March 1982, rather than the original acquisition cost dating from, say, 1975, or whenever. There are fairly detailed and complicated rules governing the rebasing to 31 March 1982 values, especially where the assets were held on 6 April 1965, or where the asset was acquired from someone who had held over an earlier gain (see p.87). However, the basic rule (allowing rebasing to 1982) helps to simplify most CGT calculations, and often to reduce the tax payable.

Rebasing assets to reduce tax
1975: Jim purchases shares for £2,000
31 March 1982: shares worth £6,000
1992: Jim sells the shares for £9,000
By electing for the 31 March 1982 base value of £6,000, Jim's gain (ignoring indexation) will be £3,000 (i.e. £9,000–£6,000), rather than a gain of £7,000 (the overall gain since 1975).

C

Indexation Allowance

This allowance simply allows the effect of inflation to be taken into account during the period of your owning an asset. If, for example, you acquired some shares seven years ago for £10,000 and sold them today for £20,000, you would have a gain before indexation of £10,000. However, during those seven years, inflation has amounted to approximately 50 per cent, so the value of money has halved. The Indexation Allowance, say 50 per cent exactly, would therefore allow you to increase the cost of the shares (for CGT purposes) to £15,000, so the consequent gain would be £5,000. On these figures the gain would be covered by your annual allowance (see p.86). Suppose, however, that you had sold the shares for £10,000 (the original purchase price), the Indexation Allowance would still be available; for CGT purposes the cost would still be increased to £15,000 and you would therefore have a loss of £5,000, which could be used to offset against any other gains of the same, or future, years.

If one spouse transfers assets to the other, the transfer is exempt from Capital Gains Tax, but the receiving spouse acquires the asset at the original cost of the transferring spouse, and the Indexation Allowance will be available for the full period of joint ownership.

If you inherit shares under a Will, your acquisition cost will be the probate value of the shares and the Indexation Allowance will run from the date of death.

Indexation Allowance tables are published monthly, so it is possible for you to obtain an accurate estimate of any CGT liability before you arrange to sell or give assets away.

Part disposals

If you dispose of only part of an asset, say, 500 units from a total of 1,500, the gain is calculated by reference to the apportioned cost of the part sold. In this case you have sold one third of the holding, so the gain would be calculated by reference to one third of the original cost. Where the part disposed of is very small, say, the sale of rights on a rights issue of shares, or in the case of land where the proceeds do not exceed £20,000 or one fifth of the total value, you do not need to calculate the proportionate gain. Instead, the small disposals relief allows you to deduct the proceeds from your original base cost. In this way the gain on an eventual sale will be increased by the amount of sale proceeds received now. Again, the detailed rules applied to part disposals are complicated so professional advice is essential.

The annual exemption

Apart from the indexation relief to allow for inflation, the other basic relief to which all taxpayers are entitled is the annual exemption – currently £5,500, but the amount is usually changed in the Budget each year. Husband and wife each have an annual exemption, and although trusts are generally entitled to one half of the individual exemption (i.e. £2,750), Personal Representatives have the full individual exemption of £5,500 for disposals made in the year of death and the next two tax years.

Taking advantage of the Annual Exemption

1985 – Robert acquires 1,000 shares in Hussein Kuwait Enterprises PLC for £5,000
1992 – Robert sells the shares for £14,500

Overall gain (un-indexed)	£ 9,500
Revised cost, adjusted for Indexation Allowance at 40%	£ 7,000
Net gain after indexation	£ 7,500
Personal exemption	£ 5,500
Chargeable gain	£ 2,000
CGT payable (assuming Robert is liable to tax at 25%)	£500

C

Other exemptions and reliefs

The list below summarizes the exemptions and reliefs which may eliminate or reduce the CGT liability on any disposal:

- The Annual Exemption (see above).
- A disposal to a spouse (who then acquires the asset at the donor's original acquisition cost).
- A disposal of the principal private residence.
- A disposal of other assets specifically exempted (see p.82).
- A disposal of business assets when the proceeds are used to replace the original assets (Roll-over Relief).
- Gifts where Holdover Relief applies.

> Holdover Relief enables the donor not to pay CGT on the disposal created by the gift, but to hold over, or include, the inbuilt gain so that the tax is delayed until the recipient disposes of the asset. Holdover Relief is available only for certain types of gift, such as business assets, shares in family businesses and gifts into Discretionary Trusts. Detailed rules govern Holdover Relief, so professional advice is essential.

- Disposals (whether by gift or sale) of the whole or part of a business made on retirement, but note that:
  - the taxpayer must be over 55 (or retiring due to ill health, if younger)
  - the first £150,000-worth of gains are exempt
  - on the next £450,000 worth of gains, 50 per cent are exempt
  - these limits are available both to husband and wife.
- Death (see below).

Gains arising through death

Just as death is the 'final disposal' for IHT purposes, so it is for CGT purposes, but in this case there is the consolation that no tax is payable. Furthermore, not only is the disposal free from CGT, but a beneficiary who inherits assets on a death does not acquire them at the original acquisition cost of the deceased; instead, the beneficiary's acquisition cost will generally be the probate value. In other words, the gain made by the deceased in his or her lifetime will be entirely free from CGT and the beneficiary will be liable to CGT only on any profit which he or she may make on a future sale of the asset over and above the value at death.

> 1970 – Tom buys 1,000 shares in Kinnock Holidays PLC for £5,000
> 1991 – Tom dies; the shares (now worth £25,000) are bequeathed to his son, Adam. Gain of £20,000 is 'wiped out' by Tom's death, so Adam's acquisition cost of the shares is £25,000 (probate value).
> 1994 – Adam sells shares for £30,000
> Gain is only £5,000 (£30,000–£25,000), not £25,0000 (£30,000–£5,000).

CGT on an inherited house

As any capital gain on an asset owned by the deceased at the date of death is wiped out, the PRs (or the beneficiary) acquire the asset at the probate value. In the case of a house, if the PRs subsequently sell it at a profit over the probate value, CGT would be payable by them (subject to the indexation relief and also to the PRs annual allowance – £5,000 if the sale was within two years of the end of the year in which the death occurred). If a beneficiary inherits the house direct, however, other conditions apply:

- The house will still be a chargeable asset, unless the beneficiary occupies it and it becomes his principal private residence.
- The beneficiary's acquisition date will be the date of death, and his acquisition cost is the probate value.
- On a subsequent sale by the beneficiary, CGT will be payable if the gain (after indexation) exceeds the beneficiary's annual allowance.

1.1.92 – Ben inherits a house valued at	£60,000	
1.2.92 – Ben adds a garage at a cost of	£3,000	
Ben lets the property to a tenant		
1.7.95 – Ben sells the house for	£87,000	
The CGT position is as follows:		
Proceeds of sale	£87,000	
Less expenses of selling (estate agents and		
legal fees)	£2,000	£85,000
Ben's acquisition cost (probate value)	£60,000	
Plus cost of acquiring the asset (proportion of		
the legal expenses in winding up the estate)	£1,000	
Plus capital improvements (the garage)	£3,000	
Indexation Allowances (say 25% × £64,000)	£15,000	£79,000
Total gain		£6,000
Ben's annual exemption		£5,500
Chargeable gain		£500
CGT at 25% on £500		£125

- If land is included with the house, the principal private residence exemption (when available) includes land of up to half a hectare (more, if reasonably necessary for the proper enjoyment of the house). However, this exemption will not apply if the house is sold first, leaving the land – perhaps with planning permission – to be sold later. Thus, especially where the land has development value, it should be sold before the sale of the house, or (better still) at the same time as the house, not afterwards.

• Where a married person inherits a house, especially if it is to be rented out, consider transferring the inherited house to the other spouse, particularly if he or she has no other income. For CGT purposes, the recipient acquires the house at probate value, but will have a separate CGT Allowance to set against any gains on an eventual sale. For Income Tax purposes, the rents will be taxable at the recipient's rate of tax, which will be nil, if the net rents do not exceed his or her unused Personal Allowance.

As the preceding points illustrate, the whole area of Capital Gains Tax is a highly technical one in which professional advice really is essential. For more information see Further Reading at the end of the book, and make use of the very helpful (free) leaflets issued by the Inland Revenue on all aspects of taxation.

Tax-effective investments

The term 'tax-effective' is a bit misleading. All it really means is that, for some people, the interest or income from an investment is not liable to income tax, and/or a profit on the disposal of the investment will not be liable to Capital Gains Tax.

Many tax-effective investments are described as tax-free, but don't be seduced by this. The main question to ask is, 'After taking account of any tax I will pay, what will be the net return to me from this investment?' The answer to that question often depends on your status. If you are a non-taxpayer, perhaps because your personal allowance exceeds your income, a tax-free return of 7 per cent will not be as attractive to you as a tax-paid return of 6 per cent. In the latter case you would be able to re-claim the tax deducted, so the actual return to you would be 8 per cent. An investment offering a gross income of 9 per cent would be even better, since no tax would be deducted and you would not have to bother making a tax repayment claim.

For nil-rate and standard-rate taxpayers there is little difference in practice between investments which pay gross income (when no tax is deducted) and investments which pay net income (from which tax has been deducted). A basic-rate taxpayer will end up with the same net amount of income either way, and a non-taxpayer will end up with the same gross amount of income either way.

C

Thomas, a standard-rate taxpayer, receives a dividend of £750 net, which means that the tax has already been deducted. He also receives gross interest of £1,000 on which he will eventually have to pay £250 tax. In both cases he ends up with £750; in the case of the gross interest, he has had the use of £250 for a few months longer, but he then has the unpleasant experience of having to pay a tax bill. If Thomas had not been liable to Income Tax, he would have kept the £1,000 gross interest, but would have been entitled to reclaim the £250 tax deducted from the dividend; again, he would end up with £1,000 from both investments.

It can sometimes help to regard each investment as a plant which you put in a greenhouse to help it grow more quickly, in the hopes of producing more fruit at the end of a certain period. In order to help it flourish, you should consider the tax consequences at three particular stages:

1. Entry
What is the tax consequence of making the investment, or putting it into the greenhouse? In particular, will the investment itself qualify for Income Tax relief (i.e. can you deduct it from your chargeable income)?

2. Duration
What will be the tax treatment of any income produced by the investment while it is in the greenhouse? If the greenhouse is a tax-free one, there is obviously more chance of the investment growing into a larger sum; an investment growing at 10 per cent per annum will double in value in approximately seven years; an investment growing at 7 per cent (e.g. because tax is deducted) would take over 10 years to double in value.

3. Exit
What is the tax treatment when the investment is taken out of the greenhouse (when it is sold)? In this case, the relevant tax is usually Capital Gains Tax, but in certain cases, such as single premium insurance bonds (see Chapter 7, Other variable investments), the profit may be subject to Income Tax rather than CGT.

Bill's financial adviser tells him that if he makes a pension contribution of £1,000 it will cost him only £750. The adviser explains that this is because the contribution of £1,000 will be deducted from Bill's taxable income and will therefore result in a reduction of £250 in Bill's tax liability, as shown below:

Before pension contribution		After pension contribution
£10,000	Bill's gross salary	£10,000
–	Less pension contribution	1,000
10,000		9,000
3,295	Less Personal Allowance	3,295
6,605	Taxable income	5,605
1,651.25	Income Tax at 25%	1,401.25
	Reduction in tax bill £250	

In this example, in addition to obtaining tax relief at the 'entry' stage (i.e. relief on the £1,000 investment made), the pension fund greenhouse also offers a tax-free return for the duration of the investment, so it is likely to grow at a higher rate. As a final bonus, the cash proportion of the pension which Bill will be able to take when he retires will also be free of Capital Gains Tax and Income Tax. This is why pension contributions are so often suggested as an integral part of any financial plan; from the tax point of view they enjoy freedom from tax at all three stages of entry, duration and (for the cash element of the pension) at the exit stage.

Types of investment

For tax purposes, these fall into three main categories:

1. Investments where the interest is paid gross, but is taxable (if the investor is a taxpayer). These include:

- Bank and building society accounts (for non-taxpayers who register as such).
- Gilts, i.e. Government stocks purchased through the National Savings Register.
- National Savings Bank investment accounts.
- National Savings Bank Capital Bond.
- National Savings Bank Income Bond.
- Some offshore accounts (e.g. in the Channel Islands or Isle of Man).

2. Investments where the interest is paid net, i.e. after Income Tax has been deducted. These include:

- Bank and building society accounts (unless the investor has registered as a non-taxpayer).
- Stocks and shares.
- Unit Trusts.
- Investment Trusts.
- The income portion of annuities (see Chapter 7).

3. Investments where the income is genuinely tax-free. These include:

- Tax Exempt Special Savings Accounts (TESSAs).
- Personal Equity Plans (PEPs).
- The first £70 of interest on a National Savings Bank Ordinary Account.
- The 'growth' on National Savings Certificates and SAYE schemes.

Other income-producing investments

Where the capital invested increases in value, the investor may encash part of that increase in order to provide an annual 'income', e.g:

- An investor could sell a handful of National Savings Certificates each year, leaving enough remaining certificates to equal the value of the original investment.
- An investor with a Single Premium Insurance Bond (see Chapter 7, Insurance-based investments) could ask the insurance company to surrender a percentage of the value of the bond each year. (For higher-rate taxpayers, a surrender over 5 per cent would involve further tax liability.)

Tax-saving tips to reduce Income Tax

- Ensure that you claim all the personal reliefs and allowances to which you are entitled and that you check your tax assessments.
- Consider investing in tax-free investments, especially TESSAs, National Savings Certificates, Premium Bonds, Family Bonds, Personal Equity Plans and Business Expansion Schemes, particularly if you are a higher-rate taxpayer.

- Take out a regular premium 'qualifying' life policy for at least 10 years. (Although tax relief is no longer available on the premium, the proceeds will be tax-free as long as the policy is maintained for at least seven and a half years.)

- If you are a higher-rate taxpayer with children under 18, transfer money to them on what is called a 'bare trust' – a little-known, but effective technical device to avoid income being taxed at your maximum rate. (You will need to consult a solicitor about this scheme.)

- In the case of a married couple, if one spouse does not have any income (or if it is less than the Personal Allowance of £3,295), the other spouse should transfer income-producing assets so that the receiving spouse can use his or her Personal Allowance and reclaim the tax deducted from the income.

- If one spouse is a higher-rate taxpayer (or falls into the 'Age Allowance trap', see p.77) and the other is liable for basic rate tax only, the higher-rate taxpayer should transfer income-producing assets to the lower-rate payer.

- If spouses transfer assets as suggested above, make sure the assets produce taxable income; it would be pointless to transfer assets such as National Savings Certificates or TESSAs on which the income is not liable to tax anyway.
  Note: A transfer between spouses is not just a tax reduction device; full ownership must pass so that the donor cannot recover the gifted asset in the future (e.g. in the event of a marriage breakdown). The moral, therefore is not to transfer assets just to save tax, unless you are happy to make a genuine outright gift.

- Purchase your house with a mortgage of up to £30,000, rather than rent a property.

- Where the mortgage is in joint names, re-allocate the loan interest to the spouse paying the higher rate of tax.

- Make maximum contributions to your pension plan. Perhaps pay additional voluntary contributions to an existing scheme, or take out a Personal Pension Plan if you are self-employed or not a member of an existing scheme.

- If you are in business, ensure that you claim all the business expenses to which you are entitled (e.g. a proportion of the running costs of your car or your house, if relevant).

- If you have a company car, try to exceed 18,000 business miles p.a. This will result in a lower charge to the 'scale benefit' for tax purposes.

- If you have a company car, take advice as to whether you might benefit from paying for your own petrol used on private motoring.
- Arrange for part of your salary to be paid as benefits in kind, especially if you earn under £8,500 per annum. Tax-efficient benefits include: Luncheon Vouchers, interest-free loans, share option schemes, profit-related pay schemes, pension schemes, permanent health insurance and payment in the shape of Unit Trusts rather than cash (to save National Insurance contributions).
- If you have a business, consider employing your spouse and paying her at least up to the National Insurance threshold (£2,300).
- If you are self-employed and your profits take you into higher-rate tax liability, consider operating as a company.
- If you are in business, consider a 'circular loan' arrangement (a solicitor or accountant will explain this somewhat technical scheme). This will allow you to get tax relief on money borrowed for the business, but which will release other funds (to the same value) for investment or other personal expenditure.

Tax-saving tips to reduce Capital Gains Tax

- Make use of your annual exemption (currently £5,500) for each spouse.
- Consider doing a 'Bed and Breakfast' (see below), either to take a profit and re-acquire the same shares at a higher acquisition cost (to reduce the future gain), or to have the benefit of a loss which can then be offset against other gains.

'Bed and Breakfast'

This is the practice of arranging to sell an asset (usually shares) and then buy them back the next day in a pre-arranged deal on which the expenses are therefore kept to a minimum. The result is that, for a relatively small cost, you are left holding the same shares, but your acquisition cost for future CGT purposes is not your original cost, but the cost of the 'breakfast', i.e. the cost at which you bought the shares back immediately after the sale.

- Invest in assets where the growth will be tax-free (e.g. Government stocks, National Savings Certificates, Family Bonds).
- Plan the timing of any sales; postponing a disposal by two days from 4 to 6 April can delay payment of tax on the profit by a full year.
- After obtaining confirmation from your adviser, make a formal election for the acquisition cost of your shares to be based on the value at 31 March 1982; this can save possible CGT and certainly save time and professional fees.
- If a married couple own two residences, consider transferring the second property to the spouse with the lesser assets and income, so as to obtain the benefit of his/her separate CGT allowance and lower tax liability on any income (e.g. rent) from the second property.
- Give assets to your spouse (disposal is exempt from CGT). Your spouse can then make further gifts, maybe to other family members, in addition to your own.
- If you wish to make gifts, give cash or other assets (chattels, see Glossary, p.259) which do not produce a gain.
- Make a gift of shares in your family business or company, either outright or into trust, and claim Holdover Relief so that CGT is not payable on the gift but only on the eventual disposal of the shares.
- If you wish to give other assets which have an inbuilt profit, making CGT payable on the gift, consider making the gift to a Discretionary Trust (see Chapter 14) so that Holdover Relief will still be available.
- If you are in business and over 55 (or suffering ill health), make maximum use of Retirement Relief (see p.87).
- Make gifts to charity as these are also exempt from CGT.
- Emigrate. (Non-residents are not liable to UK Capital Gains Tax.)

The last suggestion illustrates the advice given earlier that 'the tax tail should not wag the family dog'; it is not sensible to base a commercial decision purely on the tax consequences. As has often been said, a percentage of something is better than 100 per cent of nothing.

The technical nature of tax-planning makes it extremely unwise to implement any of the more complicated suggestions in this book without taking proper professional advice first.

7 Types of Investment

After outlining one or two general investment principles, this chapter takes a brief look at the very wide range of investment possibilities. The list is not intended to be a recommendation for any particular kind of investment, and is no substitute for proper advice tailored to your own circumstances.

Many people reach the point of having surplus capital to invest when in their forties or fifties. This is usually because by that time their earnings are at their maximum and liabilities (such as children) probably at a minimum. It is also often the age at which they inherit the estates of parents dying in their seventies or eighties.

Middle age is the time to plan your financial future – and therefore your investment portfolio – since retirement may be only 10 or 15 years away. Before looking at the range of investments, however, it would be sensible to consider a few basic guidelines.

Investment principles

Readers are recommended to bear in mind the following 11 principles (for which the author is indebted to investment guru John Templeton for the first three, and William Rees-Mogg, former editor of *The Times*, for the rest).

- The true objective for investors should be maximum total return after tax, commensurate with their chosen level of risk.
- To buy when others are despondently selling and to sell when the herd is greedily buying requires the greatest fortitude, but offers the greatest rewards.
- Long-term success requires flexibility, open-mindedness and a healthy degree of scepticism.
- Know yourself. Depending on your temperament, you will feel cautious or adventurous, optimistic or anxious. The deciding

force in all investment decisions will be your own personality.
- Know your own needs. All investment is concerned with providing the ability to meet future needs, known or as yet unforeseen.
- Never take a crippling risk. The principle of diversification in a portfolio of shares is well established.
- Use the judgement of experts.
- Always invest for as long a term as you can. The longer the time-scale of investment, the better the prospect.
- Always balance the portfolio (e.g. between Government stock and equities), but always keep an element of liquidity.
- Buy quality. Over time the best businesses prosper. If you buy rubbish, you are more likely to lose your whole investment.
- Fear inflation.

As 'principles' also includes ethics, you may be interested to know that your investments can reflect your personal concerns, such as a commitment to the environment or a disapproval of activities like arms manufacture and smoking. The 'green revolution' has also touched the financial world, so investors are now offered an increasing choice of investments (especially Unit Trusts, Bonds and PEPs) specializing in 'green' and 'ethical' areas. Some of these offer a positive approach, selecting companies likely to promote the environment; others (the 'ethical funds') adopt the negative approach of excluding those companies whose activities they consider unethical. Quite apart from the obvious moral appeal, the investment performance of several of these funds has been extremely good.

In making your choice you must go back to the first investment principle mentioned above and decide what level of risk you wish to take. As explained in Chapter 5, the risk/reward ratio decrees that if you want the rewards of seeing your investment keep pace with, or outstrip inflation, you must be prepared to take the risk that the value will fall rather than rise. You must also be aware that the larger the potential reward, the larger the potential risk. Before investing any money, therefore, you should weigh up the importance which you attach to the following factors:

- Security of the investment.
- Availability and ease of access to your funds.
- The taxation treatment of income and any capital profit.
- The reward (the possibility of capital growth and income growth).

- The risk.
- The costs involved.

Deciding How to Invest

Julie, aged 30, inherits a legacy of £5,000. She does not anticipate needing the legacy or any income from it in the near future. She is worried about inflation, but does not want to incur any risk at all. For her, the current issue of Index-Linked National Savings Certificates (or possibly an index-linked Government stock) would be an appropriate choice.

Robert, aged 25, inherits a legacy of £10,000. He also does not anticipate requiring the funds in the near future, but would like some extra spendable income and is prepared to take a small amount of risk in the hopes of obtaining capital growth and income growth. In his case, a Personal Equity Plan and/or investing part of the funds in Investment Trusts or Unit Trusts (see below) would be appropriate to his circumstances.

The 'risk pyramid' below shows the degree of risk attached to different types of investment, which are considered in the rest of this chapter.

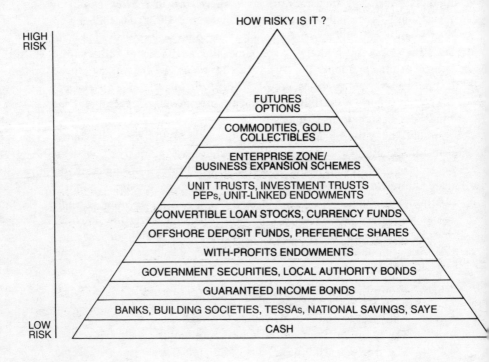

HOW RISKY IS IT ?

HIGH RISK

FUTURES OPTIONS

COMMODITIES, GOLD COLLECTIBLES

ENTERPRISE ZONE/ BUSINESS EXPANSION SCHEMES

UNIT TRUSTS, INVESTMENT TRUSTS PEPs, UNIT-LINKED ENDOWMENTS

CONVERTIBLE LOAN STOCKS, CURRENCY FUNDS

OFFSHORE DEPOSIT FUNDS, PREFERENCE SHARES

WITH-PROFITS ENDOWMENTS

GOVERNMENT SECURITIES, LOCAL AUTHORITY BONDS

GUARANTEED INCOME BONDS

BANKS, BUILDING SOCIETIES, TESSAs, NATIONAL SAVINGS, SAYE

CASH

LOW RISK

Figure 5

Deposit and cash-based investments

These investments consist of cash, so the capital is guaranteed, but the interest usually depends on current interest rates (although certain types of account may guarantee a rate for a fixed period).

Bank and building society accounts

Various types of account offer competitive rates of interest (depending on the amount and the period), and other facilities such as a cheque book or cash card.

Tax treatment
Interest is generally paid net (i.e. after deduction of tax), but non-taxpayers can arrange for interest to be paid gross. Higher-rate taxpayers must pay an extra 15 per cent on the gross amount earned.

Advantages

- Certainty of capital value.
- Easy access.
- Usually a good rate of interest.

Disadvantages

- No protection against inflation. Although the number of 'pound notes' remains constant and certain, inflation reduces the purchasing power of those pounds year after year (see pp.70–71), and there is no protection against this. As with all other fixed capital investments, the only real guarantee in the long term is that the value of the accounts will depreciate.
- The income also offers no protection against inflation. Furthermore, the income will reduce in nominal value as well as real value when interest rates fall, as the income fluctuates in line with interest rates generally.

Comment
These accounts are an ideal short-term cash home for most investors, especially when interest rates are high, and often form the core of any investment portfolio.

National Savings Bank Ordinary and Investment Accounts

These are the modern equivalent of the old Post Office savings accounts.

Tax treatment

The first £70 interest p.a. on the Ordinary Account is tax-free, but Income Tax applies over that amount. Interest on the Investment Account is paid gross (i.e. without deduction of tax), but a taxpayer still has to pay tax on it.

Advantages

- Constant capital value and no risk.
- Convenient access, especially for children and those requiring interest gross.
- Investment Account pays competitive range of interest.
- Ordinary Account also offers a range of free banking services.

Disadvantages

- No protection against inflation.
- Very low rate of interest and limits on withdrawals with Ordinary Account.
- Interest rates variable and one month's notice of withdrawal required on Investment Accounts.

Comment

Not particularly inspiring, but convenient for some, especially small investors and non-taxpayers.

TESSAs (Tax-Exempt Special Savings Accounts)

Five-year savings account (with maximum limits each year), offering tax-free return to investors over 18.

Tax treatment

Interest-free from all taxes during the five years. Investor may withdraw the net amount of the annual interest earned without affecting the tax exemption, but this will be lost if the account is closed within the five-year period.

Advantages

- The freedom from Income Tax enables investors (especially higher-rate taxpayers) to obtain an extremely attractive return on their investment.

Disadvantages

- The investment is effectively untouchable for five years.
- The account offers no protection against inflation as such, although this may be achieved if the gross interest earned is as much as the rate of inflation over the five-year period.

Comment

An attractive investment because of the tax exemption, particularly for higher-rate payers and those seeking to accumulate funds (perhaps for school fees) over the medium term.

Cash Unit Trusts

Like other Unit Trusts (see below), these are collective funds. They invest in short-term deposits and other money market funds, thereby offering a very high return, but in the shape of dividends.

Tax treatment

UK trusts pay dividends with a net 'tax credit'; offshore funds pay gross income on which investors will subsequently pay tax at their appropriate rate.

Advantages

- A high yield (often higher than banks or building societies), which can be received without tax (from an offshore fund).
- Safety; no capital risk.
- Immediate access.
- Ability to switch into other Unit Trusts at a discount.

Disadvantages

- Capital value not protected against inflation.
- The manager's charges (up to 2 per cent initial, and 0.5 per cent annual).

Comment

The generally higher return makes cash unit trusts an attractive alternative to deposits, particularly for a smaller investor seeking a high income over a short to medium period.

Foreign currency accounts

Similar to normal deposit accounts, but held in a foreign currency, whether held inside or outside the UK.

Tax treatment

Investors will be liable to tax at their appropriate rate on the sterling value of the interest received.

Advantages

- The possibility of making a capital gain if there is a fall in the exchange rate of sterling to the relevant currency.
- If the investor has a connection with the relevant country, it may be convenient to have some of the currency immediately available.

Disadvantages

- No protection against inflation.
- The additional risk of a capital loss if there is an increase in the exchange rate of sterling to the relevant currency.
- The rate of interest is often lower than on a sterling account.

Comment

Generally, not for average investors, unless they have a particular need to buy dollars, yen or whatever.

Offshore sterling accounts

Bank or building society accounts held in an offshore branch where the rate of Income Tax is very low.

Tax treatment

Investors will be liable to Income Tax at their appropriate rate on the gross amount.

Advantages

• The same as for bank and building society accounts, but with the additional advantage that interest is paid gross; they are therefore attractive to a non-taxpayer, such as a married woman with no other income.

Disadvantages

• See bank and building society accounts.

Comment

Only worth consideration by a non-taxpayer.

In the case of deposit and cash-based investments, as interest rates change regularly, it is usually a question of seeking out the best rate of return available at the time. A non-taxpayer will be looking for an investment which will pay interest gross; a taxpayer will simply be seeking the highest net return. Various publications (see Further Reading, p.263) carry details of the current returns available, the main ones also being available daily or weekly from the financial press.

Fixed interest and guaranteed investments

This section deals with investments whch offer a fixed income and those where the repayment value is guaranteed. These are particularly suitable for investors needing to know exactly how much they will receive in income each year and exactly what their capital will amount to when it is repaid. The overriding disadvantage of this type of investment is that (except for the Index-Linked Gifts, and index-linked National Savings Certificates) they offer no protection against the erosion of their real value (buying power) by inflation.

Gilts

These are securities issued by the Government which guarantee repayment of a fixed amount of capital (usually) on a fixed future date, and payment of a fixed amount of interest every six months in the meantime. There are one or two Gilts which do not have any repayment date, where the value will fluctuate with interest rates. There are also a few Gilts which are index-linked, so the income they generate is increased by the rate of inflation each year. The capital is also adjusted for inflation, so on the repayment date the capital value will have been increased by the amount of inflation during the lifetime of the stock.

Tax treatment

Income Tax is generally deducted from the interest paid, but interest will be paid gross on stocks purchased through the National Savings Register (obtainable through the Post Office). Also, any profit made on the sale or realization of Gilts is exempt from Capital Gains Tax.

Advantages

- Security; the amounts and dates of payments of the income are guaranteed, as is the capital repayment.
- The possibility of a tax-free profit when a Gilt is sold or redeemed.
- Full protection against inflation is available from the index-linked stocks, which also provide a small, but inflation-linked income.

Disadvantages

- No protection against inflation, except for index-linked stocks.
- The low initial income generated by index-linked stocks.

Comment

Particularly when interest rates are high, Gilts can provide a useful way of 'locking into' a high income with the prospect of tax-free capital gains. Index-linked Gilts offer full protection against inflation over the relevant period and are always worth consideration as part of a core holding (except for investors requiring maximum income).

Guaranteed Bonds

These are bonds issued by insurance companies, either as 'growth bonds', which guarantee a fixed rate of growth over a fixed number of years (usually between one and 10), or 'guaranteed income bonds', which guarantee the return of your capital in a fixed nmber of years, with a fixed income in the meantime. This income is usually paid annually, although some guaranteed income bonds (e.g. Midland Guaranteed Income Bonds) offer half-yearly income, and others, where over £5,000 is invested, offer monthly income at the cost of a slightly lower rate of return.

Tax treatment
This depends on the underlying contract arranged by the insurance company, which often involves annuities and/or single-premium endowment policies. Effectively, the income from the bonds can be regarded as net income, so a higher-rate taxpayer (but not a basic-rate taxpayer) will have some further tax liability.

Advantages

- A very high rate of return, often higher than building societies or any other form of guaranteed investment.
- The opportunity to lock into that high rate of return for the period chosen by the investor (up to 10 years).

Disadvantages

- No protection against inflation.
- The funds are locked in for the relevant period, unless the investor dies during that time.

Comment
A very attractive investment, especially in times of high interest rates, for those seeking high income for a two- to three-year period. Less attractive to higher-rate taxpayers or non-taxpayers.

National Savings Certificates (NSC)

Government securities issued by the Department for National Savings giving a fixed return over a fixed five-year period. The guarantee on the index-linked NSC is that the value will be adjusted by the rate of inflation plus (for the current issue) 4.5 per cent compound over the period.

Tax treatment
Proceeds entirely free of all taxes.

Advantages

- The tax exemption means that the net return of the current certificates is usually very attractive, especially to higher-rate taxpayers.
- Security; the capital value is guaranteed.
- Simplicity; no need to enter details on tax returns, etc.

- Tax-free annual 'income' can be produced by encashing certificates each year.

Disadvantages

- No protection against inflation, except on the index-linked certificates.
- To obtain the best return, the investment is effectively locked in for five years (early encashment will reduce the overall return).
- Relatively low maximum investment limit.

Comment

An attractive tax-free investment, especially for higher-rate taxpayers. The index-linked certificates could well form a core part of any investment portfolio.

Other National Savings products

As leaflets are readily available from the Post Office explaining the features of all the National Savings products, this section confines itself to giving a brief comment on only a selection.

National Savings Yearly Plan

This is a yearly savings contract offered by the Government, guaranteeing a tax-free return which is maximized if held for five years. The interest rate is guaranteed, fixed and free of all taxes, so this investment represents an attractive savings opportunity, particularly for higher-rate taxpayers.

National Savings Capital Bonds

The distinguishing feature of these bonds is that they guarantee a fixed return on which the interest is paid gross and 'compounded up' (not paid out) until a period of five years has elapsed. However, investors still pay tax annually on the interest accrued, even though they don't receive it for five years. In view of this, and the absence of any protection against inflation, these bonds are of limited benefit to most investors.

National Savings Income Bonds

On these bonds the interest is paid gross on a monthly basis, which makes them of interest to non-taxpayers. However, there is no protection against inflation, in addition to which the high minimum investment (£2,000) and the restrictions on withdrawals (three months' notice and a minimum of £1,000 per time) makes them less attractive than they might appear at first.

Children's Bonus Bonds
The tax-free return of 11.84 per cent is attractive initially, but the heavy penalty on withdrawals before the end of the five-year period, and the absence of protection against inflation, makes them less attractive than they might have been; there are certainly better opportunities elsewhere.

Premium Bonds
All investors will be familiar with ERNIE and his legal lottery. The obvious appeal is the chance of overnight riches when your number comes up, but the odds against this are extremely high, unless you hold the maximum number of bonds (£10,000). In that case, statistically you should receive around 10 prizes a year, all of which will be tax-free. This, plus the possibility of a larger prize, means that a holding of £10,000 is certainly worth consideration – at least by higher-rate payers and those who can afford to do without a guaranteed income – for the sake of a return which is much less secure but potentially more fun.

Annuities
An annuity is really the reverse of a savings plan, in that the life company receives the lump sum and the investor receives the regular payments. The investor effectively buys a regular income from the insurance company for a period consisting either of a fixed number of years, or by reference to the investor's lifetime (and that of his or her spouse as well, if required).

Taxation treatment
Each payment to the investor consists of a partial return of the capital (which is free from tax) and an interest element (which is subject to tax). A non-taxpayer can reclaim any tax deducted from the income portion, whereas a higher-rate taxpayer will be liable to an additional 15 per cent on this portion.

Advantages

- The fact that the capital portion is not subject to tax means that annuities offer a very attractive way of producing a high, frequent and guaranteed income, especially in three situations:
  (a) For the non-taxpayer (when the whole of the annuity will be tax-free).

    (b) For the older investor (say over 70) when annuity rates will be higher as the life expectancy is shorter.

    (c) When interest rates are high.

- Security. The payments are guaranteed for the relevant period. Investors who buy an annuity for life know that they will receive a regular income for the rest of their life (see below).

The Benefits of an Annuity

Beatrice, an 82-year-old widow who was not liable to tax, purchased a life annuity for £10,000. The annual amount of the annuity consisted of £2,000, of which £1,460 comprised a partial return of her capital (and was therefore tax-free) and the remaining £540 comprised interest (which in this case was tax-free as Beatrice was not liable to tax). The annuity therefore represented an annual return of 20 per cent on her original investment, and Beatrice had the security of enjoying an income of £167 per month for the rest of her life. By the time she was 85, she had received £10,000 back from the insurance company and therefore felt that she was making an excellent profit every year after that. She eventually died at the age of 102, having had the benefit and security of £167 per month for the last 20 years of her life. Of course, if she had died a year after taking out the annuity, it would have been the insurance company rather than Beatrice who made the profit.

- As the annuity produces a regular income (which can be paid quarterly or monthly if required), it can be combined with other savings plans and is especially useful in many of the packages used for such things as Inheritance Tax planning, school fees planning and retirement (see Chapters 2, 10 and 12).

Disadvantages

- The purchase of an annuity is final; investors cannot reverse the transaction and get their capital back.
- A normal annuity offers no protection against inflation, so the value of the payments will decrease in real terms as time goes by. It is possible to obtain an 'escalating' annuity which will increase each year, but this will reduce the initial level of the annuity.
- If the annuitant (the person who buys the annuity) dies sooner than expected, the total payments received may be less than the total amount which the annuitant invested. It is possible to buy a protected annuity (e.g. with a guaranteed minimum period), but again, only at the cost of a reduction in the initial payment.

Comment

Annuities are an extremely useful tool in financial planning; 'temporary' annuities (i.e. for a fixed term of, say, 10 years) can provide a useful way of funding regular savings policies, and life annuities can provide a very effective way of boosting the spendable income of elderly investors, especially those who will still have sufficient capital after buying the annuity.

Equity-based investments

In these investments the value is not guaranteed, but depends on the value of the underlying asset. A fund which invested in property, or in stocks and shares, would therefore be an 'equity-based fund'; its value would fluctuate from day to day in line with the changes in value of the properties and stocks and shares in which the fund had invested.

The term 'equities' is generally understood to be the Ordinary Shares of public companies which a private investor can buy and sell. The price of those shares is determined entirely by the laws of supply and demand. If there are more buyers than sellers, the price will go up; conversely, if there are more sellers than buyers the price will go down. The lack of guarantee means that you will often see the warning that 'prices can go down as well as up'.

So what determines whether there are more buyers than sellers? In the case of company shares, this comes down to investors' expectations of the company concerned and whether it is likely to make increasing profits. From the capital point of view, if the company continues to make increased profits, its value (and therefore the value of its shares) will increase. Similarly, from the income point of view, increased profits means that the company should be able to pay more dividends out to its shareholders; some companies have managed to increase their dividends steadily year after year. The accumulation of 'reserves' often enables companies to pay an increased dividend, even if the profit for that year is lower than for previous years.

As a result, someone who has invested in a sound, profitable company, is likely to enjoy two rewards: an increasing income each year (as the company pays out larger dividends), and an increase in the capital value of the investment as the price of the shares also increases. The following table shows how this applied to the dividends per share issued by Marks & Spencer and Shell over the last 10 years.

YEAR TO END DECEMBER 1990	MARKS & SPENCER Net Dividends (in pence per share)	SHELL Net Dividends (in pence per share)
1980	1.70	**5.50**
1981	1.90	5.90
1982	2.30	6.30
1983	2.55	7.60
1984	3.12	9.60
1985	3.40	11.70
1986	3.90	14.30
1987	4.50	16.00
1988	5.10	17.00
1989	5.60	18.40
1990	6.40	**20.10**

Table 1

So, if you had purchased 1,000 shares in Shell in 1980, your *income* in that year would have been £55 (1,000 × 5.50p). Each year the dividend would have increased, so the same investment of 1,000 shares would be producing a total £201 in income by 1990. Similarly, from the *capital* point of view, 1,000 shares in Shell would have cost £1,033 in 1980. In January 1991, those same shares would have been worth £4,530.

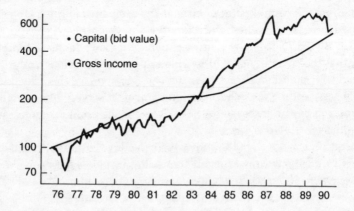

Figure 6

Shares which offer a rising income are obviously very attractive to investors, so as demand for the shares increases, the price of the shares (and therefore the capital of the investment) also rises. Figure 6 shows how the capital value of units in M & G Dividend Fund has followed the steadily rising income for the period from 1976 to 1990.

Figure 7 shows how, between 1972 and 1991, the income from a similar Unit Trust (Save & Prosper High Return Trust) has outstripped the return from a building society. It also illustrates how the building society interest has moved up and down in line with interest rates, but over the period has stayed within a narrow band, during which inflation has reduced its actual purchasing power substantially.

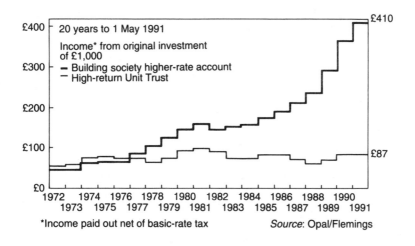

Figure 7

Finally, Figure 8 shows how the return from the FT All Share Index (the average of all shares quoted on the Stock Market) has outstripped the retail price index (effectively, the rate of inflation) over the last 25 years, and how the dividend income from the All Share Index similarly compares with the steadily increasing retail price index over this period.

Figures 6, 7 and 8 all serve to illustrate how good equities can provide protection against the ravages of inflation by offering prospects of a regularly increasing income, together with possibilities of capital growth. However, it cannot be overemphasized that neither of these attractions (income growth and capital growth) are guaranteed. Companies' profits (and therefore ultimately the dividends they pay and the value of their shares) can be affected by many things: interest rates, political

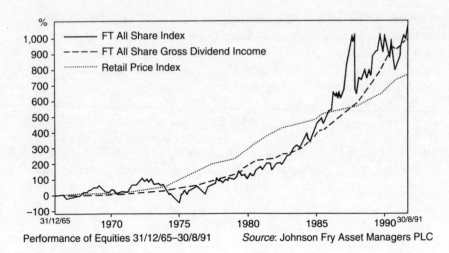

Performance of Equities 31/12/65–30/8/91　　*Source*: Johnson Fry Asset Managers PLC

Figure 8

developments, mismanagement, shrinking markets, changes in fashion
. . . Just as there are outstanding companies which have provided ample
rewards to shareholders over the years, there are equally well-known
names, such as ICI and Midland Bank, where the dividends have had to
be reduced on occasions and, even worse, other companies, such as
British & Commonwealth, Coloroll and Polly Peck, where investors lost
all their capital.

Investing in individual companies, rather than a range of companies
through a collective investment vehicle such as a Unit Trust or
Investment Trust, obviously involves a greater degree of risk. However,
the equity-based investments discussed below could well be of interest
to someone who has inherited a capital sum and is prepared to incur
some degree of risk in exchange for the prospects of outstripping
inflation and obtaining capital growth and/or income growth.

Ordinary Shares

Holders of Ordinary Shares collectively own the company and are
therefore entitled to share in its income and profits, and to share in any
surplus assets should it be wound up.

Taxation treatment

The company pays a net dividend on which basic-rate tax has been paid,
so a non-taxpayer can claim repayment of this 'tax credit'. A higher-rate

taxpayer will be liable for an additional 15 per cent. A sale of the shares will give rise to either a profit or loss for CGT purposes.

Advantages

- Prospects for unlimited capital growth.
- Prospects for obtaining a rising income.
- A vast number of quoted shares and a ready market, offering a wide choice and scope for investors, who can also follow the performance of their shares in the daily newspapers.

Disadvantages

- The main disadvantage of any equity investment is the lack of guarantee and the possibility of capital loss and/or a reduction in income.
- There are costs and expenses involved in buying and selling shares, but they are not great. Brokers' minimum commission of around £20 means that it is hardly economic to buy less than, say, £300 worth of shares.

A DIY Dealing Service

Investors who require only an economic dealing service with no professional advice, can utilize Sharelink, a computerized direct dealing service which enables them to buy or sell shares through a telephone or fax.

During 1992 the Stock Exchange will introduce TAURUS, a new computer-based system of recording all transfers and registration of shares. The practical consequence for investors will be the gradual replacement of share certificates by regular statements, similar to bank statements, and the introduction of a private investor code, equivalent to a personal identification number. However, share dealings will still be effected through a regulated broker, bank, or share dealing service such as Sharelink.

Comment

Investing in individual equities offers perhaps more interest, excitement and potential rewards, but also greater risks, than investing in a collective investment vehicle such as a Unit Trust or Investment Trust. Generally, equity investment (whether in individual shares or through a Unit Trust or Investment Trust) should be regarded as a medium- to long-term investment (say three years or more). Except in special circumstances, equities should not be bought for the short term, or with funds which may be required at short notice.

Inherited Shares: Sell or Keep?

Beneficiaries often wonder whether they should (or must) keep shares included in an estate which has been bequeathed to them. If you are in this position, you may accept the shares or ask the PRs to sell them for you and distribute the cash. Although there are no hard and fast rules, two points should be borne in mind in this situation.

First, never keep a share just because you have inherited it, or because there would be no costs or brokers' fees involved in the transfer of shares on death. A sound investment principle (in any situation, not just inheritance) is that you should only keep shares which, if you not did already own them, you would be prepared to purchase at the current price. If you would not wish to purchase that particular share at that price, you should sell it and buy another investment which you regard as a good buy. Do not keep shares just because you have them.

Second, if the shares are to be sold, you may incur Capital Gains Tax or Inheritance Tax, depending on whether the shares are sold by the PRs before distributing the estate, or whether they are acquired by you at probate value and subsequently sold. It would therefore be sensible to obtain professional advice on this before arranging for a transfer or sale of the shares.

Convertible Unsecured Loan Stocks, Preference Shares and Capital Bonds

These are an often overlooked, but nevertheless attractive, type of 'delayed' equity investment. They can offer the best of both worlds to investors, namely a fixed income and a fixed capital entitlement in their original form, but the right to 'convert' the original stock into a fixed number of Ordinary Shares at a predetermined price.

Taxation treatment
Income is paid net after tax; sales may give rise to capital gains or capital losses.

Advantages

• The main advantage of this type of holding is that it offers the greater security (and usually higher income) available from a Loan Stock or Preference Share while preserving the possibility of sharing in future capital growth and income growth through the right to convert into Ordinary Shares at some future date.

Disadvantages

- There is usually a premium payable for converting into Ordinary Shares (see box below).

In 1985 Shires Investment Trust issued some 11 per cent Convertible Loan Stock which could be converted into Ordinary Shares between 1988 and 2003 on the basis of one Ordinary Share for every £2 of Loan Stock. At that time the respective values and income from a holding of, say, £1,000 Convertible Loan Stock and 500 Ordinary Shares (into which the Loan Stock could be converted) was:

	£1,000 Convertible Loan Stock	500 Ordinary Shares
Capital value	£,1000	£800
Income	£82.50 (net)	£60 (net)

At that time, therefore, it would not have been worth converting the Loan Stock since an investor would have suffered a reduction of approximately £200 in capital value and a reduction of over £20 in income. However, since then the price of both the Loan Stock and the Ordinary Shares has increased, and in November 1991 the position was:

	£1,000 Convertible Loan Stock	500 Ordinary Shares
Capital value	£1,145	£1,125
Income	£82.50 (net)	£90 (net)

By converting, therefore, the investor would 'catch up' on the capital growth on the Ordinary Shares and would also enjoy an increased income, having had the greater security of the Loan Stock in the meantime. If the price of the Ordinary Shares had gone down rather than up, the investor would simply have retained the Loan Stock until it was repaid at full face value (i.e. £1,000) in the year 2003.

However, as compensation the Loan Stock holders receive a higher income than the holders of the Ordinary Shares.

Comment

These convertible investments often represent an attractive compromise to investors hoping for capital growth in the long run but preferring a more secure investment with a higher and more certain income in the short term.

Unit Trusts

These are 'collective investment vehicles', offering a way of investing in a wide spread of shares held by trustees and managed by professional investment managers.

Taxation treatment

The same as Ordinary Shares (as far as investors are concerned); within the fund, however, capital gains are exempt from CGT (which should help to improve the fund's performance), but investors are still liable to CGT on any profits in excess of their annual exemption.

Advantages

- Prospects of capital growth and income growth, as with Ordinary Shares.
- The risk is substantially reduced by the spread of investments.
- Professional investment management available at reasonable cost.
- Simplicity and convenience; all the normal paperwork in connection with the underlying portfolio of shares is taken care of by the managers.
- Units are easily marketable and as dealings are direct with the managers, the absence of brokers' expenses means that small holdings are not necessarily uneconomic.
- Unit Trusts are highly regulated and perhaps offer the least risky way of investing in the equity market.
- Regular monthly savings plans are available; these represent a particularly attractive, flexible and cost-effective method of building up capital on a long-term basis.

Disadvantages

- The risk factor; capital values and income can fall as well as rise, although the wide spread of investments within the fund reduces the risk substantially.
- Conversely, the wide spread of investment also reduces the chance of spectacular gains (such as may be available on a shareholding in a company which receives a takeover bid).
- Costs; in addition to the annual management charges (around 1 per cent), there is a 'bid/offer spread' of around 5 per cent. In other words, units might be 'offered' at 100p each, but if you were to sell the units on the same day, the managers would 'bid' a price of only 95p for your units.

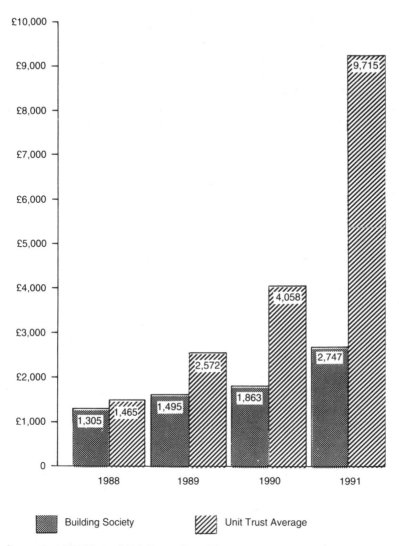

Building Society   Unit Trust Average

Source: To 1.8.91 Micropal. Unit Trust, offer to bid, net income re-invested.
Building Society ordinary share account. (Assumes that the investor pays basic-rate tax).

Figure 9

Comment

Unit Trusts represent a simple and reasonably attractive way of investing in a wide spread of equities, including overseas investments if required. They are therefore a strong candidate for inclusion in any equity-based portfolio where the investor is looking for capital growth and perhaps income growth, but with a wider spread of investments and a greater degree of security than direct investment into Ordinary Shares. However, you should still take care in selecting the appropriate Unit Trust: at the time of writing, the best-performing Unit Trust would have turned an investment of £1,000 into £7,803 over the last seven years, whereas £1,000 invested in the worst-performing Unit Trust would be worth only £242 over the same period.

Investment Trusts

These are also collective investment vehicles that enable you to invest in a wide portfolio of shares which are professionally managed. However, an Investment Trust is itself a public company whose assets consist wholly of shares in other companies.

Taxation treatment

Effectively (as far as the investor is concerned) the same as Unit Trusts.

Advantages and Disadvantages

These are also similar to those listed under Unit Trusts above. The dividend growth from most investment trusts has been impressive. For example, Figure 10 below shows the dividend record of one of the largest investment trusts, Foreign and Colonial, over the 10 years to 1989.

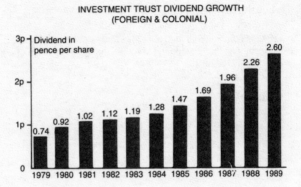

INVESTMENT TRUST DIVIDEND GROWTH
(FOREIGN & COLONIAL)

Figure 10

Equally notable has been the capital growth; over the 10 years to the end of 1990 £1,000 in an average building society account (with interest reinvested) would be worth £2,390 at the end of 10 years, but £1,000 in the *average* investment trust would have been worth £4,900 (£1,000 in the best performing trust would have been worth over £10,000). Owing to the difference in structure, however, Investment Trusts offer additional advantages which often make them a more attractive prospect to the individual investor:

- The buying costs are often lower than Unit Trusts.
- The shares of an Investment Trust sometimes stand at a discount, i.e. below the net asset value per share; in those cases, an investor buying £100 worth of shares may have £110 working for him.
- Investment Trusts are allowed to borrow (which Unit Trusts are not); the ability to obtain more funds to work for shareholders' benefit can improve the performance of the Investment Trust especially in rising markets. However, the converse can be true, especially in falling markets, or when interest rates are high. To that extent Investment Trusts have a slightly higher degree of risk than Unit Trusts.
- In the last two or three years several Investment Trusts have adopted new 'split' structures. This has enabled them to offer a much wider range of investment choice to cater for almost every requirement investors might have. These include:
  - Zero-Dividend Shares for virtually guaranteed capital growth, but with no income in the meantime;
  - Income Shares, which offer a high income with good prospects for regular future increases, but little capital growth;
  - Stepped Preference Shares, which offer a pre-determined level (usually 5 per cent compound), of annual increases in dividend, plus a pre-determined repayment value and date (for investors wanting a regularly increasing income with less risk but still some degree of capital growth).

Comment

Figure 11 (p.123) shows the difference between Investment Trusts and Unit Trusts. There is now an appropriate Investment Trust for almost every type of investor. Anyone who inherits money, some of which is to be invested for the future, should seriously consider including one or more Investment Trusts within a portfolio. Professional advice should be obtained regarding the actual selection, of course.

Personal Equity Plans (PEPs)

These represent the Government's efforts to encourage more individuals to acquire equities; a PEP is therefore a tax-free wrapping around an equity-based investment such as shares, Unit Trusts, or Investment Trusts. Because of the substantial tax advantages, certain restrictions apply:

- The current maximum investment in a PEP is £6,000 plus (from January 1992) a further £3,000 into a 'single company' PEP in any one tax year.
- The underlying investments must be UK Companies or Unit Trusts/Investment Trusts with at least 50 per cent invested in the UK. Generally, no more than £3,000 of the £6,000 can be invested in Unit Trusts or Investment Trusts (except for new issues).
- PEPs are restricted to UK residents over 18, so you can't buy PEPs for a child.

As a one-off investment, a PEP is an attractive, tax-free way of acquiring shares in individual companies, Unit Trusts or Investment Trusts, but as a series of plans, PEPs represent an extremely advantageous way of allowing you to build up a substantial tax-free fund. A couple contributing the maximum amount (£9,000 p.a. each) will, after four years, have invested £72,000 in a totally tax-free fund.

Taxation treatment

Dividends and interest on cash within the PEP are entirely free from Income Tax. All profits made within the PEP are entirely free from Capital Gains Tax.

Advantages

- Freedom from Income Tax and Capital Gains Tax should allow a greater growth rate within the fund; assuming a growth rate of 13 per cent compound, after 10 years, an initial investment of £1,000 would be worth £3,063. A regular investment of £100 per month, growing at 13 per cent, would be worth over £21,000 by the end of 10 years – in an entirely tax-free fund.
- You can invest either a lump sum or by monthly subscriptions up to the limit each year.
- Flexibility; PEPs represent ideal savings vehicles which can be used in connection with repaying a mortgage, as an alternative to a pension, or planning for school fees.
- The investment is not locked in; PEPs can be encashed at any time and a regular income can also be withdrawn if required.
- Variety; a PEP offers a wide choice of investments, so that you can have:
  - a wide spread of underlying shares (through a Unit Trust or Investment Trust);
  - a narrow spread, say half a dozen Blue Chip equities selected by the PEP managers;
  - a self-select plan, where you choose your own individual shares, or a combination, say half in a Unit Trust and half in two or three shares of your own choice.

  Environmentally aware investors can also choose a 'Green PEP', investing only in companies selected for their ethical or positive environmental approach.
- Freedom from paperwork; there is no need for you to keep records or to declare any income or profits to the taxman.

Disadvantages

- The risk element which is present in any equity-based portfolio, especially if in individual shares; equity prices can go down as well as up.
- The limitation on the underlying investments, and the restrictions of only one PEP per UK resident adult per year.
- Political vulnerability; a Labour Government would be unlikely to allow PEPs to continue in their present form.
- The manager's charges; these can be up to 6 per cent for initial charges and up to 1.5 per cent annual charge, but they are usually more than offset by the saving in Income Tax alone.

Comment

Because of freedom from tax, PEPs represent an ideal method of building up a sound equity-based portfolio in a tax-free fund, especially if it is maintained on a long-term basis; PEPs should therefore be the first consideration for any investor requiring a stake in equities. They are especially attractive to higher-rate taxpayers, but because they are politically vulnerable they should perhaps be regarded on a 'buy now while stocks last' basis.

Business Expansion Schemes (BES)

These represent another equity-based investment with tax advantages – in this case the tax relief is given on the amount invested – plus freedom from Capital Gains Tax on the proceeds of sale. The investment must be either directly into an unquoted BES company, or via a collective fund whose managers invest in several such companies.

Taxation treatment

Income Tax relief is given at the investors' highest rate on the amount invested (minimum £500, maximum £40,000) in any tax year. The investor sets the amount invested against his or her total income, so an investment of, say, £1,000 by a higher-rate taxpayer costs only £600 because the tax bill is immediately reduced by £400.

If the shares are retained for five years, no CGT is payable on any profit (which can be substantial).

Advantages

- BES offers an opportunity to get in at ground level on a new business which may flourish, with the benefit of tax relief on the original investment.
- Because of the tax advantages, there are prospects for greater growth in the value of the original investment.

INVESTMENT TRUST VERSUS UNIT TRUST

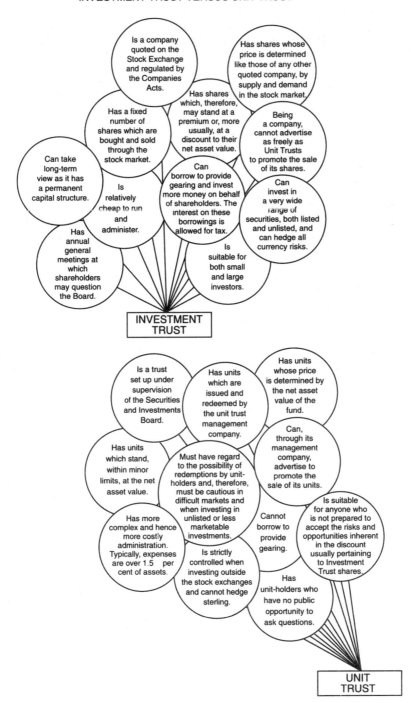

Figure 11 INVESTMENT TRUST VERSUS UNIT TRUST

Disadvantages

- There is a risk element in any equity investment, and because BES companies are generally new ventures, the risk element is often much higher. However, certain BES companies which invest in property (Assured Tenancy Schemes, often with a commitment from a housing association to buy back the properties after five years), offer greater security.
- The schemes are politically vulnerable and likely to be altered if and when there is a change of Government.
- There is a five-year 'lock-in' before the benefit of CGT relief is available.
- Relatively high management charges.
- Absence of any dividends, although some Assured Tenancy Schemes are able to pay dividends out of the rents received.
- Delay before the issue of the certificates which entitle the investor to Income Tax relief.

Comment

BES Schemes generally represent a high-risk, high-reward investment opportunity, especially attractive to the higher-rate taxpayer. However, the Assured Tenancy Schemes (while available) are also worth consideration by a basic-rate payer.

Property

Although property could be described as an equity-based investment since the price varies according to supply and demand, this particular topic is dealt with in more detail in Chapter 8. However, the following table attempts to explain the possible methods and some of the points to bear in mind.

Investing in Property		
	RESIDENTIAL	COMMERCIAL/INDUSTRIAL
Owner occupation	Principal private residence • CGT exemption • Income Tax relief on loan interest up to £30,000	Occupied by own business • Income Tax relief on loan interest no limit

Occupied by others		
A DIRECT	Protected or assured tenancies • Income Tax on rents • Manangement responsibilities • Tenants' security of tenure? • Restrictions on rent increases	Business tenancies • Income Tax • Management responsibilities • Tenants' security of tenure? • Restrictions on rent increases
B INDIRECT	• Shares in property company • Shares in Assured Tenancy BES company • Units in residential property fund	• Shares in property company • Shares in Enterprise Zone • Units in commercial property fund

Enterprise Zones

Although relatively obscure, these are certainly worth considering as an investment, particularly for higher-rate taxpayers who can afford to see their funds tied up for some years. Enterprise Zones are areas of the country where the Government has allowed 100 per cent tax allowances on buildings in order to attract industry. From the investment point of view, they effectively comprise property-based tax shelters which the investor can purchase either outright or through a syndicate. The latter is more comon for individual investors, for whom the main attraction is the tax relief on the amount invested.

Taxation treatment

Investors obtain Income Tax relief at their highest rate on the cost (or their share of the cost) of the building, not the land, so a higher-rate payer investing £10,000 in an Enterprise Zone syndicate would get £4,000 tax relief; the investment would therefore have cost only £6,000.

- Income Tax relief is also available on moneys borrowed by the investor to invest in an Enterprise Zone.
- Income Tax will be payable on the rental income received by the investor.

Advantages

- Investment in commercial property with benefit of Income Tax relief at top rate on the amount invested.

- No limit on the amount of relief (unlike BES Schemes, which are limited to £40,000).
- Prospects for capital growth.
- Investors can receive an income comprising their share of the rental.
- Income Tax relief on moneys borrowed for the investment.

Disadvantages

- Even more of a lock-in than normal property; if the building is sold within 25 years, there is a balancing charge, which would effectively cancel out much of the original tax relief, but there is a technical way round this (outside the scope of this book). Seek professional advice.
- As with other property investments, there is the risk that the value of the buildings will fall rather than rise and the (small) risk of the tenants defaulting.

Comment

A useful addition to the range of investments, particularly for a higher-rate taxpayer prepared to take a medium-term view.

Alternative investments not producing income

An inheritance might be just the thing to stimulate your interest in any of the loose collection of items that fall under the heading 'alternative investments', particularly as many of them derive from special interests or hobbies. As mentioned in Chapter 5, investments don't just consist of money and securities; a child stamp collector, for example, may well develop into a millionaire philatelist.

You can invest any amount of money in alternative investments and, provided you know what you are doing, you may be able to profit from them in terms of both money and enjoyment. Such investments can be divided into four categories:

1. Collectibles.
2. Commodities.
3. Futures and options.
4. Woodlands and agricultural land.

Collectibles

Anything collected by collectors will have a value; as long as there are buyers and sellers around, there is a market, albeit a narrow one. Generally, the more exotic the items, the narrower the market. As with Ordinary Shares, the items will range from Blue Chip to highly speculative investments, and may include any of the following:

Stamps
Fine wines
Works of art (paintings, prints, sculptures etc.)
Vintage cars
Antique furniture
Scent bottles
Oriental carpets/rugs
Toys
Books
Postcards
Ceramics
Maps
Memorabilia (e.g. Charlie Chaplin's bowler hat)
Old coins
Jewellery/diamonds
Precious metals

Most of these items are tangible and portable, and the markets in them are highly specialist. However, certain general points apply to them all.

- They are mainly long-term investments.
- They produce no income; the appeal to the investor is the prospect of capital appreciation, but even then, some turnover will be necessary. (If a Penny Black were to double in value every five years, the investor would not derive any financial benefit unless it was actually sold.)
- The markets are driven not only by supply and demand, but by other forces, such as fashion, sentiment and whim.
- High costs are often involved: on purchase, on sale, security and insurance.
- Liquidity difficulties; there can often be a delay in realizing the investment.
- For tax purposes collectibles will usually qualify as chattels so the £6,000 exemption from Capital Gains Tax will usually apply. For example, if a couple jointly built up a substantial collection of books which originally cost £10,000 but are now worth

£50,000, they could sell the collection in 'parcels', producing up to £12,000 gain per year over three or four years.

- Any collectibles left in the estate of a deceased person will have to be valued at the market value and will be liable to Inheritance Tax. Collectibles therefore represent suitable items to be given away by wealthy elderly collectors who wish to reduce their Inheritance Tax. First, it is sensible to give away items which are likely to appreciate in value; second, the investor will not suffer any loss of income if the assets given away did not produce any income; and third, it should also be possible to avoid Capital Gains Tax on the gift.

Investing in collectibles

You should invest in these types of assets only if you are personally interested and acquire a knowledge of the relevant markets. The main reward in investing in collectibles can be the interest and enjoyment obtained, rather than the financial profit, although often both are available.

Go for quality rather than quantity, as this offers more investment potential, not to mention the saving in time and space.

Finally, maintain proper protection for the assets, such as insurance and alarm systems.

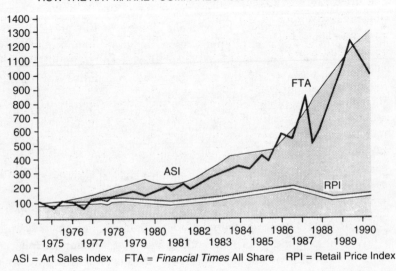

HOW THE ART MARKET COMPARES TO STOCKS AND SHARES

ASI = Art Sales Index   FTA = *Financial Times* All Share   RPI = Retail Price Index

Commodities

These may be broadly defined as articles of trade and commerce, and are usually split into 'soft' commodities, such as coffee and sugar, and 'hard' commodities, such as copper and tin. The price fluctuates according to supply and demand. From the investment point of view, the most common (but riskiest) way to invest is via the Futures Market (see below). However, investors can buy commodities direct or (more usually) can buy shares via either a commodity syndicate (managed by commodity brokers) or via a Unit Trust investing in commodities, which gives a wider spread of risk.

Even so, as tax (either Income Tax or CGT) will be payable on profits made by the investor – and as the risk element is very high – commodity investment should be left to the very wealthy who are prepared to accept that high degree of risk.

Futures and Options

These are effectively tradable bets on which way the markets in certain items or commodities will go over a fixed future period. Investors who consider that a share or a standard commodity (such as gold, coffee or even pork bellies) will be higher in, say, six months time, can buy a contract entitling them to purchase by that fixed date the share or commodity at a price fixed now (at the date of the contract). If, before the expiry date, the price has risen, the investors will sell or close their bet and take the profit, which could be many times the original stake. If the price has fallen, they will simply lose the value of their original stake. Clearly, such investments are extremely volatile and speculative, ranking only a short head above a gamble at roulette. As such, they are recommended only for sophisticated investors who can afford to lose capital.

However, an investor who does not mind an exciting ride might be interested in investing in futures via a Managed Futures Fund, which is one way of diluting the risk, especially in some managed funds which include a 'no loss guarantee'. Similarly, 'traded options' can be used as a hedge against substantial movements (up or down) in the share price of certain companies. The mechanics of futures and options are outside the scope of this book, but they may be of interest to the substantial investor who is prepared to incur more risk for the sake of larger potential rewards, or who wishes to hedge the value of his shares against exceptionally large movements in the price.

Woodlands and agricultural property

Buying a farm or a forest might seem a peculiar suggestion for investing inherited moneys. However, in the event of a large inheritance, it could be worth consideration, especially for higher-rate taxpayers, or those who have large estates and want to save Inheritance Tax.

In the case of a farm, the tax advantages only arise where you farm the land yourself, so you would have to invest time, skill and knowledge, as well as cash. Should you do this, it is possible to obtain Income Tax, CGT and IHT advantages, but the details are outside the scope of this book, and you would need detailed professional advice in any event.

In the case of a woodland, owning and working it yourself is not necessarily out of the question, especially as it is possible to subcontract much of the management to a forestry consultant. However, it is more usual to invest indirectly through a forestry investment syndicate. This will still enable the investor to obtain Income Tax, CGT and IHT advantages, but these will reduce after 5 April 1993 when woodlands become tax neutral for Income Tax purposes (there will be no Income Tax relief on the costs, but no Income Tax liability on the proceeds of sale of the timber). Timber is the UK's fourth biggest import (currently in excess of £7,000 million p.a.) and demand is anticipated to continue exceeding supply. It is reasonable therefore to anticipate steady growth, both in the value of timber and in the value of the land on which it grows.

Advantages

- Woodlands should be regarded as a long-term investment.
- After 1993 income from the sales of timber will not be liable to Income Tax or CGT.
- There are IHT advantages in owning woodlands; they are treated as a business so that the Business Property Relief will usually produce a 50 per cent reduction in valuation for IHT purposes.
- Amenity benefits in kind, such as rights to shooting, fishing and walking.
- Government grants are available towards the cost of planting.

Disadvantages

- After 1993 there will be no Income Tax relief on expenses (which can be substantial).
- No income from the investment, until the first sale of 'thinnings', many years after the original planting.

- Marketability; there can be substantial delays in realizing the investment.

Comment

Especially in view of the tax advantages, woodlands can represent a very attractive long-term investment for higher-rate taxpayers. Also the minimum investment (through a syndicate) is not excessive – say around £5,000, as compared with, say, £50,000 which would be the absolute minimum for a direct purchase of woodland of any worthwhile size.

Insurance-based Investments

Although investments linked to insurance policies do offer life insurance cover, this is an incidental bonus and not the main point of the contract. The important thing is the underlying investment, which just happens to be 'clothed' in an insurance policy. The distinction between these unitized funds (where the fund is divided into units and each policy holder is allocated a proportionate number of the units to his or her policy) and other collective investments, such as Unit Trusts and Investment Trusts, is in the tax treatment rather than in the underlying purpose of the funds. Contributions to insurance-based investments will consist of premiums which will be either *regular* (payable for a set number of years) or *single* (lump sum investments).

The insurance funds themselves will be either *with profits*, which means they are guaranteed not to fall in value and will attract an annual bonus and often a terminal bonus as well, or *unit-linked*, where the premium is invested in one of several funds, such as an equity fund, a property fund or an international fund. Units in the fund are then allocated to the policy and the value of the policy will fluctuate with the rise or fall in the value of the units.

Choosing the appropriate insurance-based investment is therefore a question of perming any two from four, as follows:

A regular premium with-profits policy.

A regular premium unit-linked policy.

A single premium with-profits policy.

A single premium unit-linked policy.

In each case the investor pays money (the premium) to the insurance company, who invest it in the appropriate fund (with profit or the relevant unit-linked fund), in which the investor participates via the policy or (in the case of a single premium policy) the bond. On a with-profit policy or bond the investor waits for the annual and terminal bonuses to be allocated, but knows that the value cannot fall. On a unit-linked policy the investor knows that the value of the policy will fluctuate according to the variation in the price of the units, which can be followed in the financial press.

Single-Premium Bonds

Let us look first at lump sum insurance-based investments – Single Premium Bonds. Although effectively a collective investment, similar to a Unit Trust or Investment Trust in intention, there are important differences.

Life Cover
The insurance bonds carry life cover, but this is usually limited to 100 per cent or 150 per cent of the initial investment – effectively a guarantee of money back in the event of death. Unit Trusts and Investment Trusts do not include life cover.

Initial Expenses
The initial charges on an insurance bond are often 5 or 6 per cent, plus 1 per cent per annum management charges. The charges on a Unit Trust are usually lower, and lower still on an Investment Trust.

Tax within the Fund
Income Tax and Capital Gains Tax are both payable at 25 per cent on income and capital gains within the insurance company's fund. Unit Trusts and Investment Trusts are exempt from Capital Gains Tax, which should enable them to produce a better growth rate within the fund.

Tax on Income received by the Investor
Unit Trusts and Investment Trusts deduct tax at 25 per cent from their income; investors receive a tax credit for this amount and, if they are liable to higher rates, they pay higher-rate tax on the gross amount. With a single premium bond, however, any income consists of a partial encashment – 'withdrawal' from the policy – to which these rules apply:

- If the withdrawal is less than 5 per cent, there is no tax liability at all, even for higher-rate taxpayers.
- If the withdrawal is more than 5 per cent, there is no liability on a basic-rate taxpayer, but there will be some Income Tax liability on a higher-rate taxpayer.
- The 5 per cent per annum exemption is cumulative, so if investors do not make a withdrawal one year, they could withdraw 10

per cent without tax liability the next year. After 20 years any further withdrawals may be taxable on a higher-rate taxpayer, but investors normally liable to higher-rate tax can choose to encash their policy in a year when they are liable only at basic rates.

Tax Position on Encashing the Investment

An investor who encashes a Unit Trust or Investment Trust pays Capital Gains Tax if the profit (after indexation relief) exceeds the annual allowance (currently £5,500). With a ᴗingle Premium Bond the investor is not liable to CGT, but may be liable to higher-rate income tax. The profit on the bond is divided by the number of years for which the bond has been held. This figure is then added to the investor's income for the year of encashment. If the total exceeds the basic-rate threshold (currently £23,700), the investor is liable to higher-rate tax on the profit. If the basic-rate threshold is not exceeded, a basic-rate taxpayer has no tax liability on encashing the bond.

On balance, the above differences suggest that Unit Trusts or Investment Trusts would be a better choice, especially for a basic-rate taxpayer, but the single premium insurance bonds offer other things which may appeal more to certain investors.

Advantages

- An insurance bond offers a wide choice of funds, including in many cases a with-profits fund, which cannot fall in value and can only increase as the annual bonuses are declared. Several funds also offer a terminal bonus.
- Switching (transferring from one fund to another) is simpler and cheaper; often the first switch is free, with a small fixed charge of £15 or so for subsequent switches. In a unit trust or investment trust, switching involves selling the units (with possible CGT consequences) and reinvesting, with at least part of the normal bid/offer spread being incurred in the case of unit trusts.
- Roll-up facility: higher-rate taxpayers can allow their profits to remain in the bond and so defer or avoid tax on the profits. In times of uncertainty they could ask the fund managers to switch their investment from the equity fund, for example, into the cash fund, but without incurring any personal tax liability at that stage. Also a higher-rate taxpayer could invest funds in the bond which would accumulate after being taxed at 25 per cent; the

investor could then delay encashing the bond until, for example, after retirement, when he or she might be only a basic-rate taxpayer so that the proceeds would also be free of tax.

- For the purposes of age allowance, withdrawals from a Single Premium Bond do not count as income, so they will not bring the investor within the Age Allowance trap (see p.77).

Comment

Single Premium Bonds can be quite attractive to higher-rate taxpayers. Investors can allow gains to 'roll up' within the fund, taxed only at 25 per cent, which is attractive to higher rate taxpayers; however, any losses on a sale of the bond cannot be offset against other gains of the investor.

Those bonds can provide a tax-efficient income by withdrawing up to 5 per cent of the value each year.

This means that they can also be useful 'feeders' (i.e. investments which can 'feed' regular annual or monthly payments) into other savings contracts, such as a 10-year qualifying policy (see below) to provide school fees, or a Capital Conversion Plan (see Chapter 10) to save Inheritance Tax.

Several Single Premium Bonds have recently been issued with a 'no loss guarantee', which effectively means that on the repayment date (typically in five years' time) the investor will receive at least as much as the amount of the original investment, even if prices have fallen. This type of guarantee obviously reduces the risk element in any equity-based investment, but as the guarantee has to be paid for, it also reduces the reward element as well, in that the investor will forfeit a small proportion of any capital growth as the price for having the guarantee. Fine for ultra-cautious investors who are prepared to sacrifice some growth prospects in order to limit their possible losses.

Broker Bonds

These are effectively Single Premium Bonds which are under the control or management of a particular professional adviser or broker. The broker levies an extra charge for managing the funds on the basis that this additional tier of management is likely to produce a better performance, perhaps by switching the funds more actively. Many people, however, are cynical about the value of introducing another tier of management, and the performance figures do not make it clear whether Broker Bonds do produce a sufficiently better performance to warrant the additional costs incurred.

Regular Premium Insurance Policies and Qualifying Policies

Regular premium simply means that the investors commit themselves to paying a regular amount to the insurance company over a fixed period, usually a number of years. If the fund is with profits, it cannot reduce in value, as the value increases by the annual bonuses, which are guaranteed and cannot be taken away. They may also increase by the terminal bonus applied to the policy. If the fund is unit-linked, the value of the policy will depend entirely on the value of the fund to which it is linked.

Most regular policies will be Qualifying Life Policies. For a Qualifying Life Policy premiums must be payable for at least 10 years and certain other conditions must apply, the effect of which is, broadly, to ensure that the policy offers a minimum amount of death cover, and is not just a savings plan disguised as a life policy. The advantage of a Qualifying Life Policy is that it is tax-free on its surrender, assignment or maturity. If the premium-paying period is less than 10 years, the policy will be a Non-Qualifying Policy, which means that the proceeds will not enjoy the same freedom from tax (see p.133) applicable to Single Premium Bonds. A common Qualifying Life Policy is an Endowment Policy, which provides life cover at a much more generous level than Investment Bonds, and an investment element to provide a worthwhile lump sum at the end of the fixed term.

With-profits policies are therefore sound investment vehicles for the cautious investor prepared to undertake a long-term savings plan. Unit-linked policies are slightly less certain, offering better growth prospects but more risk. In either case, you should not really effect a policy unless you check the surrender penalties first and are confident that you will be able to keep up the payments for the full period.

Because of their nature, Endowment Policies (whether with profits or unit-linked) represent a popular way of ensuring the repayment of mortgage loans, but they are not necessarily the best means of doing so. Statistics show that over 70 per cent of Endowment Policies are surrendered before their maturity date, and the surrender value is low.

Surrendering an Endowment Policy

- Don't; if possible, obtain the funds elsewhere as the cost is likely to be less than the cost of surrendering a policy.
- If the intention is merely to avoid paying the premiums, make the policy paid up rather than surrendering it; this means it will at least continue to qualify for bonuses on the paid-up value.
- If you have no alternative and need the funds, arrange to sell it

through one of the specialist auction houses; this will probably produce a substantially larger sum than you would obtain from surrendering the policy (see Second-hand policies below).

If you have inherited funds which you are seeking to reinvest, a Qualifying Life Policy, such as an Endowment Policy, is worth considering, but see Chapter 10 on Financial Packages; you may be better off with separate contracts to cover your investment requirements and your life cover requirements. Endowment Policies are a bit like music centres – they offer the convenience of an all-in-one package, but the person who takes the trouble to buy a separate tuner, amplifier, CD and speakers may end up with a much more impressive purchase. Similarly, an investor needing both life cover and investment returns might be better advised to obtain them separately – perhaps term cover for life protection and a series of Personal Equity Plans for investment – rather than go for the package deal.

Second-hand Policies

This is another little-known investment with fairly low risk, but it has considerable attractions as a savings vehicle to produce a capital sum in a fixed number of years. The investment simply consists of buying an existing policy on the life of someone else ('the Assured'). An Assured who wishes to encash his or her policy or cannot afford to keep it going can either surrender the policy or arrange to sell it through one of the few firms specializing in this area.

Case History

In May 1978 Julie took out a 20-year With-Profits Endowment Policy with Standard Life for a basic sum assured of £5,000 at an annual premium of £300. By December 1991 (when Julie has paid £4,200) she wishes to surrender the policy. The insurance company quotes her a surrender value of £8,200. Julie arranges to sell the policy through one of the specialist firms. They obtain for her a price of £10,800 – £2,600 more than she would have received by surrendering the policy.

The purchaser, Robert, now owns the policy on Julie's life. Provided he continues to pay the premiums of £300 for the remaining seven years of the policy, when the policy matures in May 1998, he will receive the full maturity value together with all accrued bonuses and any terminal bonus. Realistically, Robert could expect to receive a sum in excess of £30,000 (depending on the future bonus rates declared by the insurance company). On these figures, he would have made an attractive profit on his outlay of £10,800 purchase price plus £2,100 (seven premiums of £300 each) – a return of over 14.5 per cent.

C

Advantages

From the seller's point of view:

- Greater profit than simply surrendering the policy.

From the buyer's point of view:

- A secure investment with good growth prospects and a high net return.
- A known maturity date, although the policy could be resold before then, if required.
- The profit will be subject to Capital Gains Tax, but the individual's annual allowance will be available, plus the opportunity to arrange for any losses to offset the gains at the appropriate time.

Comment

Quite an attractive investment opportunity for anyone seeking a pure capital growth investment over a fixed number of years. It could also be useful in planning such things as school fees.

Friendly Society Bonds

These are essentially the same as Qualifying Policies offered by insurance companies, but with the substantial added advantage of total freedom from tax. However, because of this unique tax advantage, there are limitations on the amount of contributions. These have just been increased to £18 per month or £200 a year for any individual under the age of 70, including children.

Taxation

The funds *within* the policy are exempt from all taxes. The investor is not liable to Income Tax or Capital Gains Tax on encashing the bond after 10 years. Inheritance Tax advantages are also available where the bond is held in trust for a nominated beneficiary.

Advantages

- Total freedom from tax within the fund means that it should be able to produce a better grwoth performance over the years. One particular fund launched in 1976 has produced an annual growth rate of 17.3 per cent tax-free.
- Total freedom from Income Tax and Capital Gains Tax for the investor.

- Flexibility; after the 10 years the investor can leave the funds to grow tax-free, can encash the bond free of all taxes, or can choose to take a tax-free income.
- Investors sometimes have a choice of funds into which their premiums are paid: a managed equity fund, fixed interest securities, or a combination.
- Permanent health insurance (see Chapter 9) can also be included.
- Death benefit can be easily nominated in favour of a child or grandchild.
- Bonds are now available for husband, wife and children, so a family of four could save up to £800 a year in this tax-free fund.

Disadvantages

- The same risk element that applies to all equity-based investments.
- The low limits on contributions; on the other hand the maximum investment of £18 per month is lower than the minimum regular contribution on most PEPs.
- The long-term nature of the investment (minimum 10 years).
- Very high penalties on encashment during the 10-year term; surrender value is limited to a return of the premiums paid.

Comment

Now that Friendly Society policies are available for children as well as adults, these bonds represent an ideal way of getting started with a regular savings plan; their simplicity and freedom from tax must make them the first choice for most families where there is sufficient money to afford the low monthly premiums. For grandparents they can represent an attractive opportunity of providing for grandchildren. For parents they can be particularly useful for providing a capital sum in the future, perhaps for school fees.

It is also possible to purchase all 10 years of instalments in advance by buying an annuity; in other words, a lump sum investment now purchases an annuity which meets the annual premiums of £200 for the next 10 years. This could be worth considering when interest rates are high, but otherwise you are probably better off paying the normal regular premiums to fund this tax-free investment.

Annuities

Although mentioned earlier as guaranteed investments, it is worth remembering, particularly when interest rates are high, that it might be worth purchasing an annuity, either as an end in its own right, or as part of another investment or tax-saving scheme.

In the former, a purchased life annuity can offer a high, tax-efficient, and guaranteed income for the remaining lifetime of the investor (called the 'annuitant'). It can be of particular benefit to an elderly annuitant, especially one in good health and therefore with a good life expectancy. In this case a Dynamic Annuity (which will provide regular increases) or a with-profits annuity would also be worth considering, despite the reduction in the starting level of the annuity payments.

As a means to an end, annuities also offer a tax-efficient and convenient way of funding regular payments into other investments such as Friendly Society Bonds (to produce a tax-free sum after 10 years), and Qualifying Life Policies (which can help to avoid Inheritance Tax by producing a tax-free sum on death, which would be held in trust for the annuitant's family and would therefore not be included in the annuitant's estate for tax purposes).

Pensions

As the structure and different types of pensions are dealt with in Chapter 12, Planning Your Retirement, the purpose of mentioning pensions here is simply to remind the reader that if you do have surplus funds as a result of an inheritance, one of the most sensible and tax efficient investments you can make will be to top up your existing pension arrangements, or, if you have not already done so, take out a new pension plan. The sooner you start, the correspondingly larger the value of the pension fund when you retire.

The box below shows the cost of delaying the commencement date of pension contributions. It is based on contributions of £1,000 per annum paid by individuals at four different ages.

The Cumulative Value of A Pension Fund

Age when payment started	Accumulated value of fund at age 65
44 years 11 months	£145,607
49 years 11 months	£76,545
54 years 11 months	£32,200
59 years 11 months	£9,223

Source: Equitable Life Assurance Society

It might be thought that delaying the start date by five years would simply reduce the value of the pension fund by £5,000, plus five years' loss of interest. Of course, this is not the case. The Fund has lost not just the last five years' worth of contributions and interest, it has lost the benefit of having those funds growing tax-free over the whole of the savings period. In the above example, if the individual had started contributing at age 45 rather than 50, the additional £5,000 which would have been growing in the fund by the time he was 50 would have created an extra £70,000 by the time he reached retirement age.

Pension funds are one of the few investments to enjoy freedom from tax at all three relevant stages – entry, duration and exit. Income Tax relief at the highest rate is available on the amount contributed (subject to the allowable limits). The fund enjoys total exemption from Income Tax and Capital Gains Tax, and there is no CGT or other tax liability on the cash element of the pension. However, the investor can withdraw only a small proportion of the fund in cash; on maturity the bulk of the accumulated pension fund must be used to buy a pension (or annuity).

The net result is that, from the inheritance point of view, an investment in your own pension scheme must be one of the most sensible ways of investing inherited moneys. In addition, the cost of delay reinforces the tax reasons for putting extra pension contributions near the top of the list of possible investments.

Lump sum investments and regular payment investments

Of the previous investments mentioned so far, some can be purchased only by lump sum (e.g. Gilts, National Saving Certificates, Ordinary Shares), some are available only by regular payments (e.g. Endowment Policies, Friendly Society Bonds), and some are available both for lump sum purchases and for regular payments (e.g. Unit Trusts, Investment Trusts).

Inheriting money usually means that you will have a lump sum available for investment, but this can also provide an opportunity to start a regular savings scheme or regular payments plan. Such plans do have certain distinct advantages:

- It is no bad thing to develop the habit of regular saving; the regular saver will be less vulnerable generally and is more likely to have extra funds when they are needed.
- It is a fact that what you don't have, you don't miss; someone who regularly saves, say, £20 a month will generally have come to regard his or her spendable income as £20 less. The monthly

disappearance of £20 from the bank account is treated as if it were a phone bill or mortgage repayment, with the vital difference that, after a few years, compound growth will have helped to produce a sum of several thousand pounds.

- Many of the tax advantages – and some of the most effective investments – are available only on regular payment plans, such as Qualifying Life Policies, Friendly Society Bonds, S.A.Y.E. and pension schemes.

- Regular payment plans can offer an attractive way of avoiding Inheritance Tax. For example, regular payments into a life policy held in trust for the family will decrease the estate (and therefore the IHT liability) of the investor, while at the same time producing a substantial capital sum for the family which will also be exempt from IHT.

- Particularly for those who do not wish to be bothered with standing orders or who don't like having commitments, regular payments can be purchased in advance by means of an annuity (see Chapter 7). Annuities can offer an effective way of investing inherited capital, especially from your own Inheritance Tax planning point of view; buying an annuity immediately reduces the value of your own estate (and therefore your potential IHT liability), in addition to providing the regular payments required for whatever puprose. Alternatively, you could keep the capital in a separate building society account, which would simply be earmarked to fund the regular monthly or annual payments into the appropriate plan. In this way you would retain ownership of the remaining capital which would be feeding the regular payment plan.

- Regular payments into equity-based investments (such as PEPs, Unit Trusts and Investment Trusts) will help to even out the peaks and troughs in the stock market; if prices fall, perhaps on adverse political or economic news, the regular investment simply purchases so many more units or shares while prices are low.

- By buying more shares when prices are low (a process called 'pound cost averaging'), you will on average end up having paid less for your shares at the end of the period than the arithmetical average (between the lowest price and the highest price) in the same period.

- Regular savings plans can also provide an opportunity to earn interest on interest (compound growth). For example, many Investment Trusts and Unit Trusts offer regular savings plans which allow individual investors to deal direct with the Investment Trust managers and purchase shares at a minimum of expense, and to arrange for the dividends on the shares to be reinvested in the plan, thus producing compound growth. For a quick ready-reference guide see pp. 144–146.

● One of the main drawbacks to long-term regular savings plans, such as Endowment Policies, is the cost of premature determination. Just as you should never go into a room without noticing where the exit is, so it would be unwise to undertake any investment without ascertaining first how easy it will be to encash, and second any penalties attaching to early encashment. It is all very well signing up for an Endowment Policy with a company which has consistently produced the best returns over 10, 15 and 20 years, but this won't be much good if the company is only able to do so by over-penalizing those policy-holders who need to surrender the policies before the end of the original term. (Apparently less than half of all Endowment Policy holders retain their policies until the maturity date, so the price of locking yourself in – and the surrender penalty – is a most important factor to establish before you commit yourself to any regular savings plan.) Some plans (especially pension contracts) will allow a suspension of premiums without penalty, so they can be re-started at a later date.

Note: Never enter into any long-term commitment without checking on the penalty position and if possible making arrangements (perhaps through insurance) for the premium to be continued even if your circumstances change.

Becoming a 'Name' at Lloyds

In 1991 there was considerable publicity about one particular investment which had been relatively little known until then – the possibility of becoming a 'Name' at Lloyds. A Name is just another word for 'member' – in this case, membership of a Lloyds underwriting syndicate, which is a group of wealthy individuals who 'underwrite' insured risks for a fee or premium. Underwriting simply involves spreading the liability for a particular risk among a wide range of people who collectively accept responsibility for paying out if the insured risk happens. The members share between themselves the income of the syndicate, which consists of:

● any profits from the underwriting activities;

- investment income (and any capital gains) on the invested premiums received;
- investment income (and any capital gains) on the deposits which the syndicate requires from its members, who have to produce evidence of sufficient personal wealth.

The main attraction of becoming a Name is the ability to make your capital work twice for you. In other words, on an investment of, say, £100,000 you would receive both the normal interest (or dividend income) *plus* any return from the underwriting activities supported by your investment. Over the years this has produced a profitable return in excess of 16 per cent on average.

However, in addition to sharing the profits, members are also liable for any losses made by their syndicate; and as events in 1991 illustrated, the risk factor is extremely high, even with 'stop loss' insurance available. The fact that so many Names had to pay out substantial amounts to cover the losses made by their syndicates in 1988 has served to highlight the risk involved in becoming a Name, and probably deterred many would-be members. Furthermore, the risk is far-reaching, as Names are liable down to their last penny. As a result, it is not really sensible to consider becoming a Name at Lloyds unless you have very substantial assets – say, over a million pounds with at least £250,000 in cash. Taking the cynical view, if you have or inherit assets of this amount, you will probably have sufficient to provide for yourself in any event, so why be greedy and expose yourself to unnecessary risk?

Table 2

INVESTMENT COMPARISON CHART

Key: √ = Yes × = No (√) = Generally yes, but not always (×) = Generally no, but not always
F = Fixed G = Gross N = Net N/A = Not applicable TF = Tax-free

INVESTMENT	Lump sum	Regular contributions	Tax relief on contributions	Life cover included	Return of capital guaranteed?	Profit on encashment liable to tax?	Income	Frequency of income	Income paid	COMMENT
DEPOSIT & CASH-BASED Bank/Building Society	√	√	×	×	√	N/A	√ according to interest rates	Usually twice a year	N (G on request)	Monthly interest available
National Savings Bank (ordinary account)	√	√	×	×	√	N/A	F	Yearly	£70 TF then N	Maximum £10,000
National Savings Bank (investment account)	√	√	×	×	√	N/A	√ according to interest rates	Yearly	G	Maximum £25,000 One month's notice for withdrawals
TESSA	√	√	×	×	√	N/A	√	Roll-up (can be taken annually)	TF*	*Provided retained for 5 years £9000 maximum
Cash Unit Trust	√	√	×	×	√	CGT	√	Usually twice a year	N	
Foreign Currency Account	√	(√)	×	×	×	CGT	√	Usually twice a year	—	
Offshore Sterling Account	√	(√)	×	×	√	N/A	√	Usually twice a year	G	Income can be 'rolled up'
FIXED-INTEREST & GUARANTEED										
Gilts	√	×	×	×	√ on redemption	×	F	Twice a year	N (unless through savings register)	
Loan Stocks	√	×	×	×	√	×	F	Twice a year	N	
Preference Shares	√	×	×	×	(√) Unless company goes bust	CGT	F	Usually twice a year	N	
Gilt Unit Trusts	√	√	×	×	×	√	F	Usually twice a year	G	

INVESTMENT COMPARISON CHART

INVESTMENT	Lump sum	Regular contri-butions	Tax relief on contri-butions	Life cover included	Return of capital guaranteed?	Profit on encash-ment liable to tax?	Income	Frequency of income	Income paid	COMMENT
Local Authority Bonds	✓	×	×	×	✓	✓	F	Twice a year	N	
Guaranteed Bonds	✓	×	×	✓	✓	Higher-rate Income Tax only	F	Annual or Monthly	N	
National Savings Yearly Plan	×	✓	×	×	✓	×	(F)	8.5% p.a. 'rolled up'	TF	5-year plan Minimum £20 per month Maximum £200 per month
National Savings Certificates	✓	×	×	×	✓	×	Guaranteed growth 'rolled up'		TF	36th issue (5 years) yields 8½% Maximum investment £10,000 Index-linked 5th issue offers inflation + 4½% Maximum investment £10,000
National Savings Income Bonds	✓	×	×	×	✓	N/A	✓ according to interest rates	Monthly	G	Minimum investment £2,000 Maximum investment £25,000 3 months' notice for repayment
Natonal Savings Capital Bonds	✓	×	×	×	✓	×	F	Added to capital	G	Tax payable each year on interest added to bond, for 5 years Minimum £100 Maximum £100,000,
S.A.Y.E.	×	✓	×	×	✓	×	F	Added to capital	TF	Available to employees to fund share option schemes
National Savings Children's Bonus Bonds	✓	×	×	×	✓	N/A	F	Added to capital	TF	Minimum £25 Maximum £1000, 5% interest + tax-free bonus if held for
Premium Bonds	✓	×	×	×	✓	×	N/A	N/A	N/A	5 years (11.84% overall)
Annuities	✓	×	×	×	×	N/A	F or increasing	Choice of frequency	Capital portion exempt Income portion N	Can obtain guarantee for minimum period Can obtain increasing income

INVESTMENT COMPARISON CHART

INVESTMENT EQUITY-BASED	Lump sum	Regular contributions	Tax relief on contributions	Life cover included	Return of capital guaranteed?	Profit on encashment liable to tax?	Income	Frequency of income	Income paid	COMMENT
Ordinary Shares	✓	×	×	×	×	✓ (subject to CGT allowance)	✓	Usually twice a year	N	
Convertible Loan stocks	✓	×	×	×	(✓)	✓ (subject to CGT allowance)	F	Twice a year	N	
Unit Trusts	✓		×	×	×	✓ (subject to CGT allowance)	✓	Usually twice a year	N	
Investment Trusts (Ordinary Shares)	✓		×	×	×	✓ (subject to CGT allowance)	✓		N	
Investment Trust 'split' Zero dividend	✓	×	×	×	✓	✓ (subject to CGT allowance)	—	—	—	
Investment Trust 'split' Stepped Preference	✓	×	×	×	Sometimes	✓ (subject to CGT allowance)	F annual increases	2 or 4 times a year	N	
Investment Trust 'split' Income Shares	✓	×	×	×	×	✓ (subject to CGT allowance)	✓		N	
PEPs	✓	✓	×	×	×	×	✓	Available as received	TF	Maximum £6,000 p.a. plus £3,000 'single company' PEP
BES	✓	×	✓	×	×	×	—	—	(N)	Income sometimes available 5-year 'lock-in'
Property (Direct investment)	✓	×	×	×	×	✓ (unless principal private residence)	✓	As agreed with Tenant	G	
Enterprise Zones	✓	×	✓	×	×	✓	F until rent increase	Usually quarterly	G	
Endowment Policies (with-profits)	(✓)	✓	×	✓	✓	(×)	Regular-premium policies: N/A		(TF) for basic rate	Possible higher rate tax liability on profit from single premium policies **Note:** Watch surrender penalties on early termination of regular-premium policies
Endowment Policies (unit-linked)	(✓)	✓	×	✓	×	(×)	Single-premium policies:up to 5% p.a. tax-free		(TF) for basic rate	

8 Investing in Property

Direct and Indirect Investment in UK Property

Property (land/buildings) can be regarded as equity-based because the value fluctuates according to supply and demand. Broadly, property investments are either residential, or commercial/industrial.

Residential property can either be owner-occupied or tenanted ('investment property'). As land is a finite commodity – and with a continuing shortage of housing – it is reasonable to assume that demand will continue to outstrip supply, so over the years residential property may remain an attractive investment. Those with a large inheritance might consider regarding this as an opportunity to move up-market, or to invest by improving their existing property. Alternatively, they might wish to purchase rented property as an investment, either direct or via a fund.

Commercial/Industrial property can also be owner-occupied (for the purposes of your own business), or investment property (rented out to others). Similarly, the investor can invest direct in one or more specific properties, or can invest indirectly via a fund, such as shares in a property company, or purchase a single premium property bond (see Chapter 7, Insurance-based investments).

Taxation treatment
This depends on how the investor invests. With *direct investment* Income Tax is payable on gross rents after deducting expenses for such things as repairs and insurance. CGT is payable on any profit, unless the property qualifies for principal private residence exemption. If the property is purchased with a loan, tax relief is available on the interest if it is a qualifying loan (up to £30,000 to buy or improve your own residence), or a loan to buy property which is commercially let for at least 26 weeks per annum and available for letting at other times.

Principal private residence exemption (when available) means that no

Capital Gains Tax is payable on any gain ensuing from resale (see Chapter 4). There is also Income Tax relief on mortgage interest (as explained above). The two tax reliefs combine to make one's own house a worthwhile investment.

With *indirect investment* (via a share in a property company or a Single Premium Bond) there are no particular tax consequences. Income Tax will have been paid at the basic rate on dividends received from shares in a property company. In the case of a Single Premium (property) Bond, withdrawals up to 5 per cent p.a. will be free of tax, and profits on encashing the bond will also be tax-free to a basic-rate taxpayer; a higher-rate taxpayer will have some further Income Tax liability on withdrawals over 5 per cent and/or any profit on encashing the bond.

Advantages

- Buying your own house gives two significant tax advantages: Income Tax relief on loan interest and freedom from Capital Gains Tax.
- Capital growth; land is finite – they are not making any more, so demand is likely to exceed supply. It is reasonable to assume that property prices will continue to appreciate.
- Income growth; rents are also likely to increase, thus providing an increasing income from rented property, whether residential or commercial.

Disadvantages

- The risk factor; as demonstrated in 1990, property prices can fall as well as rise.
- Your investment is tied up; it can take a much longer time to sell, particularly in a stagnant property market.
- Expenses; buying and selling property involves agent's fees, surveyor's fees, legal fees, stamp duty, land registry fees, and so on, which can eat into the profit.
- Running costs, such as repairs and insurance.
- On investment properties there is the inconvenience of rent collection and the risk of non-payment.
- Political vulnerability, especially on rented residential property; a future Government could reinstate security of tenure, making it difficult for a landlord to recover possession, and/or it could impose limitations on rent increases.

Comment

All those who inherit money and do not already own their home would certainly be well advised to consider buying. Others who already own their home should consider paying off the mortgage (see Chapter 5, Paying off debts). Existing home-owners might consider investing inherited funds in purchasing other property as a useful addition to their portfolio (collection of investments). However, unless you have both the time and personal knowledge, an investment in property is probably best effected indirectly, through the shares of a property company or a single premium property bond rather than buying property direct and renting out.

Foreign Property

For many people it would be tempting to invest their inheritance in a dream villa on the Costa Blanca – a source of pleasure for the family in the summer months and a source of income for the rest of the year. Holiday homes abroad can indeed be a sound investment, especially where the location is good (i.e. pleasant climate, good facilities and political stability). However, there are substantial risks (in addition to the obvious ones of physical distance and language barriers), such as the possibility of exchange control being reintroduced and the necessity of guaranteeing proper title to the property.

> **Case History**
> Edward purchased his ideal villa in the Dordogne a few years ago for what he thought was a bargain price of £16,000. It appeared less of a bargain, however, when he had to pay out another £24,000 to acquire the right for all the main services to be connected and for the title to be completed when the vendor went bankrupt.

C

Questions to ask before buying abroad

- What is the climate like outside the summer months?
- What facilities are there in the area and what future developments are likely?
- How well do I know the area?
- Do I know a good local lawyer and local agent so that I could be certain of what I am buying?
- If I occupy the property, say, four weeks a year, what will I do with it for the remainder of the year?

- How will I find tenants for the property and am I prepared to take on the necessary paperwork and administrative arrangements?
- Is there someone local who will keep an eye on the property for me?
- Am I looking only for a short-term holiday investment, or might I consider retiring here?
- What is the market for this type of property, and how easily could I resell it?

If your answers to these questions are favourable, an inheritance might be just the way to enable you to achieve this particular dream. If all you want is a good summer or winter holiday in a place of your own, there are other alternatives which might achieve the same result but which involve less outlay, less bother and less risk (see below).

Other Syndicated Property Investments

As stated earlier, investment does not have to be only for financial gain; the two investments following could well produce a financial return, but they are undertaken primarily for the physical enjoyment they provide.

Time-Sharing

With time-sharing you own in perpetuity a fixed period (two weeks, for example) in a particular property anywhere in the world, usually in an established holiday area.

Advantages

- Guaranteed availability of rent-free quality holiday accommodation in a place of your choice year after year, without the burden of maintenance, insurance, and so on.
- Cheaper than buying a holiday home outright; individual weeks are available from £5,000 upwards.
- The weeks can be exchanged with owners of different weeks in other properties, so you might be able to swap your two weeks in Todmorden in February for one week in the Algarve in August.

Disadvantages

- Some time-sharing developments employ offensive high-pressure sales tactics to attract investors.
- You are basically tied to the same place and the same time each year, but exchanges are possible.
- Fees are payable on arranging an exchange.
- The annual maintenance charge is fixed and payable, whether or not you make use of your time-share each year.
- You may find it a difficult or lengthy process to dispose of your time-share.
- The sale may involve a financial loss.

Comment

A time-share in an attractive resort with reputable managers can offer a flexible and economic alternative to buying a foreign property, but watch the costs and the 'exit route'.

Holiday Property Bond

This is effectively a Single Premium Bond (see Chapter 7, Insurance-based investments), namely an insurance policy with a novel twist. The fund invests just over half the net premiums in up-market apartments and villas in a range of popular holiday areas all over the world, and just under half in a portfolio of bonds and other investments to produce an income within the fund. The investor receives one point for every pound invested, so someone who invests £5,000 would receive 5,000 points. Those points are then available each year to purchase rent-free occupation in any of the fund's properties at any time of year. (The number of points varies according to the size of property and the time of year. Thus, around 11,000 points would be required for a week in a large luxury villa on the Costa Blanca in August, but a week in a two-bedroom Austrian chalet in the skiing season would require around 5,500 points, and a week in a one-bedroomed apartment in a French château in Brittany in November could require less than 2,000 points.)

Advantages

- Availability of rent-free, up-market holiday accommodation, without the burden of maintenance or insurance, in a place of your choice.
- With a minimum outlay of £2,000, it is substantially cheaper than buying a holiday home.

- Flexibility; investors are not tied to the same time and same place, but are free to select the resort of their choice at the time of their choice; no exchange fees payable.
- The points are increased each year so that they broadly keep up with the increase in the value of the properties.
- Points which are not used one year can be taken over to the next year, so investors do not lose out if they do not utilize their holiday points one year.
- No fixed annual charge; investors simply pay a user charge only as and when they occupy the property.
- The investment includes insurance, so a cash refund is guaranteed on the death of an investor.
- The 28-day rule allows investors to take a holiday within 28 days of booking at the cost only of the user charge, but without using up any of the points.
- Easy exit route; investors simply sell their units back to the fund managers at the prevailing price, which is quoted in the financial press.

Disadvantages

- Booking the properties is on a first come, first served basis, so there is no guarantee that investors will be able to obtain their first choice of location.
- High up-front initial charges (approximately 20 per cent).
- The value of the investment will depend on the value of the underlying properties and securities, with the normal risk; there is no guarantee that investors will get their money back.

Comment

Certainly for the less sophisticated and/or smaller investor, time-sharing and Holiday Property Bonds offer perhaps a more practicable, less expensive and less risky alternative to buying a holiday home abroad. The key point for anyone who has inherited a substantial sum is to establish what they really want, perhaps lining up all the possible choices mentioned in this book and then allocating an order of preference.

9 Insurance

Life Insurance: Protection or Investment?

Although this book is mainly concerned with the investment of inherited moneys, 'investment' is interpreted in the wider sense of spending your money in anticipation of a return; the return might be in pounds and pence, in an experience, to provide enjoyment (such as a holiday home), or in protection or peace of mind. The last option is the one dealt with in this chapter.

Protection insurance may be divided into two types: life insurance and other (non-life) insurance. This section concentrates on life insurance, which can again be broken down into policies where the main pupose is to provide an *investment vehicle*, and the life cover is incidental, and policies where the main purpose is to provide a minimum sum in the event of death.

Advantages of insurance as investment

- In-built life cover is only sufficient to provide a 'money back guarantee' in the event of death.
- A wide spread of investments coupled with professional management, with a correspondingly reduced risk factor.
- The ability to switch between funds.
- During the policy, the income accumulates and the life company settles all Income Tax and CGT liabilities at 25 per cent.
- 'Withdrawals' from the policies can provide a tax-free income.
- Encashment can provide a tax-free profit for a basic-rate tax-payer.

Investment policies can therefore represent a reasonably simple and tax-efficient type of investment vehicle, especially for higher-rate taxpayers.

Life policies geared to protection rather than investment prompt the question 'Protection against what?' Obviously you cannot protect against death, but you can make provision for the adverse financial consequences of a death. Imagine the financial difficulties which could arise in the event of your sudden death:

- You are the breadwinner; your spouse is not working and you have a young family – how will they cope?
- Your children have just started at a private school; how will the remaining fees be paid?
- Your spouse is unable to work; where will his/her income come from?
- Your spouse is too old/busy/incompetent to look after the house or the children; who will pay for the necessary help?
- You are unmarried and looking after a widowed parent who lives with you; what will happen to him or her?
- You have a mortgage liability and other debts totalling £80,000; how will these be repaid?
- You are the managing director and major shareholder in a family company; what will happen to the business?
- You are a key person in a company which depends on your special skills; how will it replace you?
- You run your own business and employ 14 people who depend on you for their livelihood; what will happen to them?
- You are in partnership with a long-standing colleague who wants to retire; how can the business continue and how can he withdraw his money?

Your death in any of these circumstances could have disastrous consequences. In each case, however, the consequences could be substantially reduced, if not eliminated, by protective life insurance cover. In some cases, such as the children's school fees, only temporary cover would be needed; this would be met by 'term' insurance cover. In other cases, the cover would be needed for the rest of your life – 'whole life' cover.

Most people are substantially under-insured. The recent award of £230,000 damages to the family of a Channel Tunnel worker is not as substantial as it sounds; this was the sum which the court decided would be required to compensate the family for the loss of his income. To replace an income of say, £20,000 would need a capital sum of over £250,000, more if inflation is to be taken into account. Nor is it just the breadwinner who requires cover. The Child Poverty Action Group recently estimated that the real cost of replacing a 'non-working wife and mother' could be as much as £365 a week (£19,000 a year) – a sobering thought.

There are several reasons why most of us are uninsured. First, we don't think about the need for adequate life cover. (Well, you can now.) Second, we don't like spending money when we get nothing back. (What about your peace of mind and security for those dependent on you?) Third, it costs too much. (The cost of pure cover is much less than you would think; for example, a 30-year-old male could obtain life cover of over £250,000 for around £30 per month.)

An inheritance provides the ideal opportunity to make sure you have the right type and level of insurance cover for your circumstances and to provide protection for those dependent on you. As a very rough rule of thumb, you should consider insurance cover equal to 10 times your salary. However, it is best to seek professional advice on life insurance matters.

Different types of life policy

Although all the following policies comprise insurance cover which will provide funds on a death, there are different types of cover for different situation. A professional adviser will provide full details.

Whole Life Assurance

This simply provides for the sum assured to be paid on the policy-holder's death, or in the case of a 'joint and last survivor' policy, to be paid on the death of the survivor. With-Profits policies will cost more than non-profit policies since the death benefit will be increased by the bonuses declared each year during the policy.

Endowment Policies

With these policies the sum assured is payable on the specified maturity date, or on death (if it occurs earlier). These policies are often used as the vehicles for repaying a mortgage debt; they can also be written on a last survivor basis, and can be with profits or unit-linked.

Low-Cost Life Assurance

By taking into account the anticipated bonuses, this type of policy provides a guaranteed level of cover but at a lower cost than 'normal' whole life assurance. (The amount payable is also likely to be lower.)

Term Assurance

This is one of the cheapest forms of 'pure' insurance cover and can be added to other types of policy if required in order to boost the protection element for the relevant period. The policy expires at the end of the chosen term, although for a small extra premium it is possible for the policy to be 'convertible' (that is, converted into an Endowment or Whole Life Policy without further medical evidence of good health). Similarly, the policy can provide for the sum assured to decrease or increase each year at a predetermined rate and can include an option for the insured to renew the term cover without evidence of health. To give an idea of the low cost of such policies, a 40-year-old father with two teenage children could take out £100,000 worth of convertible renewable term cover for the next 10 years at a cost of around £16 per month.

Accidental Death Cover

This contingency cover is even cheaper than term assurance cover, because the risk of being killed in an accident is so small. However, it is still worth considering, especially for a young or fit person, since if they were to die in the next few years, it would be more likely to be as a result of an accident.

Family Income Benefit Policies

In these cases, the death benefit is payable by regular (usually monthly) instalments for the remainder of the original term of the policy, rather than by lump sum. These policies are particularly useful in connection with family protection.

Practical Tips on Life Insurance

- Do not be tempted to sign up for a life policy on the basis of an attractive personalized letter sent to you directly by an insurance company, perhaps offering you such irresistible incentives as a carriage clock, a personal organizer or a solar-powered calculator. Such policies will not necessarily be bad investments, but they may not be a sensible investment for you, especially if they involve a long-term savings period. If you are attracted by the pot of gold they offer, don't respond to the direct mail advertisement; instead, consult a financial adviser, who will be able to advise on the advantages and disadvantages of the policy (including any penalty on early surrender) and perhaps obtain a more suitable or attractive quotation without incurring any additional costs.
- If you are self-employed, or if you are not a member of a company pension scheme, you can tack life cover on to a personal pension, which will offer the added advantage of tax relief on the premiums. (A member of a company pension should be able to nominate in favour of his family the death benefit payable under the scheme.)
- For any form of Whole Life Cover consider whether to put the policy in trust for other family members. If you don't, the policy moneys will pass under your will as part of your residuary estate, and may therefore be liable to Inheritance Tax. If the policy is written in trust for the family, the death benefit will be outside your estate and free from inheritance tax on your death.

Before considering the other risks which you might wish to insure against, it would be appropriate to mention a hybrid type of policy which is becoming increasingly popular – namely a flexible Whole Life Policy. These are regular premium policies which combine an element of protection (life cover) with an investment element (in a unit-linked fund). A particular attraction is the flexibility, which allows the insured to choose between high initial cover and a low investment element, or lower initial cover and a higher investment element.

Other risks to consider insuring against

The rationale for suggesting insurance as a possible area for investing inherited money is that an inheritance provides a golden (and possibly the only) opportunity for you to make sure that all the relevant risks are properly covered. The range of possible risks – from death to someone being bitten by your pet snake – is so wide that you could easily spend the whole of your inheritance (and the rest of your income) on insurance premiums. The following is therefore a list of the more relevant risks which can be insured against and which it would be worth at least considering. In view of limitations on space, this is really a list of reminders only, as to the extent and types of cover available; further details can be obatined from your professional adviser. These risks fall under three general headings: health, possessions and other.

Health Matters

Permanent Health Insurance
This badly named cover should really be called 'income replacement' insurance, as it is intended to replace income lost through ill health. It has been estimated that you are 17 times as likely to be injured as to be killed in an accident, and permanent health insurance must be a strong contender for anyone needing to provide proper protection.

Dread Disease Cover
With these policies the sum assured is paid out on the *diagnosis* of a dread disease, such as cancer – in other words, at a time when you can benefit from the policy moneys.

Medical Expenses
If you were to need hospital treatment and would prefer to 'go private', you would be well advised to take out medical expenses insurance. This

market is becoming more competitive and comprehensive cover for the whole family can be obtained for a few hundred pounds a year.

Hospital Cash Plan
For a much smaller cost, this type of policy simply provides a certain amount of cash for every day that you have to spend in hospital, whether private or NHS. It is really a sort of cash compensation payment for being ill.

Care in Old Age Cover
This new type of policy (initiated by Commercial Union in 1991) offers a choice between paying a regular income, or paying nursing home costs, when a disability occurs. Although not cheap, this type of policy would certainly cost less than the fees incurred in the event of a disability requiring constant medical care.

Parts of the body
If your livelihood depends on a particular talent or part of the body (e.g. a professional singer or hand model), it would be sensible to consider insuring against the financial consequences of damaging your voice or losing a finger.

Possessions
House
Your property will probably be covered through your building society's policy if you have a mortgage; this is therefore just a reminder to ensure that you have adequate cover in force, especially if you have paid off your mortgage, or if you own a second property.

Contents
It is easy to overlook the necessity of keeping your contents cover, particularly the 'all risks' section, up to date, especially if the insurance is on a 'reinstatment' rather than a 'market value' basis.

Animals
Horse-owners, dog-breeders, snake-charmers and the like will need to make sure that these expensive commodities are properly insured.

Car
Although basic insurance is obligatory under the Road Traffic Act, an inheritance may enable you to increase the level of your cover (comprehensive rather than third party), and even buy a new car as well.

Other Risks

Travel and Holiday Cover

Rather than take out separate cover with a tour operator every time you go abroad, regular travellers should consider an annual premium policy (such as those available through Wexas or American Express), which provide year-round cover against all the usual risks.

Third Party Liability

Check your home cover to make sure you are insured against liability to someone else who might be injured on your premises or as a result of your carelessness.

Pets

Every family with a household pet should have one of the comprehensive insurance policies available from any of the dozen specialists in this field.

Legal Expenses

The cost of litigation means that it is only the very rich (or the poor, who qualify for Legal Aid) who can afford to go to court to pursue their rights or defend themselves. Just as you can insure against medical expenses, it is now possible to take out insurance against legal costs for most types of legal work (especially those involving litigation) for around £100 a year.

Maintenance Protection

Divorced or separated spouses who rely on maintenance payments from their husband/wife can now insure this income against the risk of the death of the payer.

One-off risks

These include such things as rain at your daughter's wedding.

If you think that any of the above might be relevant to your circumstances, it will not cost you anything just to obtain a quotation; the odds are that the premium cost will be less than you might imagine.

One final piece of advice in connection with insurances is that, as with pensions, you can't start too soon. The younger you start, the cheaper the cover, and the better placed you will be later — whether to reassure a prospective parent-in-law that your fiancée will be well provided for, to establish another way of repaying your mortgage, to provide funds which you could use as security for a loan in the future, or simply to provide peace of mind and security for your family/partner/employees. An inheritance should be regarded as the means of ensuring that all your insurance requirements are brought up to date, so review them now, as soon as you have read this chapter.

10 Financial Packages Unravelled

Insurance companies and financial planners are in the business of selling, but it can take close study and determination to unravel the true nature of the packages they offer. In most cases the packages are just a combination of straightforward contracts under fancy names, such as 'School Fees Plan' and 'Capital Preservation Plan'. This chapter takes a clear look at what they offer.

School Fees Plan

Although it might appear unique, this type of plan is simply a clever piece of marketing. Planning to cover school fees involves no more than choosing the appropriate savings or investment vehicles so that funds will be available at a specified future date, when they can be withdrawn three times a year.

Do not be seduced by school fees plans which claim to save you large sums of money, say, over £10,000, by producing £18,000 worth of fees (starting in nine years' time and spread over seven years) for an outlay of only £8,000 invested now. Although the maths may be correct, you haven't actually saved anything like as much as £10,000. In fact, you would be nearly as well off if you had simply left the £8,000 in a building society account. In that event, merely as a result of the accumulating interest, it would have grown (depending on interest rates) to around £16,000 in nine years' time. Even when you start to make withdrawals at the beginning of each term, you would still continue to receive interest on the reducing capital.

Although investing money in a building society is a perfectly valid school fees plan, there are drawbacks. First, the actual return would depend on interest rates in the meantime, and second, there would be no protection against inflation, which would certainly increase the fees being charged, but not make a corresponding increase in the value of your capital.

For those wishing to educate their children privately, the real question is simply, 'Where can I put my funds to produce the largest sum which I can draw on three times a year, leaving the remainder to continue growing/earning interest?' In other words, what investment vehicle is likely to provide the highest net return over the relevant period of years?

School fees plans tend to utilize investments which will either offer prospects of capital growth (e.g. With Profit policies, Single Premium Bonds, Unit Trusts, Investment Trusts and PEPs) or guaranteed investments, such as gilts and deferred annuities, or a combination of both. The best selection of investments will depend on:

- The length of time before the fees become payable.
- The amount of fees required.
- The tax position and assets of the payer.
- Whether the fees can be provided out of capital or are to be provided out of income.

With regard to the amount, it has recently been estimated that the total fees required to educate privately a child born today will be in the region of £150,000. However, as the old saying goes, 'If you think education is expensive, try ignorance.' Before you groan and pass on to the next chapter, it must be said that such a target can be achieved, especially if inherited wealth is available.

Most school fees plans assume that fees will be paid either out of income on a regular savings basis, out of capital, or a combination of the two. Where fees are to be generated by savings from income, it is usually a case of using either Qualifying Life Policies (especially where these can be arranged more than seven and a half years in advance of the required date), or using other regular savings plans, such as those discussed in Chapter 7. These include:

A deferred annuity
– funded by monthly premiums and guaranteeing a fixed level of income at a future date.
Friendly Society policies
– tax-free sums after 10 years.
PEPs
– tax-free growth, but short-term volatility.
TESSAs
– tax-free sums after five years.
Unit Trust and/or Investment Trust savings plans
– prospects of capital growth, but volatile, especially in the short term. With all income plans it is also sensible to take out life cover in order to

provide the extra funds required in the event of your death. For example, term assurance cover for a 45-year-old male, which would provide an initial cover of £50,000 for the first three years (reducing to £30,000 in the fourth year, £10,000 in the fifth year and then terminating), would cost under £10 per month.

Inheriting moneys would give the opportunity of funding school fees by the second method – out of capital. Again, this boils down to trying to obtain the highest net return from an appropriate range of investments from which the interest and/or capital growth will compound up over the relevant period until the fees are required.

Over a medium- or long-term period (say, over five years), equity-linked funds clearly offer better prospects for capital growth (although with some degree of risk, and no guarantees), and tax-free funds, such as TESSAs or National Savings Certificates, will obviously produce more growth than taxed investments. There is no single right answer; capital available from an inheritance could be applied in any of the following ways to meet the school fees payable at a future date:

Composition fee
– a sum paid in advance direct to the school concerned. However, you should check the position if the child does not eventually attend the school for any reason.

A charitable education trust
– thanks to its charitable status, this is tax-free both to the investor and on the child, but the capital is tied up. Advice also needs to be taken regarding possible IHT consequences. As an approximate guide, a capital contribution of about £17,500 might provide a total of around £40,000-worth of fees payable over a five-year period commencing in seven years' time.

Second-hand endowment policies
– maturing at the appropriate dates (see Chapter 7).

Single Premium Bonds
– either with profit or unit-linked.

Unit Trusts/Investment Trusts
– no guarantee, but possibilities of greater growth, at least over the longer term.

National Savings Certificates/Zero-Dividend Preference Shares/Gilts
– these investments would provide a guaranteed sum at the appropriate future date.

If the school fees are required sooner rather than later, and if no other funds are available, you may have to borrow the money (perhaps on the security of an existing policy), then repay the loan during (or even after) the time when the child attends the school. Absence of tax relief on the borrowing makes this an expensive option.

Do not forget that school fees offer a good opportunity for financial assistance from grandparents. If you have grandchildren for whom a private education is planned, you should consider making lifetime gifts either direct to your grandchilden, or into a trust for their benefit (see Chapter 14). Such gifts can be one of the most effective and appreciated methods of helping your family, in addition to reducing your estate for IHT purposes.

Capital Conversion Plans

The purpose of this particular package is to produce a tax-free income for higher-rate taxpayers; as such, this type of investment could be of interest if you have inherited capital – especially if the inheritance has given you the honour of becoming a higher-rate taxpayer.

A Capital Conversion Plan is simply a 10-year Qualifying Life Policy (either with profits or unit-linked), the premiums for which are paid by a 'funding vehicle', such as an annuity or Single Premium Bond.

C

Capital Conversion Plan Case History

Don, aged 54, inherits £50,000. He invests £40,000 in a Single Premium Bond, from which tax-free withdrawals of £2,000 p.a. are paid into a regular premium, unit-linked Qualifying Policy. The Single Premium Bond is reducing by £2,000 p.a., while the Qualifying Policy is building up by the same amount (plus the interest and any growth from the underlying units). After 10 years, Don can encash the Qualifying Policy for, say, £34,000 entirely free of all tax liability. In addition, Don can continue to make tax-free 5 per cent withdrawals from any remaining funds in the original Single Premium Bond.

The advantage of this type of package is that the proceeds of the Qualifying Life Policy are entirely tax free after seven and a half years, so the investor can encash the policy free of any income tax or capital gains tax liability. Using a Single Premium Bond to fund the premiums also enables a higher-rate taxpayer to take advantage of the rule allowing 5 per cent withdrawals tax free. (Against that, a higher-rate payer would be liable to Income Tax on any withdrawals over 5 per cent, or on any profit when surrendering the Single Premium Bond, in addition to tax penalties on early termination of the scheme.)

It must be stressed that capital conversion plans need not involve the expense of buying a specially named package from an insurance company; you or your financial adviser could quite easily construct your own capital conversion plan by taking out a Qualifying Life Policy in the usual way, and then arranging for the premiums to be funded by the periodic encashment of other types of investment (Equities, Unit Trusts, Gilts, PEPs, National Savings Certificates), some of which could be more tax-efficient than a Single Premium Bond or an annuity.

'Back-to-Back' Policies and other Fancy Packages

The term 'back-to-back' applies to various packages used mostly for mitigating Inheritance Tax, basically by transferring capital in such a way that, on the investor's death, the capital taken out of the estate will reappear in a separate policy held in trust for the family, free of IHT. These plans come under several fancy brand names – Abbey Life Wealth Preservation Plan, Providence Capitol Capital Preservation Plan and suchlike – but most have a similar structure.

Capital Preservation Plans

These packages generally consist of an annuity which provides the monthly/annual instalments for a Whole Life Policy, the benefit of which is held in trust for the investor's family so that the value will be outside the investor's estate.

The payment of premiums into the Whole Life Policy constitutes a series of gifts, but generally, the amount of the premium would be covered by the annual exemption (£3,000). Even if this were not the case, the premiums might still qualify for the separate exemption for 'regular payments made out of net income' (see Chapter 2, Lifetime Gifts).

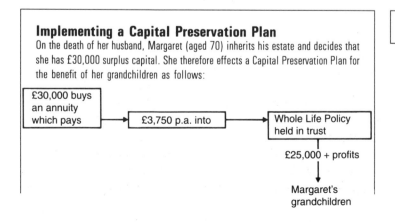

Implementing a Capital Preservation Plan

On the death of her husband, Margaret (aged 70) inherits his estate and decides that she has £30,000 surplus capital. She therefore effects a Capital Preservation Plan for the benefit of her grandchildren as follows:

£30,000 buys an annuity which pays → £3,750 p.a. into → Whole Life Policy held in trust → £25,000 + profits → Margaret's grandchildren

C

> There is a double benefit in that Margaret's estate is reduced by £30,000 (reducing her IHT liability by £12,000), and the grandchildren receive £25,000 plus any further growth in the value of the Whole Life Policy (e.g. bonuses).

Instead of an annuity, some schemes (such as the M & G Retained Income Scheme) use a Single Premium Bond from which regular withdrawals provide the income which feeds the Whole Life Policy, which is held in trust for the investor's family and will therefore be outside his estate. On the investor's death, the Whole Life Policy produces the sum assured (plus any growth) free of Inheritance Tax for the family, and the estate receives the value of any remaining units in the Single Premium Bond. This is perhaps more flexible than the annuity-based plan because the investor retains ownership and control of the capital sum which is used to produce the amounts required for the premiums.

Note: For technical reasons it is normally advisable for the Whole Life Policy (which is to be held in trust) to be issued by a different company from the one providing the annuity. Because of this potential tax trap, professional advice in this area is essential.

Gift and Loan Scheme

This package is again aimed at saving Inheritance Tax, and, as its name suggests, is a combination of a (small) gift into trust for the family, followed by a loan to the trustees. The trustees invest the loan in, say, a Single Premium Bond, the benefit of which is also held in trust for the family.

> ## Implementing a Gift and Loan Scheme
> Rod (aged 60) inherits £50,000. He invests £3,000 in a Single Premium Bond held in trust for his children, and then lends £47,000 to the trustees, who invest this in a second Investment Bond. If Rod wants to receive an income, withdrawals (up to 5 per cent tax free) out of the second bond can be paid to him and treated as repayments on account of his original loan. In this way the bonds and all the growth accruing within them are outside Rod's estate. The value of the asset remaining in his estate – the balance of the loan – is frozen, and reduces with each payment back to Rod, which he simply regards as spendable income.

Although these various financial packages may sound complicated at first, there is really nothing mysterious about them; you are simply being offered a combination of two or more investment products which you could arrange for yourself with the right assistance and advice.

11 Going Offshore

This chapter concerns itself with the overseas investment of money (offshore equity and cash investment), overseas property having been discussed in Chapter 8. Although you could certainly buy individual equity shares in Europe, the United States or Japan, most people wanting to invest outside the UK would be advised to do so only through a professionally managed fund (similar to a Unit Trust). Many UK institutions run such funds in the Channel Islands, the Isle of Man, or more exotic tax havens such as the Cayman Islands, from where they invest in sterling, other currencies, equities or government securities.

Why invest abroad?

The reasons for investing an inheritance overseas are numerous:

- To avoid the reintroduction of Exchange Control, to escape a possible Wealth Tax, or to 'shelter' income which would otherwise be taxed at an even higher rate.
- As a 'currency hedge'. For example, if the value of sterling were to fall against another currency, an investment in that other currency would appreciate by the amount of the fall in sterling.
- In anticipation of emigration.
- To shelter a higher-rate taxpayer's income which would otherwise be taxable, particularly if he were likely to become a basic-rate taxpayer in the future, perhaps following retirement.
- To give a gross income to a non-taxpayer (although this is now possible in the UK).

Many people are understandably wary of going offshore. The reputation of some offshore institutions is not of the best; the physical separation and lack of control is obviously a deterrent, and generally speaking, there is already a sufficiently wide range of investment and tax-saving opportunities in the UK. In the absence of special reasons, offshore investments will not be of particular interest to the average UK investor. However, the following points may be of relevance to some readers.

Offshore Sterling Funds

These are similar to UK sterling funds, such as bank accounts.

Advantages

- The interest is paid gross and can be accumulated so that, after a few years, the compound effect can produce a substantial benefit.
- Accounts managed in the Channel Islands or Isle of Man by branches of UK institutions (governed by the Securities and Investments Board) provide the additional security of good marketability, and cover from the Compensation Fund.

Disadvantages

- The investor pays tax at the highest rate on any income actually received, whether partial withdrawals or on final encashment of a roll-up fund, but by delaying the encashment the fund can be accumulated into a much larger amount.

Currency Funds

These are similar to sterling funds, but invest in a wide range of other currencies.

Advantages

- The investor obtains the benefit of a 'sterling hedge', with the potential for capital gain if the chosen currency appreciates against sterling.
- The investor has a wide choice of different currencies, or may opt for the Managed Currency Fund, where the fund manager decides which currencies to invest in.
- Switches between different currencies can be made freely.

Disadvantages

- There is a risk of loss if the chosen currency falls against sterling.

Offshore Trusts

These are simply trusts (see Chapter 14) which are administered by trustees situated offshore (usually in the Isle of Man or Channel Islands).

Advantages

- The opportunity of delaying or saving Income Tax (rather than CGT), especially where the amounts in question are substantial. As the UK Revenue cannot collect tax from offshore trustees, Offshore Trusts are still used to obtain the cash-flow benefit of rolling up gross interest until required, say, until tax rates are reduced in the UK, or perhaps until a beneficiary emigrates and can then receive the rolled-up income free of UK tax. Alternatively, offshore trustees could distribute gross incomes to UK beneficiaries who were not liable to pay tax – perhaps grandchildren who have not used up their personal allowance.

Disadvantages

- The inevitable feeling of loss of control by the investor.
- Dependency on unknown and remote trustees.
- The expense; most offshore trusts would cost well in excess of £1,000 p.a. to run.   -
- Vulnerability to further UK tax legislation under different governments.

The regulations are so complicated and the pitfalls so many and varied that if you do wish to invest your capital outside the UK, you should not take any steps without first consulting a qualified adviser experienced in this particular area.

12 Planning Your Retirement

As illustrated on page 139, you can't start a pension too soon. The longer you wait before making provision for your retirement, the harder it will be to produce an adequate income.

It is perhaps encouraging, but also sobering, to realize that 50 per cent of all males over 60 will live until they are 80, and 50 per cent of all females currently over 55 will live to be older than 85. There is therefore a substantial period for which provision must be made. Living expenses do not stop just because a job does. Although commuting and mortgage expenses may be reduced, other expenses (perhaps leisure and travel) will be increased, not to mention the effect of losing such perks as a company car.

Retirement considerations

These fall under three broad categories:

- Your future residence requirements.
- Your future health requirements.
- Your anticipated financial requirements.

Each of the above will require money and that money can only come from your capital or your income. For most retired people income consists only of the investment income produced by their capital and their pension income. This chapter is about increasing both of these.

If you do nothing about a private pension, on retirement you will receive only your State pensions. These are:

Basic (flat-rate) State Pension Scheme
– currently £52.00 per week for each person who has made enough National Insurance contributions, or £31.25 for a wife who has not contributed.

State Earnings-Related Pension Scheme (SERPS)

which provides an additional pension based on pay between 'band earnings' for National Insurance purposes, currently between £52 and £390 per week. Because of the cost, the pension benefits payable under SERPS are to be substantially reduced for all those retiring after March in the year 2000. Given this, it is now possible for individuals to contract out of SERPS, either by joining a contracted out pension scheme or by arranging their own personal pension plan (see below).

The question is: will you and your family be able to manage purely on the State Pension benefits (which is all you will receive, if you make no further provision, and if you are not already a member of an Occupational Pension Scheme)? If you would not be able to manage on the State benefits, it is vital to make some additional provision now, when the funds are available. An inheritance provides the ideal opportunity to do this, either by making additional contributions to your existing pension arrangements, or by supplementing your existing pension in one of the ways described later in this chapter.

Whichever route you adopt, do remember that the sooner you start, the better, and the more you pay in, the more you will get out.

Pensions

The word 'pension' is a convenient term for describing post-retirement income. Although they are very tax-effective, pensions are by no means the only way of obtaining such income. The main consideration is how to accumulate the largest amount of capital by your chosen retirement date so as to provide as much post-retirement income as possible.

Savings made via a private pension scheme are likely to produce a larger sum than normal savings because they enjoy three distinct tax advantages:

1. Tax relief on the contributions going into the scheme.
2. Freedom from Income Tax and Capital Gains Tax on the investments while within the scheme.
3. Freedom from Capital Gains Tax on the cash withdrawn from the scheme when you reach retirement.

These three attributes obviously give pension contributions a head start over other forms of saving which do not enjoy the same advantages. However, you should not overlook the drawbacks of investing further funds in a private pension scheme, as opposed to the alternative methods outlined later for other ways of providing post-retirement income.

Disadvantages of adding to private pensions

- Your contributions are effectively locked in and cannot generally be withdrawn before retirement age.
- On retirement only a small proportion can be withdrawn in cash; the bulk of the benefit has to be taken in the form of income.
- The benefit stops on your death, or on your spouse's death, if you have opted for a widow's pension.
- You are liable to Income Tax on the pension income you receive.
- There are limits on the amount which you can contribute to a pension scheme – broadly, 15 per cent of income for an employee, or between $17\frac{1}{2}$ and 40 per cent for the self-employed, depending on age and subject to an overall 'capping'.

At this stage, assuming that you have inherited funds and do wish to apply part of the money to increasing your pension, the avenues open to you will depend on whether you are already a member of an occupational pension scheme; the self-employed, of course, are not.

Members of an Existing Occupational Pension Scheme

If you are in this category, you effectively have four ways of increasing your pension:

1. Top up your existing scheme with an Additional Voluntary Contribution (AVC). Your contributions will obtain the benefit of the three tax reliefs mentioned above, and you are not entering into any long-term commitment as you will be able to suspend the AVCs whenever you want. However, there is a maximum limit on the amount you can contribute (15 per cent, including AVCs) and your total pension benefits, including AVCs, must not exceed Inland Revenue limits.

2. Top up your existing contributions with additional contributions to a 'free-standing' scheme (FSAVC); this is purchased privately from an insurance company or building society of your choice, and provided your FSAVCs do not exceed £200 per month, there are no particular restrictions. If the contributions are over £200 per month, the pension provider will

need details of all your existing scheme benefits. FSAVCs are particularly suitable for employees who have a relatively short length of service – frequent job changers, early leavers and suchlike.

Both AVCs and FSAVCs provide a very tax-efficient method of saving, but neither of them can provide lump sum cash benefits; they should be regarded as a means of supplementing income only.

3. Opt out of membership of your occupational scheme and transfer the benefit into a Personal Pension Plan (PPP, see below). Generally speaking, this is not usually advisable, and you should take professional advice in any event.

4. Pursue an alternative method of providing post-retirement income (see p. 175).

Non-members of an Occupational Scheme and the Self-Employed

Individuals in this category can continue to contribute to SERPS, but generally speaking, this would only be worthwhile for males over 50 or females over 42. Most people who are not already a member of an occupational scheme would be better advised to pursue one of the following choices:

1. Continue contributing the maximum amount to any Retirement Annuity Pension already taken out before July 1988.

2. Pursue one of the other ways of producing post-retirement income (see Chapter 12).

3. Opt out of SERPS and take out a Personal Pension Plan. This is essentially a private scheme of your own, which has the following features:
   - Full tax relief on the contributions paid in. This means that a contribution of £1,000 would cost a higher-rate taxpayer only £600.
   - Freedom from Income Tax and Capital Gains Tax within the fund.
   - Freedom from Capital Gains Tax on the cash you can withdraw on retirement.
   - Choice of investment contracts within the fund; it can be with profits, unit-linked, cash-based, or a combination of these things, with the freedom to change the allocation of future contributions.

- Flexibility – contributions can be made on a regular monthly or annual basis, or periodically on a one-off basis.
- You are not tied to the same provider of a PPP; you could take out a plan with a different provider each year.
- A PPP is fully portable; you can take it with you, even if you change jobs.
- On retirement you can take up to 25 per cent of the fund as a tax-free cash lump sum. The remainder must be used to purchase an annuity (an annual income), but you can buy an increasing annuity, which will be lower to start with but will increase automatically each year.

As with AVCs, there is a time limit on the amount which can be contributed each year to a PPP; up to age 35, the limit is 17.5 per cent of earnings (subject to a 'cap' of currently £71,400); if you are over 35, the limit increases at various age bands, up to 40 per cent of capped earnings between ages 61 and 74.

Whether you are making a FSAVC or PPP contribution, you have the same choice between a unit-linked fund, a deposit-based fund, or a with-profits fund.

A unit-linked fund
is like a Unit Trust; the value is linked directly to the value of the underlying stocks and shares. The value will therefore fluctuate, but the longer the period before retirement, the better the prospects for substantial growth in the fund.

A with-profits fund
is like an Endowment Policy; a minimum value is guaranteed and the value can only increase each year as bonuses are declared.

A deposit- or cash-based fund
offers the least risk, but also the least potential, as it is simply like watching funds build up in a bank account; however, the interest is tax-free.

For most people, the practical solution is to combine a choice of funds – perhaps 50 per cent of contributions going into an equity fund or managed fund, and 50 per cent into a with-profits fund. With many contracts, you can then switch into a cash fund shortly before retirement in order to reduce the risk over the last two or three years before retirement. Again, professional advice in this field is essential.

Other Ways of Providing Post-Retirement Income

The fundamental objective is to accumulate the maximum capital value so you can receive a sufficient post-retirement income. There is no reason why you should not use any of the investments described in Chapter 7. Some of the investments entail regular contributions, such as Friendly Society Bonds, Qualifying Life Policies and the National Savings Yearly Plan; others entail lump sum contributions, which can be repeated. Again, the best policy, in order to provide both flexibility and a spread of risks, is to combine several of the investment possibilities.

Personal Equity Plans (PEPs)

It can be argued that taking out a PEP each year is a very effective way of providing for post-retirement income:

- The maximum contributions (currently £9,000 p.a. per person) compare favourably with the limits on contributions to a PPP or FSAVC.
- Although there is no tax relief on the contributions (unlike an FSAVC or PPP), there is freedom from Income Tax on the income withdrawn from a PEP – a very real advantage.
- Income can be taken at any time, even before retirement; with a PPP or FSAVC, income cannot be taken before age 50 at the earliest.
- You retain full access to all your capital in a PEP, as compared to 25 per cent in a PPP and none at all in a FSAVC.
- The money in a PEP will still be there when an investor (and his spouse) have died; a PPP or FSAVC ceases on death.

Other Savings Vehicles

The table following summarizes some of the advantages and features of various investment vehicles, any of which – or a combination of which – could be used to accumulate a capital sum by your intended retirement date.

Table 3

COMPARISON OF FUNDING PLANS FOR RETIREMENT

	FSAVC (Free-standing Additional Voluntary Contribution)	PPP (Personal Pension Plan)	PEP (Personal Equity Plan)	TESSA	UNIT TRUST/ INVESTMENT TRUST	QUALIFYING POLICY (ENDOWMENT)
Limits on contribution?	15% total earnings	17½–40% of net relevant income	£6,000 p.a. + £3,000 single company	£9,000 over 5 years	None	None
Tax relief on contribution?	✓	✓	✗	✗	✗	✗
Freedom from tax within the fund?	✓	✓	✓			✗
Cash available on retirement?	✗	25% of fund	100%	100%	100%	100%
Freedom from CGT on cash withdrawn?	N/A	✓	✓	✓	✓ (up to allowance)	✓
Freedom from Income Tax on post-retirement income?	✗	✗	✓	✗	✗	✗
Minimum lock-in period?	Until retirement	Until retirement after 50	✗	5 years	✗	No, but penalty on early surrender of with-profits policy
Early access to funds possible	✗	✗	✓	✓ (tax liability if within 5 years)	✓	
Effect of death before retirement?	Death benefit	Refund of contributions or value of units	Current value repaid to estate	As PEP	As PEP	Sum assured payable to estate (or to beneficiaries if under trust)
Effect of death after retirement?	Income ceases	Income ceases; capital remains in estate	Capital remains in estate	As PEP	As PEP	As PEP

Home Income Plans

Although not strictly an investment – and therefore not something you can consider for investing inherited moneys – Home Income Plans are worth a brief mention for two reasons. First, they can serve as a useful way for the elderly to boost their post-retirement income, and second, if the elderly do increase their income in this way, they may consequently have surplus funds with which to make gifts, say, to grandchildren.

There are two basic types of Home Income Plans – loan-based and sale-based.

In the *loan-based plan* the home-owners borrow up to £30,000 on the security of their house and use the loan to buy an annuity. The annuity provides a high, regular and guaranteed income which will more than cover the net interest due on the loan, and leave a surplus income in the hands of the home-owners. When the home-owners die, the mortgage is a debt which will reduce the value of the survivor's estate (and possibly save IHT if the estate is above the threshold).

In the *sale-based plan* the home-owners sell the house to an insurance company, which then allows them to continue living in it rent-free for the rest of their lives. As it may be some years before the insurance company is able to obtain vacant possession, the price paid for the house is lower than its vacant possession market value. However, the home-owners at least have the benefit of substantial cash in hand and can then boost their income, perhaps by buying an annuity.

> **Note:** There has been much adverse publicity about the use of Single Premium Bonds (instead of an annuity) to generate income. As there is no guarantee, and the capital value of the bonds can fall as well as rise, substantial losses have been sustained in some cases. In view of these things, the use of bonds in Home Income Plans is not recommended.

In both cases, mortgaging the house, or disposing of it, will reduce the size of inheritance available for the family, so Home Income Plans are not really suitable for those who want (or feel obliged) to leave an inheritance for their family. However, in the right circumstances, a Home Income Plan can be a useful way of enabling the occupier to unlock the financial value tied up in the house, but this is not a step to be undertaken lightly or without professional advice.

13 Helping Others

Inheritance often provides an ideal opportunity for helping others – individuals or charities – particularly if it leaves you with surplus capital or surplus income. Making a gift in your lifetime benefits both parties to the gift: you can enjoy the satisfaction of helping someone at a time when the help is most needed, and the recipient can benefit by having access to the funds immediately, rather than having to wait until after your death.

If the gift is made to relatives, the family as a whole will also benefit in the long term as the reduction in your estate may well entail a corresponding reduction in the amount of Inheritance Tax eventually paid.

Before making a gift

- How much can you afford to give away, and should it be a one-off or a series of regular gifts?
- What will be the tax consequences of the gift for (a) the giver and (b) the recipient?
- What will be the subject matter of the gift – cash or in kind?
- What will be the form of the gift – an outright lump sum – a gift to a nominee or a gift into trust?

Do remember that helping others does not necessarily mean giving assets or cash to them; you might choose to help an individual, for example, by providing benefit in kind, such as a much-needed holiday, or an interest-free loan.

Giving to Charity

Giving to charity is generally understood to mean giving to an organization which is officially registered with the Charity Commission. To achieve official charitable status the organization must be involved in at least one of the following activities:

- The relief of poverty.
- The advancement of education.
- The advancement of religion.
- Other purposes beneficial to the community.

A charity does not *have* to be registered to be bona fide; you could, if you liked, give a Deed of Covenant to a local amenity group (provided their aims fell within the definition of 'charitable' given above) and still obtain tax relief on your donations. However, registration is conclusive evidence of charitable status, and as gifts must be to a particular charity rather than to charity in general, it is usually better to choose a specific registered organization.

Non-specific charitable gifts

If you wish to benefit charities under your Will, but don't want to be tied down to specific ones, you could always leave the benefit to such charities as your executors decide within, say, two years of your death. This could be followed by a 'gift over in default' (a long-stop gift if the executors fail to choose a charity). This could be to a specific charity or, probably better, to the Charities Aid Foundation (see below). You could then keep a letter with your Will, outlining your wishes concerning the choice of charity.

The Charities Aid Foundation (CAF)

This is a registered charity which exists for the purpose of encouraging and distributing donations to other registered charities, either at its own discretion, or to charities nominated by the donor.

A facility of particular interest to many donors is the CAF Charitable Account Scheme; you simply send a donation to the CAF and a Charitable Account is opened in your name. If the donation is over £600, it will be immediately increased by the Income Tax which the CAF can recover. (There is no tax relief on gifts under £600.) The account is similar to a bank account, but instead of a cheque book, you receive charity vouchers, which can be personalized or anonymous. You can then issue these vouchers, like cheques, to whichever charities you wish to support. For tax purposes, however, the gift was made when you sent the original donation to the CAF, and this can be topped up at any time.

The CAF is therefore a useful vehicle for spontaneous giving. It is happy to advise on any aspects of charitable giving, and also provides an investment management service for charities, including two tax-exempt Unit Trust funds.

Tax consequences for the donor

In order to encourage gifts to charity, the government grants generous concessions to the donor and to the charity. These apply both to regular gifts (made by a Deed of Covenant) and to one-off lump-sum gifts over £600 (under the recently introduced Gift Aid scheme).

Income Tax
Regular gifts by a Deed of Covenant (which must last for at least three years) qualify for tax relief at the donor's highest rate. A covenanted payment of £100 gross, therefore, would cost a higher-rate taxpayer only £60 a year.

Lump-sum gifts of over £600 also qualify for tax relief under Gift Aid; this means that a one-off gift of £800 would 'cost' only £480 to a higher-rate taxpayer.

Capital Gains Tax and Inheritance Tax
Gifts to charities do not count as chargeable disposals, so they are exempt from CGT and IHT.

Tax consequences for the donee
Charities are generally exempt from tax and can therefore reclaim the Income Tax deducted by the donor, whether under a Deed of Covenant or under the Gift Aid scheme (see Case History, p. 182). The charity obtains the repayment by presenting a Tax Deduction Certificate to its inspector of taxes. (This certificate, signed by the donor, is normally provided by the charity.)

The subject matter of the gift

As transfers to a charity are exempt from CGT and IHT, it does not make much difference whether shares or cash are transferred, although the latter is easier for practical purposes. However, if you leave a benefit under your Will to a specific charity, and if your estate includes some investments which would fit in with the charity's own investment portfolio, the charity can ask your executors to transfer some of the investments up to the value of the legacy or benefit stated in your Will.

Once the charity has received the gift, it can invest any surplus funds in order to obtain the maximum gross return; this is because charities are also exempt from Income Tax and Capital Gains Tax on their investments.

How to give – outright gift or Trust?

Deeds of Covenant

Charities welcome regular gifts by Deed of Covenant, since this assures them of a regular flow of income, and they are also able to increase the value of the gift by obtaining repayment of the tax deducted by the donor.

Outright gifts

If you do not wish to bother with a regular commitment and would rather just write out one single cheque, there are still two ways in which the charity can increase the value of the gift by obtaining a tax repayment:

1. Under the Deposited Loan scheme the donor writes out one cheque as an advance loan for the total amount of the covenanted payments, which the charity then draws off each year. There are technical traps here for the uninitiated, so professional advice is recommended.
2. Under the Gift Aid scheme, charities can reclaim tax on donations over £600. If the donation is under £600, the donor will not obtain tax relief and the charity will not be able to reclaim any.

If you cannot afford (or do not wish) to give £600 to individual charities, a popular solution is to give £600 to the Charities Aid Foundation (see p. 179); this will qualify as a charitable gift, with all the tax benefits, and you can then use the Charitable Account vouchers to make a series of smaller gifts over any period of time to your chosen individual charities.

Charitable trusts

Yet another way to give to charity is to establish your own charitable trust. This allows you to put your surplus funds into particular projects or areas of activity that interest you. As long as the project or activity falls within the definition of 'charitable' (see p. 179), you can set up a charitable trust to promote these activities. For example, if you are concerned about the poverty and lack of facilities in a certain local area (or, indeed, anywhere in the world), you could establish the 'Fred Bloggs

Charitable Trust for the Relief of Poverty'. Once registered (for which you would need professional assistance), a gift of £600 to the Fred Bloggs Trust would enable the trustees to obtain the tax reliefs and help to fulfil the trust's objectives.

If you establish a charitable trust in your lifetime, you can leave further legacies or benefits to it by your Will. Both a lifetime gift and the benefit under the Will will be exempt from Inheritance Tax and will reduce the IHT payable on the remainder of your estate.

Finally, even if you do not wish to support a particular project or activity, it could still be worth considering setting up your own charitable trust (either in your lifetime, or by your Will) with the object of supporting any *other* registered charity – a sort of private alternative to the Charities Aid Foundation, to whom the funds could be distributed by your charity in any event. If the trustees are chosen by you, you would have the benefit of more personalized control and distribution of the funds, in addition to the pleasure of knowing that your name on the charitable trust would be a form of permanent memorial – something the world could remember you by.

Setting Up a Charitable Trust

Sue Hainsworth (a basic-rate taxpayer) inherits £50,000 from her father's estate. As she has sufficient assets of her own and no dependants, she establishes the Sue Hainsworth Charitable Trust with £20,000 (the gift is exempt from IHT) and appoints herself, her husband Wally, and the family solicitor, as trustees of the trust. As the gift qualifies for tax relief under Gift Aid, the Income Tax position is as follows:

Gross gift from Sue (before tax relief available under Gift Aid)	£26,667
Basic rate tax deducted	£6,667
Net cost of gift to Sue	£20,000
Charity reclaims tax deducted (£6,667) and receives	£26,667

Wally (a higher-rate taxpayer) then covenants to pay the trustees £1,000 p.a. gross for four years. Income Tax effect:

Gross amount	£1,000
Less tax at basic rate (25 per cent)	£250
Amount paid over by Wally	£750

As Wally is a higher-rate taxpayer, he can claim tax relief on a further £150, so the net cost to him is only £600 p.a.

Gifts to Individuals

Unlike Deeds of Covenant to charities, there is no Income Tax relief on Deeds of Covenant to individuals; a gift to an individual is simply an act of generosity out of net income or capital. Clearly, an inheritance is an ideal opportunity to make such gifts. Once you have established the amount of surplus, the amount of the intended gift and the persons whom you wish to benefit, it only remains to ascertain the tax-consequences and the method of giving.

Note: The following points apply to *all* individuals, but there are special rules affecting gifts to one's own minor children; these are explained below.

Tax consequences for the donor

Income Tax

Generally, a gift has no Income Tax consequences except in one important situation – where you make a gift to your own children under the age of 18. In such cases, if the child receives more than £100 gross income from assets originally provided by either parent, the income over £100 p.a. is treated for Income Tax purposes as if it were the parents' income.

The Income Tax Trap

Derek (a higher-rate taxpayer) inherits £40,000. He puts £10,000 in a building society account for his son Timothy. The gross interest in the first year amounts to £1,000, i.e. £900 more than the £100 limit. £900 is therefore added to Derek's income, and he then pays £360 Income Tax (at 40 per cent) on this interest.

C

There are several ways round this Income Tax trap:

- Give only a small amount so that the income is less than £100 p.a.
- Persuade someone else (e.g. grandparents) to give the assets.
- Ensure that the funds are invested where they do not produce taxable income (e.g. National Savings Certificates, Family Bonds, Zero-Dividend Preference Shares, Single Premium Bonds, etc). This option is often the best solution.

Capital Gains Tax

CGT is never a problem on cash gifts; it raises its head only where the gift is a disposal of a chargeable asset on which there is an inbuilt gain in excess of the Annual Allowance, and after allowing for inflation (see Chapter 6).

Inheritance Tax

This is the tax which causes the most confusion. As IHT is chargeable on all disposals, it includes a Gifts Tax as well as Death Duties; death is simply the 'final gift'. For more details, consult Chapter 2 on IHT, particularly the list of exempt gifts on p. 22.

Getting the Best of IHT Exemptions

John and Evelyn are in their late sixties, with a joint estate worth £300,000. As a result of an inheritance, they want to benefit their family (two children and eight grandchildren under 18) in addition to four godchildren and two close friends. Every year John and Evelyn can each make the following gifts with no IHT complications at all:

- £3,000 between, say, the children (John could give £3,000 to his son and Evelyn £3,000 to her daughter).
- £250 to each grandchild, godchild and friend (i.e. 14 × £250).
- A gift on the occasion of any marriage (£5,000 to a child, £2,500 to a grandchild, and £1,000 to anyone else).
- A series of regular gifts (without limit, as long as they are all out of net surplus income).
- Gifts to charity without limit.
- All the above gifts would be exempt from IHT; if they were made in cash, there would also be no CGT problems.

Suppose, however, John and Evelyn were to exceed the limits by giving £10,000 to each child (i.e. £7,000 over the exempt amount of £3,000 per donor) and £400 to each grandchild (i.e. £150 over the exempt amount of £250 per donee). The consequences would be as follows:

Exceeding IHT Exemptions

John would have exceeded his annual exemption by £8,200 (£7,000 + £1,200 [8 × 150]). John would therefore have made a Potentially Exempt Transfer (PET, see p. 22) of £8,200. No IHT would be payable at the time; this amount would simply go on record. If John survived for seven years, the PET would drop out altogether. If John were to die within seven years, this £8,200 would be brought into account in calculating any IHT on his estate.

This example highlights three important aspects of IHT:

- No IHT is payable at the time of the gift; a gift to an individual which exceeds the annual exemption will be a PET. The tax will only be payable if the donor dies within seven years.
- If the total of the estate, including gifts made within the previous seven years, does not exceed the IHT threshold (£140,000), or if it is not chargeable, perhaps because it passes to an exempt beneficiary such as a spouse or a charity, no IHT is payable in any event.
- If the donor's estate is liable to IHT, the tax attributable to the gift is payable by the donee. It can therefore be sensible for the donee to insure the donor's life for the estimated amount of IHT payable by the donee. The relevant policy would usually be a seven-year decreasing term insurance (see Chapter 9).

One final point for a donor to remember: if you are entitled to an inheritance and want to use it to help others rather than yourself, remember the advantages of using a Deed of Variation to alter the estate from which your inheritance comes (see Chapter 1). This avoids the gift becoming a disposal by yourself and will possibly save IHT in the event of your own death). Do remember, however, that the Deed of Variation will not get round the Income Tax trap if you simply transfer the funds direct to your own minor child (see p. 183). Generally speaking it is safer for the Deed of Variation to pass the benefit either to an adult child or to grandchildren.

Tax consequences for the donee

At the time of writing, the tax position for the donee is straightforward, although the Labour Party has suggested replacing Inheritance Tax with a Capital Receipts Tax, which would tax the donee. The current situation is as follows.

Income Tax
There is no Income Tax payable on the gift. Normal Income Tax liability arises on any income produced by it, so the choice of investment becomes relevant.

Capital Gains Tax
There is no CGT on the donee.

Inheritance Tax

Generally, there is no IHT on the recipient unless the gift is a PET which subsequently becomes chargeable (because the donor dies within seven years and his estate plus the gift exceeds the IHT threshold). As mentioned earlier, the relevant proportion of IHT in this case would be payable by the donee, who should therefore consider insuring the donor's life.

Subject matter of the gift

If the gift is made from inherited funds, it is often in cash, so there will be no problems (except for the Income Tax trap regarding gifts to your own children under 18), and the possible future IHT liability if the donor dies within seven years. (This may be avoided if the donor has executed a Deed of Variation of the original estate.)

However, there is no reason why the gift should not be in kind – stocks and shares or personal effects. In these cases the principles are the same as those mentioned earlier, but there are three additional points to note:

- Capital Gains Tax may become relevant where the subject matter of the gift has a market value which exceeds the acquisition cost (as increased by indexation relief) by more than the donor's CGT allowance (£5,500). No CGT is payable on chattels which have a predictable life of less than 50 years, or where the market value at the date of gift does not exceed £6,000. If the chattel has a life of over 50 years and is worth over £6,000, CGT can be restricted to five-thirds of the excess value over £6,000.

Cash or Kind?

Phillip inherits his father's estate, consisting entirely of cash. He uses this to make the following gifts to his three children:

- To Adam – £8,000 cash.
- To Ben – £8,000-worth of shares (acquisition cost £1,500 in 1983).
- To Toby – £1,500 cash and oil paintings which cost £500 originally but are now worth £6,500.

The tax position is as follows:

CGT

- Gift to Adam – No CGT.
- Gift to Ben – Indexation allowance increases the cost to around £2,400, so gain exempt under £5,500.

- Gift to Toby – CGT restricted to £1,000 ($\frac{5}{3}$ × £6,600–£6,000).

IHT

Total value of gifts (£24,000) exceeds annual allowance (£3,000) and small gift allowance (3 × 250) by £20,250. This goes on Phillip's IHT record, but drops out if he survives seven years. In this case, if Phillip had executed a Deed of Variation altering the distribution of his father's estate so as to provide for three legacies of £8,000 direct to each grandchild, he would have avoided all the CGT and IHT problems.

Income Tax

When making a gift to your own minor child, do remember the Income Tax trap, which means you will be taxed on income over £100. In such cases, it is sensible to choose an asset which will minimize or avoid this tax liability. A parent wanting to give (or redirect by Deed of Variation out of a grandparent's estate) to a minor child should consider the following types of investments which would avoid producing taxable income: National Savings Certificates, Friendly Society Policies, Zero-Dividend Preference Shares, Premium Bonds, Single Premium Insurance Bonds and Index-Linked Gilts.

The house

Where the gift is a house, say, from parents to children, there are two points to watch:

1.   If the transfer is to avoid IHT, it is important that the parents do not reserve a benefit, such as continuing to live in the house (see Chapter 2, GROBs). There are technical schemes to avoid the reservation of benefit rules, but professional advice is essential.
2.   If the house is transferred immediately before the donor goes into a local authority nursing home, for example, the local authority has the power to disregard the gift when assessing the contribution due from the patient. Nursing home fees will not be waived unless the gift was effected at least, say, two years earlier.

The form of the gift – Outright, Trust, or Nominee?

In most cases an outright gift is preferred; it is neater, cheaper and both parties have the satisfaction of seeing the donee enjoying the benefit of the gift. However, there are sometimes special reasons for not wanting this, usually where the donee is not able, not well enough or cannot be trusted to deal with the funds properly. This could apply to any of the following:

A young child.

A handicapped person.

A bankrupt.

A spendthrift.

Someone who is vulnerable or impressionable, or perhaps married to someone whom the donor might not trust or wish to benefit.

In such cases the donor may wish to protect the gift by not burdening the donee with the immediate control and responsibility for it, or by reducing the donee's ability to squander it.

Protecting a gift

- Carefully choose the form of the gift. A gift of cash is the easiest to waste. A gift of National Savings Certificates, stocks and shares, or an insurance policy can still be turned into cash, but with more effort and initiative on the part of the donee.

- Make a nominee arrangement. A nominee simply puts his or her name on the passbook or certificate in place of the name of the actual owner; often the nominee will include a 'designation' after his surname (e.g. the initials of the owner) to show that a nominee arrangement applies. This is particularly useful in the case of children or handicapped people; all their investments can be in the name of parents, for example, designated with the children's initials. The nominee then has practical control over the investment, including the ability to encash it, but legally it belongs to the beneficiary. On reaching full entitlement, the beneficiary could call for the funds to be transferred into his own name.

- Set up a trust. This can offer the maximum protection and is usually the solution where there is some reason why the beneficiary should not have personal control over his investments. Effectively, trusts are simply 'slow-motion gifts' under the control of caretakers, who are responsible for the administration of the trust, looking after the assets and the interests of all the beneficiaries. Trusts are dealt with in more detail in Chapter 14.

Interest-free loans

As mentioned at the beginning of this chapter, helping others does not necessarily mean giving money away. Although a gift will be more effective for IHT purposes, there may be reasons why you want to help someone but do not want to let go of the strings completely; for example, you may be uncertain of your own future requirements, you may want the funds back, or you may not be certain what the recipient will do with the gift. In these cases, instead of making a gift, you can make a loan, which can be with or without interest. The recipient will have use of the funds – any income or growth obtained from them will belong to him – but the capital remains owing to you (unless you cancel the loan). You can cancel the loan in your lifetime, either outright or by stages. The cancellation will, of course, amount to a gift by you. Any remaining amount still owing at the date of your death will be an asset in your estate.

Note: Any transfer of funds must be either a loan or a gift. To avoid uncertainty, it will be sensible to have a letter or written memorandum confirming whether the transfer is a gift or a loan, and, if the latter, any terms as to interest or repayment. The best written evidence is called a promissory note; this is simply a legally binding IOU which a solicitor would prepare for a nominal charge.

Investments for children

The opportunities and tax consequences of using an inheritance to give away money to those whom you might wish to help (usually children) have been explained, but do remember the following points:

- Where the donor is a parent of a minor child, avoid the Income Tax trap by choosing investments which do not produce a chargeable income.
- All children now have their own Personal Allowance, so until their income exceeds £3,295, they will not be liable to tax. It is therefore often suggested that children's money should be invested only in accounts where the interest is paid gross. This is presumably on the basis that reclaiming tax is difficult, time-consuming or expensive. Do not be put off; nothing could be further from the truth. Reclaiming tax on behalf of a child involves completing a fairly straightforward form (obtainable from your inspector of taxes); this task is made even easier if a solicitor, accountant or bank's trustee department has already

started the ball rolling by completing the first year's form. To choose an investment on the basis of whether the interest is paid without deduction of tax is letting the tax tail wag the investment dog, and not to be advised.

As with adults, the choice of investments for children depends on the age, circumstances and requirements of the individual child. The following suggestions are therefore intended purely as a rough guide. A fuller explanation of each of the following investments and the tax consequences is contained in Chapter 7.

Short-term investments – Immediate access

- Bank account or building society account – these offer reasonably high interest, immediate access and a variety of 'freebies', such as cash incentives, vouchers or gifts.
- National Savings Accounts – offer convenience of operating through the Post Office, but very low interest on Ordinary Account, and one month's notice is required on Investment Account.

Medium-term investments (say, 4–8 years)

Lump sum investments

- National Savings Certificates – guaranteed rate if held for five years; no income; tax-free growth.
- National Savings Income Bonds – minimum £2,000; variable interest but paid gross, and monthly.
- National Savings Capital Bonds – five-year contract; interest paid gross but added to capital, so full benefit not available until end of fifth year.
- Children's Bonus Bonds – new five-year contract; maximum £1,000; funds available on one month's notice; 5 per cent per annum paid for first five years, but large bonus of 47.36 per cent on fifth anniversary, producing overall return of 11.84 per cent.
- TESSAs – up to £9,000 over five years; interest tax-free if left to accumulate over five-year period.
- Premium Bonds – no interest, monthly prizes free of all tax, but not really worth holding less than maximum of £10,000.

- Gilts – interest paid gross if purchased through National Savings Register.

Regular savings

- National Savings Yearly Plan – monthly savings plan offering tax-free return of 9.5 per cent compound if retained for five years.
- Unit Trust Savings Plan/Investment Trust Savings Plan – no guarantees, but good prospects for capital growth and income growth over the longer term. Risk of loss over shorter periods.

Longer-term investments (say, over 8 years)

It is over the longer term that inflation becomes a major factor in investment decisions. At an annual rate of only 7 per cent, a £1,000 legacy would be worth (in real terms) under £500 in 10 years' time. For this reason equity-based investments should certainly be considered in any long-term savings plan for children.

Lump sum investments

- Units in a Unit Trust – probably a UK general trust rather than one of the more exotic ones.
- Ordinary Shares in an Investment Trust.
- Zero-Dividend Preference Shares in a 'split-level' Investment Trust – sounds very technical, but well worth considering for virtually guaranteed capital growth.
- Convertible Stocks – these are less risky than individual shares, generally with higher income, but still with prospects of capital growth.
- A selection of individual stocks and shares – higher degree of risk, but possibly greater degree of interest, as well as more growth potential.
- Index-linked Gilts – a choice of repayment dates, plus the probability of keeping pace with inflation.

Regular savings

Particularly over the long term, starting a regular savings plan is an excellent way of encouraging a child to learn how to save, in addition to building up what could be a very substantial sum for the child's future.

- Friendly Society Bonds – minimum 10 years, but free from all taxes; equity-based investments offer prospect of capital growth; after 10 years, can leave the funds to accumulate further, tax free.
- Unit Trust Regular Savings Plans/Investment Trust Regular Savings Plans. Good prospects of capital growth and income growth (child can reclaim tax deducted). Plans can be stopped and restarted at any time.
- With Profits Endowment Policy/Unit-linked Endowment Policy – minimum 10-year savings with insurance cover, usually on the life of the parent; funds bear tax during the period, but the proceeds will be tax free; different maturity dates can be chosen to meet differing requirements.

Regular savings plans for children can build up substantial capital through the generosity of grandparents. A covenant from grandparents in favour of a newborn grandchild can be used to fund the premium on, say, a 21-year Endowment Policy on the parent's life held in trust for the child. Although covenants no longer provide any tax advantages, they can establish that the gifts (i.e. the covenanted payments) are sufficiently regular to qualify as regular payments out of the donor's net income, so as to be exempt from IHT on the grandparents' death.

If the father dies before the child is 21, the insurance proceeds would provide a substantial fund to help look after the rest of the child's education and upbringing. If the father survives until the child is 21, the maturity value of the policy will provide a substantial fund out of which the child would then be able to start a new savings plan, perhaps effecting further policies or PEPs which could be encashed at specified future times. Alternatively, the fund could be used to provide further benefits for the child's own family in due course.

If savings are accumulated in this way for a total period of, say, 40 years, the result will vividly illustrate the 'miracle of compound interest'; for example, an investment of £100 per month started by a grandparent for a newborn child, and then continued by the child between the ages of 21 and 40, would produce (assuming a constant growth rate of 12 per cent) the staggering total of just under £1 million by the time the child is 40. Even allowing for inflation, the availability of such a sum at age 40 could be invaluable, whether to reduce a mortgage, assist with school fees, help the family business, set up a new family trust or whatever.

Where children are concerned, especially over the longer term, family trusts can often provide a solution to all sorts of problems, practical as well as financial, as will be seen from the next chapter.

14 Trusts

A trust can be regarded as a suspended or slow-motion gift, as it allows assets to be set aside for the future benefit of one or more persons, including children not yet born. In many cases the beneficiary gains access to the trust fund on reaching a particular age (often 18 or 25) or on marrying. In the meantime, the trust fund (which can be in any form – cash, property, investments, or an insurance policy) is under the control of trustees, who act as caretakers with specific duties and responsibilities. The trustees are the legal owners of the trust fund, but they hold it for the benefit of the beneficiaries and can deal with it only in accordance with the terms of the trust. If a trustee fails in his responsibilities, perhaps by using the fund for his own benefit, he would be in breach of trust and personally liable.

Trusts are established either by a lifetime Deed or by Will, and the person who sets up the trust is called the settlor. In the case of a lifetime trust, the settlor can also be a trustee, which allows him to retain a say in the management of the trust and in the investment policy.

Trustees

Ideally, there should be no less than two trustees, and no more than four, all of whom must be over 18. Alternatively, a corporate trustee (such as a bank's Trustee Department) can act as a sole trustee, or jointly with an individual. Trustees are under a general obligation to use the utmost diligence in carrying out their duties – this includes avoiding losses, if possible, and keeping proper accounts – and they are personally liable to the beneficiaries for any losses caused by their default. Given the importance of their role, the choice of trustees is vitally important.

The ideal trustees

- Must be entirely trustworthy.

- Ideally, live locally and have a reasonable personal knowledge of the family affairs.
- At least one of them should have some technical expertise in trust and tax administration.

Trusts can represent a most convenient way of dealing with family assets, both in your lifetime and after the death of you and your spouse. Although an outright gift of money may be simpler and cheaper, it may not always be appropriate; trusts offer a more flexible alternative, often with considerable tax advantages. Look at the following range of financial problems:

- How can a successful businessman provide for his disabled son?
- How do concerned parents help their daughter financially without making her a target for fortune-hunters?
- How can a grandparent provide for her grandchildren equally, without worrying about their inheriting too much too soon?
- How does a husband ensure that if his (younger) wife remarries after his death, there is no risk of his assets passing through to the new husband to the exclusion of his own children?

A trust can provide the answer to all these (and many other) problems.

Advantages of Using Trusts

- To look after or provide for someone who is unable to look after himself, perhaps through mental or physical disability.
- To protect beneficiaries against themselves – e.g. a spendthrift, a daughter who has married a money-grabber, or a beneficiary who is vulnerable to the influence of others.
- To protect family assets against the claims of creditors, but not to defraud them.
- To benefit young children who are not yet able to look after themselves.
- To facilitate the provision of funds when and where they may be needed – e.g. school fees, or to protect business interests, perhaps on the death of a partner or fellow shareholder.
- To save tax – possibly the most important reason of all. Trusts are separate entities, so transferring funds into them can produce a saving in all three major taxes.

Income Tax

Depending on the type of trust, trustees are taxed at 25 per cent, or in some cases 35 per cent, which can compare favourably with an individual's top rate of 40 per cent.

Capital Gains Tax

Trustees have a separate allowance of half the individual's allowance (currently £2,750) and are liable to CGT at only 25 per cent (or 35 per cent in some cases).

Inheritance Tax

If a settlor transfers assets into a trust from which he cannot obtain any further benefit, this will count as a gift, even though the funds may not be paid over to the beneficiaries until much later. Depending on the type of trust, it will either be a *Potentially Exempt Transfer* (so no Inheritance Tax would be payable unless the settlor died within seven years of setting up the trust), or a *Chargeable Transfer* (when IHT would be payable only if the transfer exceeds £140,000). In either event, the full IHT exemption (currently £140,000) would become available again after seven years if there had been no other substantial gifts in the meantime.

So if you inherit money, but do not require the full amount of the inheritance for your own use, it would be sensible to unload some of the surplus at a time when you are likely to survive for at least seven years. But what if you do not feel that it would be appropriate to make immediate gifts, perhaps because the family members are still too young, or you would simply prefer to provide for their future rather than releasing funds to them now? It is in this sort of situation that trusts have a unique part to play.

Types of Trust

All trusts should be individually tailored to the circumstances. As the legal and taxation aspects are extremely involved, professional advice is essential. However, there are two basic types of trust:

- Interest in Possession Trusts.
- No Interest in Possession Trusts (including Discretionary Trusts and Accumulation and Maintenance Trusts).

Interest in Possession Trusts

These allow at least one beneficiary an immediate right to receive any income as it arises. For example, a wife might leave her estate in trust for the income to be paid to her husband during his lifetime, or she might leave her house in trust for her husband to live there during his lifetime; after her death the estate would be divided between her children. In this case the trust would be created by the wife's Will, her trustees would be the legal owners of the house, and her husband (who would be entitled to receive the income and occupy the house) is called the 'life tenant'.

Where the trust consists of a life policy, it is common to have an Interest in Possession Trust for the benefit of the other family members, who then become entitled to the trust fund (the policy moneys) immediately on the death of the life insured. This is a common arrangement in Inheritance Tax planning.

Putting a Life Policy in Trust

In 1991 Tom (aged 58) effects a Whole Life Policy (with profits) on his life for £50,000. The annual premium is £2,860 p.a. Tom appoints his wife and solicitors as trustees. Payment of each premium is techincally a gift, but there is no IHT problem, as it is covered by the 'normal expenditure out of income' exemption for IHT purposes. (Alternatively, the premium would also be covered by the £3,000 p.a. exemption).

When Tom dies in 1996, the policy proceeds of, say, £65,000 are outside his estate, and therefore free of IHT, thereby saving £26,000 for the family. The proceeds are payable immediately to the trustees (without the need for Probate), who then distribute the proceeds to Tom's family in accordance with the terms of the original Trust Deed.

C

It is also common, especially where the trust relates to an insurance policy, to have a Flexible Trust. Although one or more particular beneficiary has an interest in possession, the trustees are given a Power of Appointment, namely the ability to switch all or part of the income away from the particular beneficiary and to distribute it between a range of alternative beneficiaries.

No Interest in Possession Trusts

These are trusts where none of the beneficiaries are entitled to the income as it arises; it is up to the trustees whether they distribute the income or leave it to accumulate. There are two main types of trust within this category:

Discretionary Trusts

These allow the trustees full discretion on whether to accumulate the income or distribute it. In the latter case they are free to choose the beneficiary, to decide how much and when he or she should be paid, and whether out of capital or income. This is an extremely flexible arrangement which can be most useful if, for example, it is not clear how things will work out – whether the children will make happy marriages, for instance. This is the most flexible type of trust, but it does have two slight tax disadvantages:

Income Tax

The trustees pay an additional 10 per cent income tax surcharge, i.e. a total of 35 per cent on trust income.

Inheritance Tax

To prevent funds from accumulating tax-free for too long, there is a small periodic charge to IHT every 10 years, and an exit charge when funds are finally transferred out of the trust.

In practice, the additional IHT liability is not substantial; it only arises if the value of the trust funds exceeds the IHT threshold (£140,000), and is a relatively small price to pay for the great flexibility offered by Discretionary Trusts.

Accumulation and Maintenance (A & M) Trusts

This is really a narrower sort of Discretionary Trust. The trust funds must either be accumulated, or used for the education and maintenance of the beneficiaries, who must become entitled to either capital or income by the time they are 25. This type of A & M Trust has the same Income Tax and Capital Gains treatment as Discretionary Trusts, but it does have specific Inheritance Tax advantages in that there is no periodic charge or exit charge. An A & M Trust is therefore a reasonably flexible, particularly useful and tax-efficient way of providing for the education and assistance of younger family members, especially grandchildren.

Tax Treatment

The tax treatment of trusts is too complicated and technical to explain in detail in this book; but as trusts are so important in financial planning generally, and in organizing gifts of money particularly, there follows a very simplified tax guide to the two main types of trust already discussed.

Interest in Possession Trusts

Income Tax

The trust income belongs to the life tenant and is taxed as part of his or her income.

Capital Gains Tax

The lifetime transfer of funds to trustees is a disposal by the settlor, so CGT will be payable if the assets transferred do not consist of cash, and if they carry a gain (after indexation relief) in excess of the settlor's allowance. If the trust arises under the settlor's Will, i.e. on his death, there is no CGT. Subsequent disposals by the trustees will be subject to CGT if the gain exceeds the trustees' allowance (£2,750).

Inheritance Tax

The transfer to the trust is again a disposal by the settlor and, as such, a PET; but if the life tenant is the settlor's spouse, the transfer is exempt. The subsequent death of the life tenant is also a disposal and, for IHT purposes, the life tenant is treated as the owner of the trust funds, so their value is added to the value of the life tenant's own estate.

Interest in Possession Trusts and IHT `C`

Lucy is the life tenant of her late husband's estate, which is held in trust for her during her lifetime. In 1992 Lucy dies. The trust assets are worth £100,000. Lucy's own estate (mainly her house) is worth £80,000. For IHT purposes, the two are added together. The total of £180,000 exceeds the threshold by £40,000. The IHT liability (40% £40,000) is therefore £16,000. This is paid proportionately by the trust (10/18ths) and by the life tenant's estate (8/18ths).

Discretionary Trusts and A & M Trusts

Income Tax

The income belongs to the trustees, who pay an extra 10 per cent tax, making a total of 35 per cent. However, if they pay out the income to a beneficiary, it is then taxed as the beneficiary's income, but after taking into account the tax paid by the trustees.

Establishing a Discretionary Trust `C`

Alan establishes a Discretionary Trust for the benefit of his children and grandchildren.

Gross income in year one	£1,000
Tax payable by the trustees:	£350
Net income of trust:	£650

The trustees divide the income between Alan's two grandchildren, Richard and Amanda. They each receive £325 cash and a tax certificate showing that £175 tax has been deducted (half of the £350 paid by the trustees). If this is the children's only income, it will be covered by their Personal Allowances, so they would each be able to reclaim the full amount of £175.

Capital Gains Tax

There are two occasions on which CGT may be payable:

- On the creation of a lifetime trust. If the settlor gives assets with an inbuilt gain in excess of his allowance, CGT will payable. CGT will not be a problem on the creation of a trust if the trust fund consists of cash, or if the trust arises under a Will.
- On any disposal by the trustees. If the trustees sell a trust asset, or distribute any of the trust assets to a beneficiary, this will be a disposal, so CGT will be payable on any gain in excess of the trustees' allowance.

Inheritance Tax

In this case, Discretionary Trusts and A & M Trusts are treated differently. With a Discretionary Trust there are three occasions when IHT may be payable:

- Entry charge – setting up a Discretionary Trust is a chargeable disposal, so IHT will be payable if the amount exceeds the threshold of £140,000.
- Duration – Discretionary Trusts are liable to a small periodic charge every 10 years.
- Exit charge – there will be a further disposal when the trust is wound up, unless the value is under the IHT threshold.

An A & M Trust enjoys more favourable treatment for IHT purposes:

- Setting up a lifetime A & M Trust is not a chargeable transfer, but a potentially exempt transfer, so there will be no IHT unless the settlor dies within seven years, even if the value of the trust exceeds £140,000.
- There is no periodic charge or exit charge.

The Cost of Trusts

After extolling the virtues of using trusts, especially for gifts within the family, the only real disadvantage is the expense involved in setting up and running them. This is because of two factors. First, the administrative requirements, especially the necessity of maintaining accounts, filing tax returns and providing tax certificates, can be a burden. Second, there is a heavy degree of personal responsibility on the trustees, who must supervise the trust investments, deal with the beneficiaries, comply with all the rules and accept personal liability for any loss.

Given these two factors, it is usually advisable for the trustees to include at least one professional (a solicitor, accountant or bank Trustee Department). This will mean a minimum cost of several hundred pounds a year for a straightforward trust. (Many professional trustees, and all corporate trustees, charge on a percentage basis, say, 1 per cent p.a. of the value of the trust assets, often with a minium fee of £1,000 or £2,000 p.a.)

Nonetheless, professional fees should be regarded as money well spent when the result can be of great benefit to the family. If the assets are substantial, the costs can often be outweighed by the saving in tax, not to mention the greater peace of mind derived from the flexibility and the knowledge that Aunt Agatha's inheritance is being properly looked after for the benefit of young or financially naive beneficiaries.

One final word of warning – do not attempt to set up and run a trust unaided; the technical expertise required makes it essential to obtain proper professional advice on all the legal and taxation aspects involved.

15 Obtaining Professional Advice

The desirability and, in some cases, necessity of obtaining professional advice on financial matters has been stressed throughout this book. Technical details, procedural requirements and taxation consequences are just a few of the reasons for doing so, but there is only one reason for not doing so – the question of costs. Yes, professional advice does cost money, but except in the most straightforward or low-value cases, where it may not be cost-effective, the outlay is usually more than offset by the security and peace of mind obtained, by the tax saved, or both. Note too that in many cases the commission generated on the purchase of certain investments or life insurance products means that there will be no additional cost to the investor (see p. 212).

Take care not to be seduced by direct mailshots: 'For only x pounds per month you could be a millionaire by the time you are 55.' No matter how attractive the product may sound, it will rarely be better – and will often be much worse – than another (and perhaps more appropriate) product from another company, and which a professional adviser would be able to arrange for you (see Practical Tips, p. 156).

Going it alone

It is quite possible for you to wind up Aunt Agatha's estate, invest your own inheritance and perhaps even effect a trust for the benefit of the next generation, just as you could fill your own teeth, or service your own boiler, but it would be a foolhardy person who attempted any of these tasks without professional advice. In most cases, at no extra cost, you are likely to obtain a more appropriate investment and more advantageous result.

Having said that, there is certainly scope for intrepid investors who would prefer the DIY approach to undertake the management of their own investment portfolio at least. In this case, the first thing they need to acquire is knowledge, and there is no shortage of good books and magazines on investment matters (see Further Reading, p. 263). With the aid of such publications, you may well devlop an interest in investments and be able to decide which particular ones you require. If you are therefore an 'execution only' investor, you only need to know the best way of actually buying and selling your chosen investments.

Many investment products (building society accounts, National Savings products, Guaranteed Bonds, TESSAs) are available direct from the suppliers, but most insurance-based products (life policies, Single Premium Bonds, annuities) and most Stock Exchange investments, Unit Trusts and Investment Trusts are best purchased through authorized intermediaries. However, in the case of equities, Unit Trusts and Investment Trusts there is no reason why you should not purchase them direct if you are confident in your choice of investment and aware of all the risks. (Note that there are many 'tip sheets' relating to shares. They range from the authoritative *Investors Chronicle* to the racy *Penny Share Guide*; but remember that no one, not even the editor of the *Financial Times*, can forecast the movement of share prices. The prices fluctuate according to supply and demand and any 'good buy' of a particular share is only the other side of the vendor's 'good sell'.)

In the case of the Unit Trusts, these can be purchased or sold direct. The telephone numbers of the trust managers are quoted in the financial papers. When you telephone and request the current price, they will usually quote two prices – a 'bid' and an 'offer' price, for example, 95p bid, 100p offer. In other words, if you purchased 1,000 units today at the offered price of 100p, they would cost you £1,000. If you sold the units tomorrow at the same bid the price of 95p you would receive only £950. This bid/offer spread is where the managers make their money.

In the case of stocks and shares (including Investment Trusts) most investors find it convenient to deal through stockbrokers, especially provincial ones whose commission rates tend to be less than London brokers. They are also more willing to take on small private investors.

Brokers generally offer three levels of service (with corresponding levels of charges):

Execution only service

This is the 'cheap and cheerful' approach, where the broker simply completes the deal, but without offering any advice. Minimum commissions range from £10 to £40.

'Dealing with advice' service

Advice is offered, but a slightly higher fee is payable.

Portfolio management service

Brokers look after your investments in their name, dealing with most of the paperwork and administration. The service can either be 'advisory', where the brokers consult you before dealing, or 'discretionary', where they act on their own initiative. This level of service involves an annual management fee.

Alternatives to stockbrokers

Share Link
This is a no-frills dealing service set up by British Telecom and Birmingham stockbrokers Albert E. Sharp. Dealings by telephone, post or Prestel. Low commission (minimum £20).

Banks
All major clearing banks offer a share-dealing service, with minimum commissions of between 1.5 and 1.65 per cent on the first £7,000 or so invested. (Minimum commissions range between £20 and £30.)

Building societies
An increasing number of building societies offer similar dealing facilities to banks, with commission rates and minimum commission in the same range. If you don't already know a broker, it is worth shopping around.

In 1992 TAURUS will be introduced (see p. 113). This computerized method of transferring shares will do away with share certificates and transfer forms, and replace them with statements. Every investor will have a unique personal identification number for every holding. TAURUS may or may not save paper, but it will certainly increase the importance of record-keeping.

For the rest of this chapter, it is assumed that you do not wish to pursue the DIY approach, but would prefer to use the services of a professional adviser or intermediary. Whatever path you opt for, do remember the golden rules for investors (see Chapter 7), and particularly note the following:

- Beware of greed, and don't overlook the risk/reward ratio; if something looks too good to be true, it probably is.
- In equities generally stick to Blue Chips (the large, established companies).
- In Unit Trusts or Single Premium Bonds, unless you can afford to lose part of your capital, avoid the more speculative sectors (Japanese Recovery Funds, Emerging Market Trusts, Commodity Funds, etc.) and invest in the larger, more general funds with established track records.

Investor Protection and the Financial Services Act (FSA)

One of the main purposes of the Financial Services Act was to increase and improve protection for investors, not least by regulating all investment advisers and (at least in theory) making it harder for 'cowboys' to remain on the scene. The most notable achievement so far has been an increase in government bodies with fancy names like the Securities Investment Board (SIB), exceeded only by the increase in paperwork, record-keeping and (consequently) cost to the investor. However, although the regulations are constantly being amended, the new framework introduced by the Act is still in place. This puts the SIB at the top of the heap, and under it are the various governing bodies which supervise the activities of all institutions and individuals involved in investments – from the single private investment adviser to the largest insurance company. The structure is as follows:

Securities & Investment Board
(SIB)

Recognized professional bodies,   Self-regulatory organizations,
e.g. Law Society, Institute of   e.g. FIMBRA, LAUTRO
Chartered Accountants

Individual members   Individual members

The new system imposes a stringent set of rules on its members. For example, it is a criminal offence for any person to undertake investment business (give investment advice, or manage or deal in investments) unless they are authorized by the appropriate governing body. (There are various governing bodies for different types of advisers, but they all impose similar minimum requirements.)

The system also stipulates that all intermediaries and investment advisers must be either 'tied representatives' (i.e. agents of one particular insurance company) or independent. This distinction is called 'polarization'. Tied representatives act for the insurance company, while independent advisers act for you, the individual investor client. All advisers must make clear to which category they belong so that investors know what they are dealing with.

All investment advisers must abide by certain codes of conduct and minimum standards laid down by the appropriate governing body. For example, they are under the following duties:

- To know their client; the adviser must establish sufficient facts to ensure that the advice will be appropriate and that only suitable investments are recommended.

- Not to mislead or persuade someone to invest in any particular investment.
- To compensate for financial loss or negligence (most carry insurance cover).
- To keep records of advice given and to supply details of all investments purchased or sold.
- To give the best advice; this is effectively a question of knowing the client's circumstances and requirements, and then selecting the most suitable investment and on the best terms available.

All investment advisers must provide their clients with a 'buyer's guide', confirming whether they are tied agents or independent, and giving details of the service to be provided.

Types of Adviser

If you are seeking advice on investment, you can go to any one or more of the following advisers (presented here in alphabetical order):

Accountant
Bank manager
Bank investment department
Independent Financial Adviser (IFA)
Insurance broker
Insurance company representative
Merchant banker
Solicitor
Stockbroker

All the above must be authorized and regulated under the Financial Services Act, but as mentioned earlier, there is a fundamental distinction between tied and independent advisers.

Tied Agents

Tied agents are representatives, usually of an insurance company. Therefore they can sell only the products of that company and must make it clear that they are doing so. They are backed by the resources of the relevant financial institution. All the major banks and most of the building societies (except for the Bradford & Bingley) are tied, so they sell only the policies issued by the company to which they are tied.

Advantages

- Security and confidence in the wealth of resources behind such advisers; you know who you are dealing with.

Disadvantages

- As tied agents can sell only the products of their parent company, it will not always be the best, most suitable or cost-effective product. If you require term assurance cover, for example, a tied agent would be restricted to a term policy issued by his own insurance company, and the premium might be substantially more than one obtained for the same amount of cover from a more competitive company.
- Tied agents are not required to disclose the amount of commission which they receive from their insurance company, so it can be more difficult for the investor to establish how much of every £100 will be invested and how much goes in administrative expenses.

Independent Financial Advisers (IFAs)

Independent advisers act for the client and are under a duty to select the best product for him or her. All insurance brokers, some building societies, most stockbrokers, all accountants and all solicitors (if authorized to do investment business) are independent; they offer independent advice and are not allowed to recommend or sell the products of one company exclusively. Independent advisers are legally obliged to give the best advice, i.e. recommend the most suitable product for a particular investor's circumstances on the best terms available.

Advantages

- An independent financial adviser is not biased in favour of any particular office of product; he is under a duty to ascertain all the relevant information so that he can recommend the best policy for the investor. He is also bound to disclose any commissions he receives.

Disadvantages

- There is the risk of loss if an IFA absconds or goes bankrupt (see Compensation).

Many IFAs display the Independent Financial Adviser logo. While this does not guarantee quality, it does ensure that the investor will receive independent advice and that the recommended product will be chosen from a range of suppliers.

Choosing the right adviser

This is really a question of 'horses for courses' – what kind of advice do you need? The distinction between the various types of adviser is becoming increasingly blurred, but the following table suggests factors you might like to take into account.

Adviser	Advantages	Disadvantages
Accountant	Expertise in taxation. Must be independent. Low level of risk. Professional negligence cover. Costs reduced by commissions received.	Less familiarity with non-taxation aspects.
Bank	Specialist resources available. Permanence. Minimal risk. Maximum security.	Often more expensive. Less personal and flexible approach. Changes in personnel. If tied, restricted to one company's products.
Independent Financial Adviser (IFA)	All-round approach. May have developed expertise in any area of financial planning. Costs often covered by commission. Personal and individual service.	Doesn't necessarily have depth of resources, training or professional background. Higher level of risk, so check on experience, qualifications and compensation cover.
Insurance broker	Expertise in insurance aspects. Unless fee-charging, costs covered by commissions.	Less familiarity with non-insurance aspects (taxation, legal, investments).

Insurance company representative	Depth of resources. Minimum risk. Costs covered by commission.	No expertise in non-insurance aspects. Tied agent; no choice or comparison between different offices or different products.
Merchant bank	See bank.	See bank.
Solicitors	Specialist expertise in legal aspects (Wills, probate, trusts, tax-planning). Must be independent. Ability to take all-round view. Low risk (compulsory professional negligence cover). Costs reduced by commission where relevant.	Less familiarity with non-legal aspects.
Stockbrokers	Expertise in investments. Must be independent. Low level of risk. Costs often covered by commission.	Less familiarity with non-investment aspects. Dependence on commission gives a vested interest in active dealing.

The comments in this table are necessarily generalizations. For example, you can often find an IFA with insurance expertise, a solicitor with tax knowledge, or an accountant with trust expertise. It is also possible – and often sensible – to have one main adviser who will be able to refer to an appropriate specialist if and when needed. For example, if you have a close relationship with your accountant or bank manager, you could probably rely on either of them to recommend a solicitor to draft your Will and set up a trust, and a stockbroker to help with your share portfolio.

What should advisers offer?

Financial planning, especially dealing with an inheritance, usually involves six areas of expertise:

Wills
Probate
Trusts
Taxation
Insurance
Investments.

An adviser may have knowledge in one or two or more of these areas, but all advisers should also have four other attributes:

Common sense

All-round business knowledge

Integrity

Ability to instil trust in the client.

Most people who have inherited money would have a choice between the types of advisers already mentioned, any of whom would be able to recommend further specialists, if required. It would be unusual, but not impossible, to find one adviser who could deal adequately with every aspect of your needs. The actual choice of adviser is very much one of personal preference – there is no single right answer. However, the following general points should always apply.

Trust

is a crucial element; your adviser must have integrity and (preferably) an established reputation.

Tied or independent?

If you prefer to deal with a bank or building society with whom you already have good contacts, you should receive good service and there will be virtually no risks. If you prefer the idea of independent advice from an IFA, it is important to check the security aspects. On the other hand, you have good prospects of obtaining better value at the end of the day, since an IFA is acting exclusively for the investor, is not restricted to one product supplier and will shop around for the best solution to your particular circumstances.

Recommendations

– this is by far the best and safest way of finding a satisfactory independent adviser. The recommendation may come through one of your other advisers, a satisfied friend or colleague, or IFA Promotions Limited, which exists to help the public obtain independent advice and find a local independent adviser; a list of five or six IFAs in your immediate vicitity will be sent on request (see Useful Addresses, p. 265).

Check credentials

by asking the following questions:

- Are they authorized under the FSA to conduct investment business?
- What classes of business are they authorized to conduct and are they allowed to handle clients' money? (If not, all cheques should be made payable direct to the Unit Trust or life company.)
- What is the adviser's experience? Take up references to check his or her reputation and competence.

- How will their advice be paid for – fee or commission?
- Can you have copies of all relevant documentation?
- Does the firm carry insurance cover against professional negligence?

Be prepared

for the IFA to ask you lots of questions about your circumstances and financial affairs; if he does not, he is not doing his job properly.

Watch out for:

- Churning – recommendations to sell or cash in existing investments and re-invest when there is no necessity to do so; this may simply be to produce extra commission for the intermediary.
- Flashy lifestyle, extravagant car, etc.
- Time-dated offers – 'buy now, while stocks last'.
- Anything which makes you feel that the adviser is more interested in his commission than your financial welfare.
- Very high returns or excessively attractive investments; remember the risk/reward ratio, and beware of greed.
- Guarantees – these are only as good as the person giving them.

Who pays? Commissions explained

In brief, you do. Whether an adviser charges fees or receives commission, the net result is the same – the money comes out of your pocket. The only difference is that payment by commission feels less 'painful' than writing out a cheque. However, if you invest £10,000 in a Unit Trust, for example, the £300 commission which your adviser may receive from the Unit Trust managers has come out of your £10,000 invested. Similarly, if you take out an insurance policy, a certain percentage (quite a large one) of your initial premiums is used to cover all the administrative charges of the insurance company, including the commissions paid to their sales staff or appointed representatives.

Independent intermediaries can be broken down into two categories: those who charge you for their advice and time (accountants, solicitors and some IFAs), and those who rely only on commission (many IFAs, most insurance brokers and all stockbrokers). It can be argued that the second category are not truly independent because they will generally recommend only those offices and products which will generate commission. This means that they could not afford to recommend the often first-class products of such companies as Equitable Life since they do not pay commission.

Advisers who charge fees, however, are clearly impartial because their income is not affected by their choice of company or product; the charge will depend mainly on the time taken. If commission *is* payable, a fee-charging adviser will usually rebate it, or (if the company allows) waive the commision in return for a higher investment allocation to the policy for the benefit of the investor. Where the amounts are substantial, a fee-based adviser will often work out cheaper than a commission-dependent one.

Independent vs Tied Advisers

Consider a financial plan involving an investment of £100,000 in a Single Premium Bond, a 25-year Endowment Policy (£1,000 p.a. premium) and a Personal Pension Plan (£1,000 p.a. premium). A fee-charging adviser might spend, say, seven hours on planning, advising and implementation, for which he might charge anything up to £800 plus VAT. This sounds a lot, but looks very reasonable in comparison with the commission which could be earned on the same transaction effected by a commission-based adviser;

Investment	Typical commission
£100,000	£3,000
25-year Endowment Policy at £1,000 p.a.	£500
Personal Pension Plan at £1,000 p.a.	£300

In this example, £3,800 of the total initial investment (£102,000) has been used to cover commission, which is only one of the various expenses and adminstration costs which the investor pays up-front. There is nothing wrong with an adviser receiving commission, as long as the investor is aware of it. The crucial question should be, 'How much of my initial contribution will remain in the actual investment, and how much can I expect to receive on encashment, assuming a fixed growth rate of a certain percentage each year and allowing for all charges incurred?'

Another way of considering the commission *versus* fee question is to ask whether the adviser is selling products or selling advice. Generally speaking, if the adviser is simply selling a product, he will be paid by commission, and the investor will probably prefer this to be the case anyway. If the adviser is selling advice, which may or may not result in the sale of an actual product, it will probably be a fee-based service (perhaps with commission rebate in due course) which, again, is what the client would probably prefer.

The commission clawback trap

Watch out for commission clawback, especially the notorious '1 per cent clause'. Where commission-based advisers or salesmen sell a product like an Endowment Policy, perhaps in connection with a mortgage, they often receive commission up front from the insurance company, calculated on the basis that the premiums will be paid for several years. If the policy is surrendered or allowed to lapse, the salesman or adviser will have to refund a portion of the commission back to the insurance company. It is therefore not uncommon for brokers and tied agents to introduce a clause in their contract with the client imposing a penalty if the client allows the insurance policy to lapse within the first three years. The penalty often consists of an obligation to repay 1 per cent of the mortgage loan. This sting in the tail is perfectly legal, so the moral is: Do not sign an agreement containing this penalty clause, especially if it is in connection with a mortgage loan. There are lots more fish in the sea.

How to complain

What do you do if things go wrong, or if you are not satisfied with the way your adviser has dealt with you, or with the advice given?

- First, complain directly to the adviser's firm; under the new regulations each firm should have a compliance officer and a set complaints procedure.
- If you are still not satisfied, refer the matter to the relevant regulatory body, e.g. FIMBRA (for many investment advisers), the Law Society (for solicitors), the Institute of Chartered Accountants, and LAUTRO (for Unit Trusts and life assurance companies) – see p. 214. If the regulatory body sees fit, it may refer the complaint to the appropriate ombudsman.
- You may refer the complaint direct to the relevant ombudsman yourself (see Useful Addresses, p. 265).

In addition to the preceding ways of seeking redress, an investor has two further rights:

- Common law rights – these may be used to sue the adviser for breach of contract or negligence, for example.
- Statutory rights under the Financial Services Act – these may be used to sue an authorized firm for any breach of the Investor Protection Rules which causes loss to the investor.

The governing bodies have a wide range of powers to protect the investor, including the ability to make an order for restitution, to restrict the adviser's business and to prohibit the employment of unfit persons.

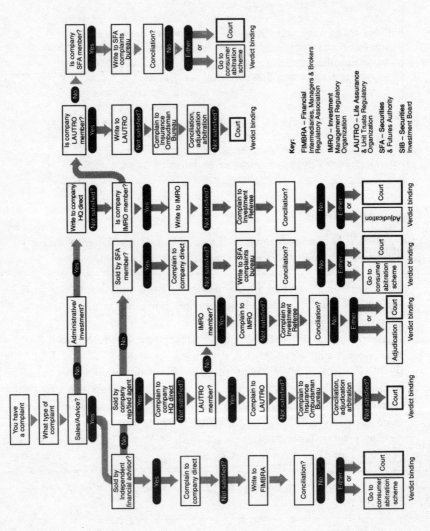

Key:

FIMBRA – Financial Intermediaries, Managers & Brokers Regulatory Association

IMRO – Investment Management Regulatory Organization

LAUTRO – Life Assurance & Unit Trusts Regulatory Organization

SFA – Securities & Futures Authority

SIB – Securities Investment Board

Source: Sunday Telegraph

Chart 2

Compensation for loss

In most cases, the complaints procedure will be sufficient to get your money back. But what if the firm itself has gone under, or the institution with whom your money is invested, so compensation or restitution is not directly available? In that event, as a last resort, you should be able to recover at least part of your loss under one of the various compensation schemes discussed below.

Banks

The Bank Deposit Protection Fund, established in 1987, provides for compensation up to 75 per cent of the first £20,000 per individual, i.e. a maximum of £15,000 per investor, irrespective of how many different accounts he or she has with the bank.

Building Societies

The Building Societies Investor Protection Fund guarantees up to 90 per cent of the first £20,000 per individual, i.e. a maximum of £18,000 per person. UK building societies also have to guarantee in full the savings of their offshore investors.

Insurance Companies

The Policy Holders Protection Board also provides for 90 per cent of the policy benefits, but with special scaling-down provisions where the benefits offered are exceptionally high. This is done in order to prevent insurance companies offering artificially high benefits purely to enable the investor to rely on the 90 per cent guarantee.

Isle of Man

Bank accounts
The 1991 regulations provide compensation of 75 per cent of the first £20,000 per individual.

Other investments
These offer 100 per cent of the first £30,000 and 90 per cent of the next £20,000; the maximum per individual is therefore £48,000.

Channel Islands and Gibraltar

There is no protection for banks and deposits, even in the case of offshore branches of UK banks. However, other investments are protected; the cover in Jersey is the same as the Isle of Man; the limits in Guernsey are slightly different – 90 per cent of the first £50,000 and 30 per cent of the next £50,000.

Investments and Financial Advisers

The Investors Compensation Scheme under the Financial Services Act provides compensation of 100 per cent on the first £30,000 of savings and 90 per cent of the next £20,000, i.e. a maximum of £48,000 per individual.

Although the complaints procedure and the compensation schemes do provide a substantial measure of protection, particularly for small investors, the newspapers are still full of stories about investors who have lost substantial sums through the fraud or incompetence of both individual and institutional advisers and investment managers. Take the following preventive measures and you can be sure such a fate will not befall you:

- Don't be talked into parting with any money until you are entirely happy about the status of the person with whom you are dealing.
- Beware of greed; are you really prepared to risk everything for the sake of that extra 1 per cent?
- Deal only with reputable advisers and managers whose references are impeccable.
- Follow the suggestions and procedures set out on pp. 210–211.

16 Possible Investment Portfolios

This chapter contains a series of case studies illustrating the types of investment portfolios it might be appropriate to consider in varying circumstances. These range from investing a legacy of £500 for a young child to dealing with the more substantial proceeds of selling a parent's house.

It must be stressed that there is no single right answer to any particular situation: 10 different experts would have no difficulty in producing 10 different solutions. The important thing is that the investment plan should take into account such factors as your age, your other assets, your tax rate, your attitude to risk, your family situation, your projected requirements and your ability to handle money, as well as the consequences of Income Tax, Capital Gains Tax and Inheritance Tax.

When considering the investment of inherited moneys, the best starting point will often be the solicitors involved in winding up the estate. If they have a financial services department, they should be able to advise on the reinvestment of the inherited funds, possibly with the involvement of an insurance broker, stockbroker, other independent financial adviser, or bank trustee department, where required.

The examples that follow are based on specific cases, but are intended only as a guide to illustrate the type of investment policy which might be appropriate. They are not intended to be specific recommendations for you, the reader. In each case, where specific investments and policies are mentioned, you can refer to Chapter 7 for further details and a brief description of the advantages and disadvantages of that particular investment; pp. 144–146 may also be a useful *aide-mémoire*.

Practical Tip

Most people have a current account, if only for reasons of convenience. However, a surprisingly large number of people (many of whom can't afford it) seem happy to throw away several hundred pounds a year, simply by leaving too much money sitting in their current accounts not earning interest. Sometimes (especially in the case of older people) they are simply not aware that it is now possible to have interest-bearing accounts with all the usual current account facilities. In other cases, it is fear of 'going into the red' which prompts people to leave substantial sums – often over £1,000 – in a current account.

If you fall in this category, you should make arrangements with your bank or building society either to switch into an interest-paying account with cheque book facilities, or to keep in your current account only as much as you are likely to spend within the next month or so. The surplus can be invested on deposit to earn interest, and you can then top up your current account every month or so. This could save you several hundred pounds a year in lost interest.

Children

Children under 18 have limited powers to enter into contracts, such as life insurance or investments, so it is rarely possible to put such things in the child's own name. (Friendly Society policies are the most common exception.) The usual solution is for the investment to be held in the parents' name (or for an insurance policy to be on a parent's life) on behalf of the child; the account or certificate is often 'designated' by including the child's initials after the parent's surname.

Investing funds for children

There are a number of factors to take into consideration.

Income Tax
– most children are non-taxpayers and will have the full Personal Allowance available, so the first £3,295 of income will be tax-free.

The Income Tax trap
– where the income is more than £100 per annum and derives from funds originally provided by the child's parents, the income will be taxable on the parents (see p. 183).

Educational requirements
– will school fees be needed?

Youth
– the period before the child attains 21 will give plenty of time for compound interest (and/or prospects for capital growth) to take effect.

Accumulation and Maintenance Trusts
(see p. 198) – for young children, these can represent excellent and

flexible vehicles to produce substantial benefits, but must be under the control of someone who is more responsible.

Generally, where a child inherits money, it is a matter of investing to accumulate funds for the future, either to generate school fees, to produce spendable income in due course, or to accumulate as large a capital sum as possible for when the child is 18 or 21 and about to start college (or get married).

Legacy of £500 to a Young Child

Aunt Agatha dies, having left a legacy of £500 to Lucy (now aged six) when she attains 18, and the remainder of her estate to Lucy's father, Sam.

C

Suggestions

---

1. If Aunt Agatha's Will does not direct the legacy to be set aside and invested, when Lucy attains 18 in 12 years' time, she will be entitled only to the sum of £500; after inflation, this will be worth only a fraction of what it is worth today. Sam therefore executes a Deed of Variation, amending Aunt Agatha's Will by providing that the legacy should be set aside and invested as a separate legacy fund (including any capital growth and all accumulated income) when she attains 18. Initially, Aunt Agatha's PRs invest the money in a building society account in their names on behalf of Lucy.

2. In view of the length of time until Lucy is 18, inflation becomes an important factor. The solicitors therefore suggest to Agatha's PRs that the £500 might be invested in a general Unit Trust, such as the M & G Dividend Fund, or an Investment Trust such as Securities Trust of Scotland Investment Trust, in the belief that these will continue to provide steady capital growth and income growth over the next 12 years. The units (or shares) are bought in the names of Lucy's parents (Sam and Janet), but designated with her initials. The income from the investment can be accumulated or paid out for Lucy's benefit, in which case she could reclaim any tax deducted from the income, as long as it does not exceed £100 per annum (see Income Tax trap, p. 183).

> ### Legacy of £2,000 to Grandchildren
> Granny leaves a legacy of £2,000 to 'each of my grandchildren living at my death'. These turn out to be Adam (18), Ben (14) and Toby (11).

Suggestions

1. As the gifts are not conditional on attaining 18, each grandchild is immediately entitled to the £2,000. Ben and Toby are too young to be able to give a valid receipt to Granny's PRs, so in their case the moneys are invested in the names of their parents, designated with the initials of the child. The parents see these legacies as an opportunity for each child to start their financial planning; they therefore arrange to open bank or building society accounts for each child, and elect for interest to be paid gross, using form IR110.

2. Adam is about to start at university; he doesn't particularly want income (which might prejudice his grant) and is happy to leave his capital for a few years, until he is likely to get married. He is also prepared to incur a certain amount of risk in the hopes of obtaining some capital growth. The solicitors winding up the estate therefore suggest investing Adam's legacy as follows:

   - Leave £1,000 in the bank or building society account on which interest is paid gross, but arrange a standing order to cover regular payments of £20 a month into a Unit Trust or Investment Trust Regular Savings Plan. This will start Adam on the savings ladder and should produce steady growth of both capital and income; Adam will also be able to reclaim the tax from the dividends.

   - Put £1,000 into Investment Trust Zero-Dividend Preference Shares, such as Scottish National Trust, which will provide guaranteed capital growth until the repayment date in 1998 (although the shares could be sold before then if required).

3. Ben is still at school and is unlikely to require the capital for at least five years. His legacy is therefore also divided between two investments – the first offering a guaranteed return and the second offering a *potentially* better return:

   - £1,000 in National Savings Children's Bonus Bonds; this will mature for £1,750 tax free at the end of five years, representing an overall return of 11.84 per cent.

   - £1,000 into a high-yielding Investment Trust or Unit Trust offering reasonable prospects of capital growth and income growth, with the added benefit of two dividends a year in the meantime, from which Ben can reclaim the tax deducted.

4. Toby is also at school, but able to take a longer-term view. His parents are concerned that the funds should be invested to obtain maximum capital growth and should not be too accessible, as Toby is really too young to deal with such a relatively large sum. His parents therefore use the £2,000 to open a building society account and arrange a standing order of £43 per month to be paid direct into two savings plans which should offer good prospects of growth over the next few years:

- £18.00 per month into a Friendly Society policy (10-year savings totally tax free).
- £25.00 per month into an Investment Trust Regular Savings Plan, with income reinvested to provide compound growth.

The building society account can be topped up with future gifts or savings, and after three years Toby's parents calculate how much would still be required to complete the regular monthly subscriptions into the Friendly Society policy. When the funds in the building society are down to that figure, Toby's parents can stop further payments into the Investment Trust Regular Savings Plan; Toby can then receive the income if required, or encash the whole or part of the accumulated funds at any time. The Friendly Society bond will mature when Toby is 21, when he can encash the policy, leave the money invested, or continue the monthly contributions himself, allowing the bond to continue growing tax free.

Legacy of £100,000 in Trust for a Young Child

Amanda (aged 7) has been left £100,000 by her grandfather in Accumulation and Maintenance Trusts (see p. 198) for when she is 21. Her parents would like to send her to a private school, while making sure that there is still something left for her if and when she gets married. The trustees of her grandfather's Will (Midland Bank Trustee Department) have full powers of investment and power to use income (and capital if necessary), as long as it is for the 'education, maintenance or benefit' of Amanda, so this will enable the trustees to use the funds to meet future school fees.

Suggestions

1. The family wishes to earmark half the trust funds specifically for Amanda's education, leaving half as a longer-term investment with a view to capital growth for when Amanda is 25.

2.   The trustees place £5,000 in a bank or building society account offering the highest interest consistent with instant access; this will serve as the main trust account to meet any future requirements for cash or professional expenses. They also place a further £5,000 in a bank account, arranging standing orders to fund various regular savings plans mentioned below.

3.   £40,000 is invested in an educational trust guaranteed scheme through the School Fees Insurance Agency on the basis that this will provide school fees of £4,533 per term for five years, starting when Amanda is 13 and increasing by 5 per cent per annum – a total of £75,147 in school fees.

4.   This leaves £50,000 to be invested so as to produce a balance between capital growth for when Amanda is 25 and some immediate income to help with living expenses. The trustees do not want all the capital locked up in case some might be needed to top up the school fees, for example. They point out that any taxable income which is not distributed to Amanda will be taxed at 35 per cent, but that she should be able to reclaim the whole of the tax deducted from any income which is actually paid to her.

5.   The following regular savings plans are therefore set up to achieve a balance of secure growth and potential growth:
   • £7,000 into a separate account to fund the maximum allowable instalments into a tax-free TESSA; £3,000 for the first year, followed by instalments of £1,800 for three years and £600 for the last year.
   • £200 p.a. into a Friendly Society policy, such as the Family Bond (minimum 10 years, totally free of all taxes).
   • £1,000 p.a. into a qualifying 15-year Endowment Policy, to produce a totally tax-free fund when Amanda is 22. In order to get the best of both worlds, the trustees effect a with-profits policy (on the life of Amanda's father) with Equitable Life and a unit-linked policy with Standard Life.
   • £1,000 p.a. into an Investment Trust Regular Savings Plan (e.g. the Dunedin Income Growth Plan) to give good prospects of capital growth and an increasing income, but with no minimum commitment in terms of years, and full flexibility.

6.   The premiums on the three policies will cost £2,200 p.a. which can be funded by standing order out of the bank or building society account (which would need to be topped up out of the other investments at suitable intervals), or by an annuity purchased in advance (worthwhile if interest rates were high).

7.   The trustees invest £10,000 in two Single Premium Bonds – one

With-Profits Bond and one Unit-linked Bond — from which withdrawals can be taken if required (see Chapter 7, Insurance-based investments).

8. The balance is invested in a portfolio consisting of:
   - Index-linked Gilts (to provide guaranteed capital growth and a small but increasing income).
   - Convertible Loan Stocks (see Chapter 7, Equity-based investments).
   - Half a dozen carefully chosen equity shares in Blue Chip companies such as Marks & Spencer, Glaxo, Reckitt & Colman, Land Securities, Shell and Unilever.

Single people

Once you have attained 18 and probably acquired some assets of your own, receiving an inheritance may provide the opportunity not just to invest for the future, but also to take account of your insurance requirements and to spend a small proportion of the inheritance on protection rather than purely on investment.

One obvious requirement is to insure your possessions (if these are not already covered on your household insurance). Life cover, although very cheap at this age, is probably not necessary just yet; but taking out an Endowment Policy, or a Unit-linked Whole Life Policy could still be an appropriate way of starting to save, especially if you anticipate getting married (when the protection element may be useful) or obtaining a mortgage (so that you would have a policy already available). Because of the high penalties on early surrender, however, you should be confident that you will be able to keep the policy going. At this age, it is also worth thinking about your other insurance requirements, such as medical expenses (which will also be cheaper, the younger you are) and Permanent Health Insurance (PHI) cover (i.e. Income Protection cover, see Chapter 9, Health matters).

If possible, you should ask your employer to pay the premiums on these insurances as a benefit in kind; if this is not possible, an inheritance may enable you to take care of these and your other insurance requirements (see Chapter 9).

Assuming that protection insurance is taken care of, this chapter concentrates on investments. At this stage, a single person is probably at college, or starting a first job. With no dependants, the main objective will usually be to accumulate the maximum capital sum with a view to providing funds when required – say, for the purchase of a house, and/or for marriage. This means making use of regular savings plans and, where money is inherited, lump sum investments.

Legacy of £25,000 for a 21-year-old Single Woman

Vanessa, 21 years old and unmarried, has just started her first job as a clerk in a firm which does not have a pension scheme. She has no immediate marriage plans, but is hoping to have settled down and bought a house by the time she is 27. On her grandfather's death, Vanessa inherits £25,000.

Suggestions

1. Vanessa pays £5,500 into her bank account for her immediate requirements, including a new car.

2. Knowing that the sooner she can start her pension provision, the larger the final pension, Vanessa invests £1,500 (15 per cent of her first year's salary) in a single-premium unit-linked pension plan recommended by her IFA. She also puts a further £3,000 in her high-interest cheque account (HICA) at the bank to make sure she has enough for a further two years' premiums at least.

3. Assuming that she may require funds for a house deposit in five years' time, Vanessa decides to divide the balance of £15,000 between investments which will offer guaranteed growth over a five-year period, and equity-based investments which carry more risk, but offer prospects of greater growth. She therefore divides the remaining £15,000 as follows;
   - £4,000 into National Savings Certificates (half in the current 36th issue and half in the index-linked issue); she anticipates a total return from these of around 9 per cent tax free.
   - £1,000 in an insurance company four-year Guaranteed Growth Bond.
   - £1,000 in a With-Profit Single Premium Insurance Bond, which cannot fall in value, and will increase in line with the profit declaration added by the insurance company each year.
   - £5,000 into a PEP, which invests half in an Investment Trust and half in a small selection of individual Blue Chip equity shares.
   - £4,000 to purchase a second-hand Endowment Policy maturing in 1997. Vanessa will have to pay annual premiums of £350 but should receive a total amount of around £11,000 if she retains the policy until 1997.

Inheritance of £80,000 for 35-year-old Bachelor   C

Alan, 35 years old and unmarried, works in a bank; he is a higher-rate taxpayer who owns his own house subject to a mortgage of £40,000. He has no immediate marital prospects. He inherits his widowed mother's estate, which consists mainly of her house. As Alan has his own property, he asks the executor of his mother's Will to sell the house, which produces £80,000 clear of expenses.

Suggestions

1. Alan pays £20,000 to the building society to reduce his own mortgage to £20,000. This obtains him full tax relief on his mortgage interest and a substantial reduction in his monthly outgoings.

2. Although his employer has a Pension scheme, Alan pays £1,000 into a free-standing AVC in order to top up his pension. He receives full tax relief on his contribution, which also offers tax-free growth within the pension fund.

3. Alan also invests £5,000 in a separate bank or building society account, which he earmarks to cover future FSAVs as soon as he is eligible, and can afford, to make them.

4. Alan pays £9,000 into a PEP; £6,000 into, for example, the Save and Prosper PEP divided between the managed fund and two shares which Alan likes to choose himself, and £3,000 into a Single Company PEP (he chooses the one run by Boots). Alan elects not to take income from the PEPs at this stage, but he can do so if he wishes to in the future.

5. Alan invests a further £7,000 in a TESSA. This is actually split into two accounts: £3,000 into a tax-free TESSA account (the maximum for the first year) and the balance into a high-interest account which feeds the remaining four years' contributions into the tax-free TESSA.

6. £10,000 divided between two BES Assured Tenancy Schemes, which Alan selects personally after reading up about them in *BEST Investment Magazine*. He chooses these particular schemes because of their greater security; the funds are invested in property, which is rented out on assured tenancies, with (in these two cases) a commitment for the property to be bought by a housing association in five years' time so that the risk is further reduced. As Alan receives tax relief at his top rate on the initial investment, the actual cost to him is only £6,000.

7. £5,000 in National Savings Certificates Index-Linked issue to

provide a guaranteed protection against inflation, plus an additional $4\frac{1}{2}$ per cent).

8. £8,000 in a portfolio of up to half a dozen Blue Chip equities, which Alan selects with the aid of his stockbroker.

9. £15,000 into a bank or building society account with a standing order to pay his contributions into four separate Regular Savings Plans, which cost a total of £4,400 p.a. (This means that Alan will have taken care of four or five years' worth of payments in advance.)

- £18 per month into a Friendly Society policy (10 years totally tax free).
- £200 per month into National Savings Yearly Plan.
- £100 per month into a Unit Trust or Investment Trust Regular Savings Plan, which can be stopped at any time.
- £50 per month into a flexible Unit-linked Whole Life Policy; at this stage, Alan chooses maximum investment content and minimum life cover, but in the future – say, if he were to marry – he could elect to increase the life cover and decrease the investment element.

Married couple without children

Once you are married, you have a dependant (your spouse), with the prospect of further dependants if you have children. Protection insurance therefore plays an important part at this stage of life. Chapter 9 contains a reminder of the additional insurance policies which should at least be considered by each spouse, especially if they receive an inheritance.

It is assumed that, on an inheritance, a small proportion is set aside to enable each spouse to bring his or her basic insurance cover up to date, including:

- Insurance of chattels and house contents.
- PHI (income protection)   } if not already provided
- Medical expenses   } for by employer.
- Life cover in trust for the other spouse.
- Family Income Benefit (FIB) cover, especially where one spouse is not working.
- Husband's insurance against incapacity of non-working wife.
- Travel and holiday cover.
- Legal expenses cover.

The following case studies assume that the extra income produced from an inheritance will be sufficient to cover any additional premiums on the above policies; the case studies therefore deal only with the suggested *investment* of inherited funds, but the reader should not overlook the importance of using an inheritance to meet the family's needs for protection, as well as investment.

If there are two incomes but no children, there are better chances of saving now than when the children arrive and the family is possibly down to one income. It is therefore vital to maximize savings and capital contributions, particularly in the light of the following factors:

- Regular Savings Plans will still be relevant, largely because of their flexibility, which allows the plan to be terminated or increased at will.
- House purchase: even if funds were available to purchase a property outright, it might be more sensible to take out a mortgage and invest the funds elsewhere, although the method of mortgage repayment becomes important. This particular point is outside the scope of this book, but the reader is strongly recommended to take independent advice before choosing.
- This is also the stage at which priority should be given to pensions. First, you are more likely to be able to make contributions now than in the future, when there are children; second, the figures on p. 139 vividly illustrate the cost of delaying pension contributions and the advantages to be gained by allowing contributions to accumulate tax free for the longest possible period of time.
- It is also essential to make Wills. Not only can the Wills provide for the possibility of future children, but if one spouse survives, inherits all the assets and subsequently dies intestate, all the assets would then pass to the family of the survivor, to the exclusion of the family of the first spouse to die – a most unfortunate (and unnecessary) result.

Inheritance of £50,000 for Childless Young Couple with Mortgage

C

Ronnie and Pam are in their late twenties, both in employment. Ronnie is self-employed and Pam works in a shop. They have a mortgage of £40,000 supported by an Endowment Policy. They do not intend to have a family for several years, but they don't want to tie their capital up for more than five years. Pam's aunt dies, leaving her estate to be divided between her three nieces. Pam's share is £50,000, which she is advised to invest as follows:

1.   £5,000 to open a new bank or building society account in joint names, to cover the insurance premiums and serve as an emergency fund for holidays, sundries and emergencies.

2.   £10,000 to reduce the mortgage to £30,000, so all the interest will qualify for tax relief, in addition to reducing the monthly outgoings.

3.   As Ronnie is self-employed, but hasn't been able to afford any pension contributions so far, his accountant confirms that he is entitled to all the unused contributions over the previous six years since he started in business. Ronnie's maximum allowable contribution would be £10,000. Pam accordingly gives Ronnie £10,000, which he uses to make single premium (i.e. one-off) contributions to two different pension providers, sensibly dividing each premium: a quarter into the With-Profits Fund, and three-quarters into the Equity Fund.

Ronnie is able to vary the premium allocation if he wants to, and to make further payments whenever he wishes. He obtains £2,500 tax relief on the £10,000 premiums now paid, so the net cost to him is only £7,500. (Ronnie invests this tax rebate in his bank/building society account to apply towards future pension payments.)

4.   Although Ronnie has wisely taken out a Family Income Benefit Policy and Pam has also insured her life for Ronnie's benefit, his only other insurance is the £40,000 With-Profits Endowment Policy taken out to repay the mortgage. Ronnie and Pam therefore each take out separate flexible 10-year Endowment Policies (which they can extend beyond 10 years if they wish) in order to combine the need for further financial protection if either of them should die, and a form of savings which will produce a tax-free cash sum any time after 10 years, which they can then use, perhaps for school fees. In each case, they divide the premiums equally between the With-Profits and the Unit-linked Managed Fund.

Total premiums of £500 p.a. each will provide approximately £4,000 cover on each life, and an estimated sum of £7,500 tax free, available for each of them in 10 years' time.

5.   Pam invests £10,000 in two PEPs of £5,000 each for herself and Ronnie. She invests her £5,000 in a New Issue Investment Trust PEP; Ronnie picks a standard PEP, with half in a Unit Trust and half in six or seven shares selected by the managers. They do not choose to receive any income from the PEP at this stage, but can do so in the future if required.

6.   £3,000 in a Single Premium Insurance Bond with a 'no loss guarantee' over five years (i.e. the value in five years' time will not be less than £3,000, even if the units fall rather than rise in price); again, Pam can withdraw 5 per cent p.a. tax free if required.

7.   Pam invests the remaining £2,000 in a Business Expansion Scheme (Assured Tenancy) Fund in the hopes of receiving a higher rate of growth over the next five years, when she will be able to realize the investment free of Capital Gains Tax.

Married couple with young children

This is perhaps the hardest stage for the family, financially at least. There may be less income (if one spouse has had to give up work) and more expenditure; having young children costs far more than childless people think it does. Protection insurance is therefore even more important for those in this category, especially if there is only one breadwinner.

This is the time when the need for capital and income is greatest, and when an inheritance is therefore particularly welcome. If the inheritance is not large, it will be a question of prioritizing and deciding where the capital is most needed:

- To reduce the mortgage debt to £30,000 or under.
- To ensure that full insurance cover is in place, specifically Term Cover (to cover all existing debts and commitments), Family Income Benefit (to provide for the family's financial needs), and PHI (to cover against loss of breadwinner's income).
- To ensure pension provision is adequate and that it includes full death benefits.
- To build up a flexible investment portfolio geared towards income or capital growth as required (see Chapter 7). Consider in particular:
   - Guaranteed Bonds, Cash Unit Trusts and Gilts if interest rates are high.
   - PEPs.
   - BES Schemes, National Savings Certificates and Index-Linked Gilts if you are a higher-rate taxpayer.
   - Equity-based collective investments, such as Investment Trusts and Unit Trusts.
- Investments specifically tailored to meet school fees.

- Additional insurances (e.g. medical fees).
- Investing for surplus income.

Married couples with young children should also ensure that they keep their Wills up to date, including the appointment of guardians (see Chapter 1); take advantage of the various ways of saving tax (see Chapter 6); and remind grandparents of the opportunity to assist financially with school fees and/or Accumulation and Maintenance Trusts.

Inheritance of Shares and £100,000 for Married Couple with Two Young Children

Richard and Liz are in their mid-thirties with two children – Charles (6) and Kirsten (4). Richard is a director of his family company, which runs its own pension scheme. He is a higher-rate taxpayer. Liz stopped working as clerk in the Revenue when Charles was born. Richard and Liz would like to send their children to private school. On the death of Richard's father (a widower) Richard and his brother inherit their father's shares in the family business and a cash sum of £100,000 from their father's pension scheme.

Suggestions

1. Richard pays £20,000 to his building society to reduce the mortgage to £30,000.
2. Although Richard has life cover under the firm's pension scheme, he has no other insurance cover. He and his brother agree that the company will take out PHI and medical expenses cover to benefit each of them. They appreciate that the premiums paid by the company will be taxable on them as benefits in kind. They also enter into an Option Agreement with regard to each other's shares in the company, backed by insurance, to ensure that the survivor would be able to buy out the shares and to provide funds for the family if either of them were to die.
3. To make sure that the school fees would be covered, Richard takes out Convertible Decreasing Term Cover for a period of 15 years, with an initial sum assured of £40,000. This will cost around only £47 p.a.
4. To protect the family financial situation, Richard and Liz each take out a Family Income Benefit Policy providing £10,000 p.a. for 20 years at an annual premium cost of approximately £170 (Richard) and £125 p.a. (Liz).

5.   As Richard's pension cover and death benefit cover is now taken care of, he can now apply his inheritance to generate as much capital as possible over the next 20 years on the basis that much of it will be needed to cover the school fees. Being a higher-rate taxpayer, he chooses investments with favourable tax treatment and decides to include regular savings plans, especially Qualifying Life Policies which will produce a tax-free sum after 10 years. Richard's investment capital is therefore applied as follows:
- £10,000 into a bank/building society account to fund £9,000 into a TESSA over the next five years, and £200 p.a. into a Friendly Society policy for the next 10 years.
- £10,000 into an insurance company unit-linked Single Premium Bond from which he encashes 5 per cent p.a. to fund premiums of £500 p.a. into a unit-linked 10-year Endowment Policy.
- £9,000 into a Personal Equity Plan (£6,000 to a managed fund and £3,000 into a Single-Company PEP).
  £5,000 into National Savings Certificates Current Issue.
- £5,000 into Index-linked Gilts to provide a guaranteed return and tax-free capital growth.
- £6,000 into two or three Unit Trusts/Investment Trusts.
- £6,000 into a Business Expansion Scheme (Property-Based Assured Tenancy Scheme).

Richard transfers the remaining £50,000 into Liz's name. As she no longer has any other taxable income, she will be able to set the whole of her Personal Allowance (£3,295) against the income produced from this gift, and will pay tax at only 25 per cent on the remainder. Liz is therefore advised to invest the £50,000 as follows:
- £10,000 into a bank/building society account paying gross interest to provide cash funds for future investments, e.g. next year's PEP.
- £5,000 in National Savings Income Bonds to provide a high monthly income on which no tax will be payable.
- £15,000 divided between high-yielding Unit Trusts and Income Shares of a split Investment Trust (see Chapter 7).
- £6,000 in a With-Profit Single Premium Insurance Bond, which can only increase in value, and from which tax-free cash withdrawals can be made whenever required.
- £5,000 in a cash Unit Trust to combine a high spendable income with immediate availability.
- £9,000 in a PEP (£6,000 in a Managed PEP and £3,000 in a Single Company one).

Richard and Liz also update their Wills, appointing guardians and incorporating a two-year mini Discretionary Trust to provide maximum flexibility.

Married couple with older children

Although this may still be a period of high outgoings, there may be more income if both spouses are earning. You will be near the height of your earning power and the emphasis is therefore changing away from the younger generation and towards your own retirement.

It will probably be possible to make savings out of income, and if you move house, this may also release further capital. If school fees have not been provided for in advance, it is still not too late. The funds could be available from existing assets, perhaps by borrowing from the pension scheme, or against the security of a life policy.

The overall strategy will be to take care of any outstanding liability for the children, while at the same time ensuring a proper foundation for your own retirement. An inheritance at this stage should enable both objectives to be achieved, possibly leaving a surplus which could be utilized to improve the quality of your lifestyle.

C

Legacy of £50,000 to Married Daughter with Teenage Children

David (45) and Carol (43) have two daughters aged 18 and 15; Sharon is about to read metalwork at Lancaster Polytechnic; Tracy is still at school. David is a divisional director of a PLC and earns £3,000 per month (plus car and pension scheme); Carol has resumed work for an estate agent, where she earns £900 per month with no perks. They have a mortgage of £30,000 on a house worth £100,000. The cost of educating Sharon and Tracy has just about exhausted their capital. Carol's father dies, leaving her a legacy of £50,000.

Suggestions

1.   David and Carol's priority is to complete the education of Sharon and Tracy, for which they calculate that they will need a total of £30,000 by the time Tracy leaves college. They therefore allocate approximately £25,000 now to provide the required total over the next six years. This is split as follows:

•   A 'composition fee' paid in advance to Tracy's school; this effectively represents the balance of the fees, discounted to take account of the fact that payment is being made in advance.

- Two or three insurance company Guaranteed Growth Bonds maturing over the next six years.
- A series of three or four Gilt-Edged Stocks maturing over the next six years.
- As interest rates are high, David purchases a Deferred Annuity, which will pay a guaranteed fixed level of fees commencing (in this case) in three years' time. This amounts to £2,000 p.a. and increases at 5 per cent p.a. over the next three years.

2. Carol and David then take care of their outstanding insurance requirements, especially PHI and FIB.

3. This leaves Carol with around £25,000, which she temporarily pays into her bank/building society account. Her adviser then confirms that, as Carol hasn't contributed to a pension scheme for the last six years, she is eligible to contribute a total of 15 per cent of her earnings over that period, and that, at her age, it will be sensible to opt out of SERPS. Carol then takes out a Personal Pension Plan, with an initial contribution of £6,000, leaving £19,000, which she divides between herself and David. They each take out a PEP for £9,000 and a Friendly Society Bond for the maximum amount of £200 p.a.

Inheritance of House and Assets Worth around £200,000 for Married Son with Teenage Children

The same facts as the case study on p. 232, but this time (a year later) David's parents die, leaving everything to him. Their estate consists of a house worth £100,000, a small block of three rented shops worth £50,000, producing £6,000 p.a. in rents (and subject to rent reviews every three years), £16,000 in the Midland bank, and a portfolio of equities worth around £40,000.

Suggestions

---

1. David and Carol's financial worries are effectively over regarding their children's education. David doesn't think that he will require all the capital he has inherited; he therefore executes a Deed of Variation, providing for the three rented shops to be put into an Accumulation and Maintenance Trust for the benefit of his children. The trustees are David, Carol and the family solicitor. For Income Tax purposes the rents will be taxable at 35 per cent on the trustees, but if they are paid out to Sharon and Tracy (once Tracy is 18), they will be able to claim most, if not all, of the tax back, assuming that they don't have

any other income. The rent itself can be used to pay the college fees.

2.   David does not want his parents' house, so he sells it for £100,000. The gain over his parents' original acquisition cost is exempt, as his parents' death created a tax-free disposal for CGT purposes.

3.   David decides to keep the equity portfolio of £40,000, but transfers the shares into Carol's name so that the dividends belong to her and will be taxed at only 25 per cent, as opposed to 40 per cent if he had kept the shares.

4.   This leaves David with £116,000 cash (the house proceeds and money in the bank). His solicitor suggests that this would be an ideal opportunity to extend the Deed of Variation and amend David's parents' Wills so as to put more funds in trust for the children. However, David and Carol feel that having worked hard all their lives, they would rather have the benefit themselves – they can always add to the trust later on perhaps when there are grandchildren. David starts by spending £6,000 on a new car for Carol, leaving £110,000 for investment. As David is still a higher-rate taxpayer, he takes advantage of most of the range of tax-free opportunities and invests a total of £70,000 (net) designed to produce maximum capital growth as follows:

● £5,000 each (for David and Carol) in the current issue of National Savings Certificates.

● £10,000 each in the current index-linked issue of National Savings Certificates.

● £9,000 each in PEPs.

● £3,000 each to meet the first instalment of TESSAs.

● £10,000 in Premium Bonds (statistically, David should win 10 prizes per year, which will be tax-free, with the always exciting possibility of landing 'the big one').

● £10,000 into BES (Assured Tenancy) Schemes; the net cost to David will be £6,000.

5.   As David is interested in property, he also invests £10,000 in a syndicated investment in an Enterprise Zone. After tax relief this costs him only £6,000, in addition to which he will receive a reasonable income from the investment.

6.   As David and Carol hope to take more holidays, they consider the possibility of buying a timeshare apartment, but eventually invest £7,000 in a Holiday Property Bond (see Chapter 8, Foreign property).

7. A keen philatelist, David spends £1,000 buying stamps.

8. Mindful of the solicitor's advice, David does arrange for gifts of £3,000 each from Carol and himself to the children, which they invest between National Savings Children's Bonus Bonds (£1,000 each) and a couple of Unit Trusts/Investment Trusts from which the dividends are ploughed back to buy further units/shares to achieve compound growths.

9. This leaves an immediate cash surplus of £12,000, which David divides between his bank account and a cash Unit Trust to provide a ready fund for future investment purposes, such as payments to the TESSAs and a contingency fund for taking up any rights issues.

The Fabulous Fifties – Pre-Retirement

By the time you are in your fifties your children will probably be self-sufficient and away from home, the mortgage may well be paid off so that outgoings are reduced, and income will be high, especially if both spouses are working. A move to a smaller house may also have released capital. In addition, with both sets of parents in their seventies or eighties, it is likely that your capital may be further increased by up to four inheritances. The fifties are therefore the age at which you should have maximum surplus income and capital.

Priorities

- Post-retirement income and pension planning.
- Making sure that all insurances are in place, especially Family Income Benefit, Permanent Health Insurance, private medical insurance and possibly the new Long-Term Care Insurance (see Chapter 9, Health Matters).
- Inheritance Tax Planning.
- Making sure your Wills are up to date.

As a general rule, your overall financial policy should be considered in relation to tax and investment consequences.

Income Tax

- Transfer assets between husband and wife to take advantage of separate taxation; reduce the differences in incomes so that more income will be taxed at nil or 25 per cent and less at 40 per cent (see Chapter 6, Income Tax). Equalizing the size of estates is also sensible from the Inheritance Tax point of view as it will provide greater security to the surviving spouse and more opportunity for saving IHT (see Chapter 2, A dozen practical points).

• A husband might be able to employ a non-earning wife in his business or as a partner; this would not only save Income Tax, but also provide further opportunities for pension contributions for the wife.

• Maximize pensions contributions for both partners; tax relief at the highest rates available on the contributions and the pension funds build up tax free.

• Utilize investments with tax advantages, such as Business Expansion Schemes, Personal Equity Plans, Woodland Syndicate Investments or purchasing a property for holiday lets, which the lower-income-earning spouse can run as a business. If the property is purchased with borrowed money, this will be a Qualifying Loan, so tax relief will be available on the loan interest (see Case Study on p. 238).

Capital Gains Tax

• Include investments which will avoid CGT problems on realization, e.g:
  – Qualifying Life Policies (see Chapter 7, Regular Premium Insurance Policies); the minimum 10-year period means that these have the added advantage of maturing when you are in your sixties, which makes them particularly relevant for retirement planning.
  – BES and PEPs.
  – Low-coupon Gilts, National Savings Certificates, etc.

Inheritance Tax

The fifties is perhaps the best time for IHT planning, making gifts and establishing trusts because there should be surplus capital and income, particularly in the event of an inheritance. You are also statistically likely to survive at least seven years, so any gifts (whether chargeable disposals or Potentially Exempt Transfers, see Chapter 2, Lifetime Gifts) will be likely to drop out of charge and escape IHT.

If you can afford it, IHT makes it sensible for both spouses to make maximum use of all the exemptions and unload as much of their estates as possible (see Chapters 13 and 14). In particular:

- Establish a Discretionary Trust; this will be a Chargeable Transfer, but no IHT will be payable up to the value of the Nil Rate Band (£140,000 per donor). After seven years the transfer 'drops out' of charge and the Nil Rate Band becomes available again, so the exercise can be repeated.
- Establish an Accumulation and Maintenance Trust; this will be a Potentially Exempt Transfer. No IHT will be payable when the trust is established; IHT would be payable only in the event of death within seven years.
  Note: The order in which these trusts are established can have important tax consequences; professional advice is therefore essential.
- Make maximum use of exempt gifts (see Chapter 2, Lifetime Gifts), especially the annual exemptions of £3,000 per donor, £250 per donee and the regular gifts out of surplus income.
- Make further gifts to individuals or an A & M Trust; these will be further PETs, and as a result each one will 'drop out' in turn after seven years.

Investment

In your fifties you should be able to afford a wide range of investments, mostly directed towards your own retirement, so on average you will be able to take a 10-year view. Investments should therefore concentrate on maximum overall return over a 10-year period, that is capital growth with or without income. The tax treatment both now and later will be relevant; you could be a higher-rate taxpayer now, but likely to be a basic-rate taxpayer after retirement. This means that the core investments may well include most of those investments listed in Chapter 7, particularly the following:

- Maximum pension contributions.
- Contributions to Qualifying Life Policies, including Capital Conversion Schemes (see Chapter 10) and Maximum Investment Plans. These may be funded either from surplus income or funded in advance by an annuity or by tax-free withdrawals of 5 per cent from a Single Premium Bond.

- PEPs, BES, National Savings and any of the other investments mentioned in the Case Study below, offering a range of advantages – guaranteed growth from some, potential growth from others, Income Tax relief on initial contributions, freedom from Income Tax during the investment period, exemption from Capital Gains Tax on eventual disposal, etc. (see Chapter 7).

A portfolio comprising these investments should ensure that when retirement age is reached, there will be sufficient capital and income to maintain and even enhance your lifestyle. However, once you have provided for sufficient 'jam tomorrow', there is no reason why you shouldn't have 'jam today'. An inheritance when in your fifties would certainly provide the opportunity to invest in some indulgences which you couldn't afford earlier, such as a new car, a cruise, a harpsichord, or an expensive hobby (see Chapter 7, Other variable investments). It is important to strike the right balance between today's needs and tomorrow's requirements; neither should be met only at the expense of the other – hence the necessity for a financial plan and proper professional advice.

The following case study represents a comprehensive situation with a wide range of suggestions, which readers can simply whittle down to those applicable in their particular situation.

Inheritance of Parents' Estates worth £860,000 for a Middle-Aged couple with Grown-up Children

John (54) is a dentist earning £35,000 p.a. His wife Angela (52) has not returned to work, even though their children are now married and living away from home. There are two grandchildren and one on the way. John's (widowed) mother lives in a bungalow inherited from her late husband, not far away from John and Angela's large house (formerly the vicarage) which is currently worth around £200,000, subject to a mortgage debt of £50,000. John has a share portfolio of £40,000, some retirement annuity policies and an Endowment Policy due to mature next year. Angela has about £6,000 in a building society account.

John's mother dies, leaving him her bungalow (worth £80,000); her death means that John also inherits his father's estate, which had been held in trust for his mother during her lifetime. After Inheritance Tax, the estate is worth around £580,000 in cash and shares, with a further £200,000 due under a 'joint life and survivor' insurance policy taken out by his father many years ago. John therefore inherits a total of £860,000 worth of assets, which he now wishes to invest with a view to:

- Providing financial security for Angela and himself for the rest of their lives.
- Saving as much Income Tax and Inheritance Tax as possible.
- Improving the quality of their lifestyle.

Suggestions

To achieve their main objectives, John and Angela are advised by their financial adviser to take the following steps (in approximate order of priority).

1. Personal insurances

To ensure that they will have sufficient income in the event of illness or death, John effects the following policies, the premiums being amply covered by his income:

- Family Income Benefit for Angela – benefit £10,000 p.a. for the next 25 years; premium cost £145 p.a.
- Permanent Health Insurance – to provide £10,000 p.a. income for the next 10 years if John were incapacitated for more than three months; monthly cost around £550.
- Private medical expenses insurance for both of them, costing about £65 per month.
- Long-term Care Insurance – in case he or Angela have to go into a private nursing home when they are older. Cover against nursing home fees of £15,000 p.a. for both of them would cost them jointly between £123 and £166 per month, depending on the type of cover chosen.

2. To save income tax

- John gives Angela £250,000 to equalize their estates and provide sufficient funds for Angela to be able to implement the suggested investment policy, including the various gifts mentioned below.
- John employs Angela as a part-time assistant in his dental practice at a salary of £10,000 p.a. This reduces his tax bill by £4,000 p.a. at a cost of less than £2,000 p.a. tax on Angela, i.e. a net saving of £2,000 p.a.
- John pays £25,000 to the building society to reduce his mortgage to £25,000; this produces the double benefit of reducing his monthly outgoings and obtaining tax relief on 100 per cent of the interest payable.
- Angela uses £50,000 of the gift from John and borrows a further £50,000 to purchase a £100,000 house in Scarborough which is being converted into flats for holiday lets. The total rents amount to around £12,000 p.a. Interest on the loan is around £6,000 p.a. Angela manages the property as a business. This gives her the following advantages:

– Full tax relief on the interest paid on the loan.
– The opportunity to set business expenses (e.g. travel, telephone, secretarial work, etc.) against the income for tax purposes.
– The opportunity for Angela to make pension contributions up to 20 per cent of her income and obtain tax relief on them.

3. To Save Inheritance Tax

- John and Angela each effect a Capital Conversion Plan with an insurance company, whereby they each purchase a Single Premium Bond for £20,000 and withdraw £1,000 p.a. (5 per cent) tax free to cover the premiums into a flexible 'joint life and survivor' policy held in trust for the children. The policy proceeds will be free of IHT on their deaths. Standard insurance cover of, say, £50,000 could be purchased with annual premiums of just over £500. Payment of these premiums by John into the trust policy would also be exempt from IHT, being regular expenditure out of surplus income. On the death of the survivor the sum of £50,000 (plus any further bonuses) will be exempt from IHT and immediately available to the children, who can use the proceeds to meet the IHT bill on the survivor's death. With a flexible policy of this nature, the benefits could be varied to provide a larger investment element and smaller protection element, or vice versa. Alternatively, annual premiums of around £1,650 could provide minimum cover of £50,000 on a 'joint life and survivor' with profits basis. The value of the policy would steadily increase year by year (depending on the profit performance), so on the survivor's death, say, 20 years later, the sum available for the children could be in excess of £150,000 – again, free of IHT.
- John executes a Deed of Variation on his mother's will, redirecting the bungalow into the names of the children, who can rent it out or sell it and keep the cash. As the gift is made under a Deed of Variation. It is deemed to be from John's mother, not from John, so there would be no further IHT, even if John died the day after making the Deed.
- John and Angela then transfer £140,000 each into a new Family Discretionary Settlement for the benefit of their children, grandchildren and any future grandchildren born within the next 21 years. They appoint the family solicitor and a bank trustee company to be the trustees. This is a chargeable transfer, but no IHT is payable as the total amount is just covered by the amount of their Nil Rate Bands (£140,000 each).

- John uses a further £100,000 to set up an Accumulation and Maintenance Trust with the same trustees for the benefit of children and grandchildren. This transfer is a PET (Potentially Exempt Transfer).
- John and Angela utilize their annual allowances of £3,000 each to make gifts between their children, plus £250 to each grandchild, which they use to fund a Baby Bond (tax-free Friendly Society policy).
- John and Angela execute new Wills with Nil-Rate Band discretionary trusts for the survivors of them and their children and grandchildren.

With this assortment of measures the total saving in Inheritance Tax if John and Angela survive seven years will be more than £200,000.

4. To Provide Post-Retirement Income

- John's accountant confirms that John has not utilized all his allowable contributions to his self-employed pension during the last six years. John therefore contributes the full unused allowance (£8,000) on which he receives £3,200 tax relief.
- Angela has two jobs: working for John as an employee at £10,000 p.a. and as a self-employed property manager earning £6,000 p.a. She is thus entitled to two pensions, one from each job.
- John sets up an Employer's Pension Scheme for Angela; his contributions do not add to Angela's taxable income, but they are still deductible from John's income and the contributions grow tax free within the pension fund.
- In addition, Angela is eligible (in her self-employed capacity) to contribute up to 20 per cent of her income (£1,200 p.a.) on which she also obtains tax relief.

The total of these three pension schemes will ensure that, after retirement, John and Angela will still have a substantial (and probably increasing) income for the rest of their lives.

5. Investments

After making the above arrangements, John and Angela still have around £350,000 remaining capital. They wish to invest this mainly to obtain maximum growth for when they retire, but also to supplement their income and enable them to pursue a reasonably luxurious lifestyle in the meantime. Although they like to travel abroad, they do not wish to purchase any foreign property. They are happy to spread their investments as widely as possible so as to reduce any risk and take advantage of the maximum number of opportunities. As John already has a reasonable Stock Exchange portfolio, the balance is invested in the following range of investments for each of them. (Spendable income from investments is taken in Angela's name to take advantage of her lower rate of Income Tax.)

- £9,000 each into PEPs.
- £20,000 each into Business Expansion Schemes, mostly Assured Tenancy Schemes with buy-back commitments in five years' time.
- £10,000 each into growth-oriented Unit Trusts/Investment Trusts, including some investing in the USA, Japan and Europe.
- £15,000 each into Investment Trust Zero-Dividend Preference Shares, to provide virtually guaranteed capital growth.
- £15,000 each into Low Coupon and Index-linked Gilts, again to provide guaranteed capital growth over five to 10 years.
- £10,000 into Index-linked National Savings Certificates.
- £5,000 into the current issue of National Savings Certificates.
- £10,000 each into Premium Bonds.
- £20,000 into Insurance Company Single Premium Bonds – half into Unit-linked Bonds, half into With-Profit Bonds.
- £10,000 into an insurance company's Deferred Income Bond; the insurance company will pay an increasing annual income after five years and repay the capital (depending on the growth rate achieved) with a small profit at the end of 10 years.
- £10,000 into an Offshore Managed Currency Fund, where interest is ploughed back and taxed only when John and Angela withdraw it, which can be after retirement when they may both be basic-rate taxpayers.
- £7,000 to purchase a Second-hand Endowment Policy due to mature in 1996, with a redemption figure of about £15,000 and a £100 annual premium payable in the meantime.
- £10,000 into an Enterprise Zone Trust, costing John £6,000 and offering an increasing income, plus prospects of capital growth over the next 10 years.

John and Angela also arrange for two or three regular savings plans, which will mature between five and 10 years later:

- £3,000 each as the first instalment into a TESSA.

- £200 p.a. each into a Friendly Society policy.
- £3,000 p.a. into 10-year Maximum Investment Insurance Policies (again split between With Profits and Unit-linked) which can be funded either out of their cash resources, or by withdrawals from some of the other investments, such as the Single Premium Bonds, PEPs or National Savings Certificates.

John and Angela invest the remaining cash in a bank or building society account in order to provide cash funds for luxuries, emergencies and holidays, to fund the instalments on the regular savings plans and pension policies, and to provide a fund for future PEPs, etc.

The result of all those measures is to produce an investment income sufficient to supplement John and Angela's earnings, with the ability to increase their income if required (perhaps by taking tax-free withdrawals from the Single Premium Bonds or from the other investments), plus reasonable prospects that at retirement age there will be a substantial amount of cash, much of which can be used to provide a tax-free income (say, from the PEPs, National Savings Certificates, Friendly Society policies and Qualifying Life Policies). If their income or capital is clearly surplus to their requirements, they can then make further gifts to the children or into either of the family trusts (after obtaining advice on the timing and the amounts).

Grandparents

Grandparents can, of course, be any age from 40 onwards, so the investment of an inheritance (say, from their own parents) will depend on each individual's financial situation, tax rates and future requirements. For investment ideas consult the appropriate chapters of this book, and the case studies preceding and following this section.

The purpose of including grandparents in this chapter is largely to illustrate the opportunties for transferring assets, saving Inheritance Tax and helping grandchildren in particular to make a start on their own investment portfolios. The emphasis is therefore more on helping grandchildren than on the choice of investments for grandparents themselves. The following case study is an illustration of the benefits which can be produced by implementing some of suggestions in Chapters 14 and 15.

Inheritance of Estate worth £130,000 for a Couple in their sixties with Grown-up Children

Norman and Val are in their early sixties when Val's mother dies, leaving a house worth £100,000 and £30,000 in a building society account. Norman and Val have sufficient capital and pension arrangements for their retirement, so they do not anticipate needing Val's inheritance. Their two children, Steven and Karen, are both in their late twenties, married, and each expecting to start a family. Despite the family solicitor pointing out the advantages of a Deed of Variation, Val and Norman do not wish to pass on the capital to children or grandchildren until Norman has retired and they can see how their children's marriages are working out.

Three years later (by which time they are too late to do a Deed of Variation), Norman has retired and Steven and Karen each have two children. Norman and Val decide that they would now like to make provision for the grandchildren, and they regard virtually the whole of Val's recent inheritance as being available for this.

Suggestions

1. The family solicitor recommends that they do not leave all the benefit only by their Wills for the following reasons:
    - If they keep the £130,000 in their estates, £52,000 of it will go to the Government in Inheritance Tax, leaving only £78,000 to benefit the grandchildren.
    - Unless the money is well invested in the meantime, inflation will eat into the real value of the funds so that £78,000 in, say, 10 years' time will be worth only a fraction of what £130,000 would be worth today.
    - If the funds are truly surplus, the grandchildren may as well have the benefit *now*, at a time when the funds will be of maximum use – perhaps for school fees, clothing, holidays, etc. – rather than in the future, when the need may be less.
    - Any income produced by the moneys given to the grandchildren will be exempt from tax (at least up to £3,295 p.a.), whereas the income on the money retained by Norman and Val will be taxed at 40 or 25 per cent.

2. After further discussion, Norman and Val agree that the £130,000 be divided between three basic schemes:
    - A trust for the benefit of all present and future grandchildren.
    - An outright transfer of capital to each grandchild to be invested immediately on their behalf.
    - A series of regular-contribution savings plans to get them on the savings ladder and build up a substantial sum for later on (school fees, university, marriage, house purchase, etc.).

Norman and Val therefore implement the suggested plan as follows:

3. £60,000 into an Accumulation and Maintenance Trust.

This will be a Potentially Exempt Transfer, i.e. no Inheritance Tax will be payable either now, or even in the event of death within 7 years. (In that case Val would simply have used up £60,000 of her £140,000 Nil Rate threshold.) The trustees are the family solicitor, their accountant and Norman and Val themselves. Under the trust each grandchild will become entitled to a proportionate share of income on attaining 25; meanwhile, the trustees can use income for the benefit of all or any of the grandchildren (e.g. paying school fees), in addition to which, capital is available if required. Part of the funds is invested in a bank or building society account to provide a cash 'cushion', with the balance invested in Equities, Unit Trusts and Investment Trusts chosen with the assistance of a stockbroker acting on a 'dealing with advice' basis.

4. £44,000 total gifts between the four grandchildren.

Again, after the first £6,000 each (the exempt allowance for last year and this year), the remaining £32,000 comprises a PET, but as the total is still under £140,000, no IHT will be payable, even on death within seven years. The £44,000 is invested in the names of the parents designated with the initials of each grandchild:

- £5,000 for each child in a bank or building society account, on which they elect for interest to be paid gross.
- £1,000 each in the new National Savings Children's Bonus Bond – each account will mature in five years' time for £1,750 tax free.
- £5,000 in an insurance company Single Premium Bond on the life of each grandchild. As the policy is on the child's life, the policies are effected with Friends Provident in their unitized With-Profits Fund. The income will admittedly be taxed at 25 per cent, but remains a sound, risk-free, long-term investment with professional management, which should offer steady growth and can probably be encashed at any time without any tax liability (as long as the child is not a higher-rate taxpayer).

5. Regular Savings Schemes

- Norman and Val each pay £3,400 to an insurance company to

purchase two 10-year annuities for each of the four grandchildren. These annuities will fund the maximum premiums of £18 per month into a tax-exempt Friendly Society Bond, such as the MIM Britannia 'Rupert Tax-free Savings Plan'. If the bond continues to achieve a growth rate of 13 per cent, after 20 years each child could anticipate £13,700 tax free, which could be left to continue growing tax free if the bond is not encashed.

- Norman and Val also set up four regular savings plans linked to Unit Trusts or Investment Trusts; premiums of £50 per month each (two from Norman, two from Val) are paid by direct debit out of a separate interest-bearing bank account which Norman and Val opened for this purpose.

- Finally, Norman and Val each execute a 21-year covenant for £500 p.a. in favour of each grandchild, with Steven and his wife, and Karen and her husband as trustees. The trustees use the £500 to meet the premiums on a 21-year Endowment Policy in trust for the relevant grandchild. If Norman or Val die during the 21 years, the balance due under the covenant would be a debt payable out of their estates. If Steven or Karen were to die during the period, the sum insured would be payable and would be available for the maintenance or benefit of the grandchild. (Although there is no Income Tax advantage in a Deed of Covenant, it is still a valid way of gifting income for a fixed period; the obligation to pay each year also establishes the covenanted payment as a regular gift out of income, so it will probably be exempt from IHT, in addition to the remaining gift exemptions.) As each grandchild attains 21 and the policy matures, he or she can effect further savings plans for which the premiums can be paid out of the proceeds of the original policy. After a further 20 years, the accumulated sum built up with the benefit of compound interest can be extremely substantial.

Summary

Norman and Val still have some surplus from the original funds, but they can of course use this for any future grandchildren, who will benefit under the Accumulation and Maintenance Trust in any event; Norman and Val could effect fresh Deeds of Covenant and Friendly Society Bonds as and when any further grandchildren arrive. The net result of implementing the preceding steps is:

- The family have saved up to £50,000 in Inheritance Tax.

- They have saved further Income Tax on whatever income is produced by the moneys gifted to the grandchildren.
- Norman and Val have provided immediate help to their own children by assisting with the cost of bringing up the grandchildren.
- They have also ensured that substantial sums will be available for the grandchildren later in their lives, but (as the bulk of the funds are held within the trust) without the very real risk of young children inheriting too much too soon.

Post-Retirement

Once you have retired, without the income and security of a job, you are entirely dependent on your pension and the income from your investments, the total of which will usually be less than your income while you were working. That is why it is so important to start early on Retirement Planning (see Chapter 13). The chief concern is usually to maintain and, if possible, increase your standard of living. Because of your change in circumstances, this is probably a good time to revise your personal balance sheet and update your budget (see p. 66) to incorporate the probable changes. These include the disappearance of the bulk of your income (from your employment). This will be partially offset by the commencement of pension income and the possible reduction in your tax rate from 40 per cent to 25 per cent.

Giving assets away (perhaps from an inheritance) to reduce IHT may well be possible, but the first prioprity must be security for yourself and your partner. There are far too many cases of elderly people being persuaded to part with assets on the basis of saving thousands of pounds in IHT, and then worrying (perhaps needlessly, but worrying nevertheless) whether they have sufficient left to cover such eventualities as nursing home fees. This is a classic example of the tax tail wagging the security dog. Far better to have too much financial security in your joint lifetimes and pay some extra IHT, than lose sleep at night worrying about your financial future.

Any inheritance received at this age should therefore be viewed as a means of enhancing your own financial security. The actual investment policy will depend on your age, state of health, life expectancy and desired lifestyle. A fit and active 65-year-old with a family will undoubtedly still require a substantial portion of his assets to be in equity-based investments in the hopes of obtaining both capital growth and income growth. An elderly person permanently resident in a nursing home will have very few needs over and above the nursing home fees, and could well be happy to have given most of his assets away. An octogenarian without dependants who simply wants to keep everything as simple as possible, would probably be best advised to buy a lifetime annuity and leave the remainder of his capital in a bank or building society account where he can see exactly what he has got, and which will be sufficient to see him through the rest of his life.

Pre-investment considerations

- Your insurance requirements should be taken care of; life and health insurances will cost more for an older life, but they should not be ruled out, especially if income can be boosted with an annuity (as it often can, particularly when interest rates are high).

- Inheritance Tax savings; there is still room (and probably time) to give away assets, especially if you are likely to survive by at least four years. Remember, at the very worst the IHT liability *cannot* be greater as a result of making a lifetime gift – it can only be reduced. If you survive a Potentially Exempt Transfer by seven years, it escapes IHT liability altogether. If you don't, the frozen value of the gift is simply added back to your estate, so the beneficiaries are *no worse off*. In fact, they will be slightly better off than if you hadn't made the gift in the first place, since the donee will at least have had the use of the money in the meantime. However, if the subject matter of the gift is shares or other assets with an inbuilt gain, the possible saving in IHT (by giving them away) may have to be weighed against the possible Capital Gains Tax liability on the gift. If the shares were not given away but remained in the estate (attracting IHT), their value for CGT purposes would be uplifted to the value at the date of death, thereby reducing the future CGT liability.

The final two case studies deal with two average situations and suggest the possible investment approach which might adopted for a recently retired couple and a widowed person living on his or her own.

Inheritance of £60,000 By a Pensioner needing more Income

Reg retired on his 65th birthday in 1992 and (wisely) exercised his lump sum option under his pension scheme. Reg was formerly a company director earning £30,000 p.a.; his wife Evelyn (now 67), retired seven years ago without a private pension, but having contributed to her own state pension. Their financial position after retirement is as follows:

			£
Capital:	House (in joint names, no mortgage)		90,000
	Savings (bank, building society, etc.)		
		(Reg)	20,000
		(Evelyn)	12,000
	Share portfolio	(Reg)	30,000
			£152,000

			p.a.
Income:	Reg's company pension		18,000
	Reg and Evelyn's state pensions		
		(£2,704 each)	5,408
	Income from investments,	(Reg)	3,500
		(Evelyn)	1,000
	Total joint income	(Gross)	£25,908

With the aid of a budget planning form (see p. 67) Reg and Evelyn estimate that their joint expenditure will amount to approximately £20,000 on average. As their net income after tax will be around £23,450, they would therefore like to receive at least £2,000 more in income. Reg's older brother dies, leaving Reg the residue of his estate, which consists of a house which Reg sells for £60,000.

Suggestions

1.   Reg and Evelyn transfer all their existing investments into their joint names and execute a declaration to the effect that they hold the income from all the joint investments on trust for Evelyn absolutely. They do this for two reasons:

Income Tax

– Reg's pension income will leave his taxable income just below the higher-rate threshold. If he and Evelyn elect for all the income now to be treated as Evelyn's, she will be able to reclaim the whole of the tax on some of the income (equal to the balance of her unused personal allowance) and will be liable at only 25 per cent on the remainder, which would otherwise have suffered tax at 40 per cent if the investment income were added to Reg's other income.

Probate

– By holding the investments in joint names, ownership will be automatically transferred to the survivor without the need for probate (and therefore without further expense or delay) on the death of either of them.

2.   They do not feel that they can afford to make any gifts to avoid Inheritance Tax, but they take out a Private Medical Expenses Plan costing around £1000 p.a. and which they estimate will be easily covered by the increase in income attributable to the new investments.

3.   With the help of his professional adviser, Reg arranges for the inherited £60,000 to be invested as outlined below (again effecting all the new investments in the joint names of himself and Evelyn, but signing a declaration for Income Tax purposes that the income belongs entirely to Evelyn). As they both have a reasonable life expectancy, and as their projected shortfall in income (with the additional insurance premiums) will be only around £3,000 p.a., Reg and Evelyn prefer not to go all out for income at the expense of possible future growth, but to have a range of investments which will provide at least £3,000 p.a. with prospects of future growth of both capital and income. The £60,000 is invested as follows:

- £10,000 in two Guaranteed Income Bonds, one maturing in three years and one in five years; they therefore lock into a fixed return of up to £1,000 p.a. guaranteed for the next few years, with income payable monthly. (The actual amount will depend on interest rates prevailing at the time of investment.)
- £10,000 in two managed PEPs (£5,000 each) to provide prospects of tax-free growth and income if required.
- £20,000 into a mixed portfolio of high-yielding Unit Trusts and Investment Trusts. Their adviser particularly recommends Investment Trust 'Stepped Preference Shares', such as River and Mercantile Stepped Preference Shares, which offer an initial yield of 5.5 per cent, but with guaranteed 5 per cent increases in income each year, until repayment in the year 2000. At that date it is planned to repay the shares at 188.6p each (as compared with the current price of around 125p) so there is a reasonable prospect of capital growth as well as the regular increases in income.

- £10,000 in National Savings Certificates Index-Linked Issue to provide tax-free guaranteed growth at 4.5 per cent more than the rate of inflation. If inflation is only 5 per cent, this will still be a return of almost 10 per cent p.a. tax free.
- £10,000 in insurance company Single Premium With-Profit Bonds, which cannot fall in value. Reg and Evelyn can obtain an income by withdrawing 5 per cent tax free, but still anticipate some growth. They can also retain the bonds or cash them in at any time.

Reg estimates that the additional income from the above programme could well exceed the £3,000 target, in which case he suggests that next year they might gradually withdraw funds from the £32,000 which they already had in their bank and building society accounts, investing them in a regular-contribution PEP in order to spread the risk and obtain the benefit of pound cost averaging. Reg and Evelyn are now much happier about the future; whatever happens, they feel that they (or the survivor) will have sufficient to meet all their foreseeable financial requirements.

Inheritance of House and £35,000-worth of Assets from Husband's Estate by a 74-Year-Old Widow Requiring Income

C

Connie (74) and Frank (76) live in their own home; the mortgage has been paid off and their married daughter (45) lives a few miles away. Connie has relied on Frank to do all the finances; their assets consist of the house in joint names (worth £100,000) and approximately £35,000 worth of savings (mostly in the bank and building society) in Frank's sole name. Frank also has a Whole Life Policy for £25,000. On Frank's death Connie inherits all his estate, so her capital now consists of a house worth £100,000 and £60,000 in cash and savings.

Her income consists of:	£ p.a.
Widow's pension from Frank's employer	6,000
State's widow's pension	2,704
Income from cash from Frank's estate, up to	(6,000)

Connie estimates that if she stays in the house, she will need a minimum of around £8,000 p.a. net to cover her normal living expenses. She accepts that if she were to move (e.g. into sheltered accommodation or into a nursing home), the proceeds of sale of the house could be invested to produce income which would just about cover the residential fees. However, Connie does not wish to move just yet. She realizes that if she were short of income, she could always use the house to generate further income (e.g. from a Home Income Plan), although she is uncertain as to the wisdom of this, having read various horror stories in the press about some of these plans.

Connie therefore places her finances in the hands of a professional adviser who has been recommended by a friend in a similar position. Connie confirms to the adviser that her main concern is to maintain her financial independence. Although she would like to feel that there would be funds left for her daughter to inherit, Connie would not object to dipping into capital if that would give her greater financial security and peace of mind. Connie is tempted to leave all the funds in the building society, but recognizing her lack of understanding of financial matters, she agrees to leave the investment in the hands of her adviser, as long as it can be kept relatively simple.

Suggestions

1.   Connie's adviser points out two disadvantages of just leaving the £60,000 in the building society:
   - Lack of protection against inflation; the cost of food, fuel and travel goes up every year, but the value of her capital would be going down (in real terms); the interest will also fluctuate up and down, which would obviously make things more difficult for Connie.
   - The Age Allowance Trap; if Connie's gross taxable income were to exceed £13,500, Connie would fall into the Age Allowance Trap and suffer tax at a marginal rate of 37.5 per cent on the excess (see Chapter 6, p. 77).

2.   As Connie does not feel obliged to provide for her daughter, and Connie is still reasonably healthy, her adviser suggests that she should invest £20,000 out of the total £60,000 to purchase an annuity. If interest rates are reasonably high (say around 11 per cent), an annuity could provide a monthly income of around £192 (increasing by 2 per cent p.a.) for the rest of Connie's life. For tax purposes only £90 of this monthly income will be taxable; the bulk of £102 per month (comprising a return of her capital) will be exempt from tax and won't count towards the Age Allowance Trap. Apart from boosting Connie's income, the purchase of an annuity will have the incidental benefit of reducing Connie's estate to below the IHT threshold of £140,000, thereby avoiding IHT on Connie's death and simplifying the probate process.

3.   Her adviser suggests leaving £10,000 in a bank or building society high interest account (with instant access) as a reserve cash fund. He suggests that Connie should divide the remaining £30,000 as follows:
   - £5,000 in Single Premium Bonds. Connie can take tax-free

withdrawals of 5 per cent, or even more if she wishes; apart from the prospects of capital growth and income growth, the withdrawals will not count as taxable income for the purposes of the Age Allowance Trap.

- £5,000 in Income Shares or Stepped Preference Shares of an Investment Trust.
- £5,000 in a Guaranteed Income Bond paying fixed monthly income for, say, five years.

As an alternative to any of the above, a PEP could also provide a tax-free and perhaps increasing income.

4.   The effect of the above would be to produce a total spendable investment income of around £5,000 p.a. which will avoid the Age Allowance Trap, be payable monthly and not reduce, with good prospects of regular increases.

Together with the increases in her pensions, Connie should therefore be able to cover all her anticipated expenditure with funds to spare and need not be worried about future increases in the cost of living. If her income needs were to increase drastically, she would still be able to resort to the house to provide further funds, perhaps through a Home Income Plan. For someone in Connie's position it is essential that she finds a financial adviser in whom she can place complete trust and who will not only look after her financial security, but also make sure that her tax affairs are kept up to date.

17 Conclusion

Having reviewed the various aspects of Wills, inheritances and investing inherited moneys, there are three final points to bring to the reader's attention.

The European Factor

Despite the undoubted effects on the investment world of the 1992 Single European Market, this book has not really tackled the question of UCITS – a sort of European equivalent of Unit Trusts. There are three reasons for this. First, it is still very early days and there is no reason to believe that European firms, European fund managers or European investments are likely to produce any unique opportunities or greater profits for the UK investor, who can already invest into Europe anyway (through UK-based Unit Trusts and Investment Trusts investing in Europe, for example).

Second, investing outside the UK involves the added dimension (and added risk) of the currency factor (see Chapter 11). Any profit on the pure investment performance could therefore be enhanced or reduced by the movement of sterling against the relevant currency.

Third, the insurance and investment opportunities in the UK are probably more advanced, comprehensive and available to individuals than those in Europe. In general the UK offers all the products and services which most investors are likely to require, and has the added advantages of security through familiarity and geographic proximity.

This book therefore concentrates on the domestic market. However, if you are interested in investing abroad, perhaps because you are working abroad or intending to retire to the sun, you should obtain the appropriate specialist advice (see Chapter 16).

The Political Factor

At the time of writing, the first General Election of the 1990s has not yet been held. If the Conservatives remain in office for the next few years, the basic content of this book is likely to remain generally valid, although the amounts of the individual allowances and reliefs will need to be adjusted in subsequent Budgets.

If a Labour Government comes into office, however, there would inevitably be changes, although perhaps not immediately. Several fundamental changes in taxation and investment matters could be forecast with reasonable certainty, so it would then be essential to obtain updated professional advice.

Possible changes under a Labour Government

Income Tax

- Top rates would be increased to 59 per cent (that is, 50 per cent Income Tax and a 9 per cent increase in National Insurance contributions).
- Personal reliefs would be amended.
- An investment income surcharge (probably 9 per cent) would be introduced.

Capital Gains Tax

- The current exemption would be reduced and the rate of CGT would be increased, probably to 50 per cent.

Inheritance Tax

- This would be amended so that gifts and inheritances would be taxed on the *recipient* at the time of receipt, rather than on the donor at the time of disposal.

Pensions

- SERPS would be revamped in order to attract a target of 5 million people back into it, including the self-employed.
- Higher-rate tax relief on pension contributions would probably be abolished.
- Personal Pension Plans would be downgraded and probably become available only for topping-up purposes.

School Fees

- The effect of removing the charitable status of many educational trusts would be to increase the amount of school fees payable.

Business Expansion Schemes

- Would be abolished and replaced with 'Growth Business Schemes', which would probably have a higher degree of risk and not permit, for example, property-based investments.

Personal Equity Plans

- Would either be abolished or the tax advantages would be reduced.

Private Medical Insurance

- The tax relief for the elderly on PMI schemes would be abolished.

Clearly these proposals would entail substantial changes in personal investment plans (and would require a new edition of this book). Meanwhile, irrespective of the outcome of the General Election, the best advice has to be to take advantage of those opportunities which currently exist; invest inheritances, make gifts and set up trusts while the funds and the opportunities are there.

The Technical Factor

Even if you have a good knowledge of financial matters, it is still wise to consult a professional adviser in connection with any aspect of inheritance or investing inherited moneys. The amount (if any) expended in fees should be repaid many times over by the quality of the advice, the peace of mind and (often) the tax advantages obtained.

A solicitor or a bank trustee department can generally be relied on to offer the most qualified and comprehensive advice in connection with Wills, probates and inheritances. When it comes to investing inherited moneys, the field is widened to include the other professionals mentioned in Chapter 15, Choosing the right adviser. The anticipated cost need not deter you; in many cases it will be covered by the commission generated from implementing the advice. It is of more importance to ensure that your funds are properly looked after. As you are probably dealing with the bulk of your worldly wealth, the final recommendation – and probably the most important of all – is that before consulting any adviser, and definitely before making any investments you should carefully re-read the chapters on investment principles and choosing the right adviser. Doing so could make you happy as well as rich.

Glossary

Administrator The equivalent of an executor, but on an intestacy, i.e. where the deceased did not leave a Will.

Affidavit A document which is legally sworn.

Assent Document by which the PRs transfer ownership of land to the beneficiary.

Assurance Protection against certainties which will eventually happen, i.e. death.

AVC Additional Voluntary Contributions to an employer's pension scheme.

Beneficiary The person entitled to a benefit under a Will or trust.

BES Business Expansion Scheme.

Blue chip companies Large, established organizations, such as ICI and Shell.

Capital Gains Tax (CGT) Tax payable on the gain or profit realized on a chargeable disposal.

Capital Taxes Office (CTO) The Revenue department responsible for dealing with Inheritance Tax.

CAR Compound Annual Return.

Chargeable transfer Transfer of assets on which CGT or IHT will be payable.

Chattels House contents, personal possessions and effects, but not cash.

Codicil A legal supplement to a Will, usually making small amendments or additions.

Deceased The person who has died.

Estate All the assets of the deceased: house, land, contents, investments, cash, etc.

Executor/Executrix The person (male/female) who executes the terms of the Will. He or she 'stands in the shoes' of the deceased and is responsible for collecting the assets, paying all debts and liabilities, and distributing the balance to the beneficiaries.

FIB Family Income Benefit.

FIMBRA Financial Intermediaries, Managers & Brokers Regulatory Association.

FSAVC Free-Standing Additional Voluntary Contributions to a separate plan offered by an independent pension provider.

Gearing Money borrowed by e.g. Investment Trusts to enhance potential returns.

Grant of Probate The court order 'proving' the Will, which gives the executors the legal authority to deal with the deceased's estate. Also called simply 'probate'.

Grant of Representation The generic term for a Grant of Probate or Letters of Administration.

GROB Gift with a Reservation of Benefit.

HICA High Interest Cheque Account.

IFA Independent Financial Adviser.

IMRO Investment Management Regulatory Organization.

Inheritance Tax (IHT) Tax payable on a transfer of assets, either by gift or on death, which is a chargeable transfer.

In specie 'In its present form'. Chattels transferred in specie are handed over as they are (in kind rather than cash) without having to be sold.

Insurance Protection against contingencies which may or may not happen.

Intestate Dying without a Will.

LAUTRO Life Assurance & Unit Trusts Regulatory Organization.

Letters of Administration A court order where there is no Will, giving the necessary authority to the administrators.

Life interest The right of an income beneficiary (life tenant) to receive the income from trust assets during his or her life.

Life tenant The beneficiary with a life interest in a trust fund.

Personal representative (PR) Another name for an executor or, where there is no Will, adminstrator.

PEP Personal Equity Plan.

PET Potentially Exempt Transfer.

PHI Permanent Health Insurance.

PPP Personal Pension Plan – available to the self-employed and those who are not members of an occupational scheme.

Power of Attorney A legal document which nominates someone (not necessarily a lawyer) to handle your affairs on your behalf.

Real property/Realty Land, including a house, as opposed to 'person-ality', which means moveable, non-land assets.

Residuary estate The remainder of the estate after all the debts, liabilities, tax and legacies have been paid. Also called the 'residue'.

Reversion An inheritance that passes to someone else (the reversioner) when the life tenant of a trust dies.

SERPS State Earnings-Related Pension Scheme.

SFA Securities and Futures Authority.

SIB Securities Investment Board – a Government body which supervises the activities of all institutions and individuals involved in investments.

TESSA Tax-Exempt Special Savings Account.

Testament Another word for a Will.

Testamentary guardian The person appointed by a Will to be responsible for a child under 18 – a 'substitute parent'.

Testator/Testatrix The person (male/female) who makes a Will.

Title Guarantee of legal ownership (property).

Trustee A legal caretaker who manages the trust assets and affairs for the benefit of the beneficiaries.

Further Reading

The following publications offer further information in specific areas of investment planning. Most are available from libraries and bookshops, but some must be ordered direct from the publisher. In these cases, an address or telephone number is provided.

Wills and Probate
Allied Dunbar Capital Taxes and Estate Planning Guide (Longman)
Help When Someone Dies (free DSS leaflet FB29)
How to Sort Out Someone's Will (Consumers' Association)
Introduction to Inheritance Tax (free Inland Revenue leaflet IHT3)
Make Your Will, (Consumers' Association)
Telegraph Willmaker (Mapin House, 4 Winsley Street, London W1N 7AR, £47.95)
Tolley's Inheritance Tax (Tolley Publishing)
What Happens When Someone Dies? (free Inland Revenue leaflet IR45)
What to Do When Someone Dies (Consumers' Association)
Wills and Probate (Consumers' Association)
Write Your Own Will, Keith Best (Paperfronts)

TAX (Income, Capital Gains and Inheritance)
Allied Dunbar Capital Taxes and Estate Planning Guide (Longman)
Allied Dunbar Tax Guide (Longman)
Daily Mail Income Tax Guide (Chapman)
Daily Telegraph Guide to Income Tax (Harper Collins)
101 Ways of Saving Tax (Telegraph Books)
Tolley's Tax Guide (Tolley Publishing)

Investments
Allied Dunbar Investment and Savings Guide (Longman)
Financial Care for Your Elderly Relatives (Allied Dunbar/Longman)
Good Retirement Guide (London)
Guide for Widows and Widowers (free Inland Revenue leaflet IR91)
Insurance Buyer's Annual Guide (Kluwer Publishing)
Investors Chronicle Beginners' Guide to Investment (Investors Chronicle)
Pensions – Your Choice (Tolley Publishing)

Personal Financial Planning Manual (Butterworths)
Personal Tax and Investment Planning 1991/2 (Tolley Publishing)
The Saver's and Investor's Guide, David Lewis (Wisebuy Publishing)
Socially Responsible Investment, Sue Ward (Directory of Social Change)
Stock Exchange Guide to Selling Shares (London Stock Exchange, tel: 071-588
   2355)
Success in Investment, R. G. Winfield (John Murray Ltd)
Unit Trusts: What Every Investor Should Know, Christopher Gilchrist
   (Woodhead Faulkner)
Your Guide to Saving for Children (Home Owners Friendly Society, Freepost,
   Harrogate)
Your New Pensions Choice (Tolley Publishing)
Your Taxes and Savings 1991/2 (Age Concern)

Financial Magazines

Financial Product Review
Investment Trust Magazine
Investors Chronicle
Money Facts Magazine
Money Magazine
Moneywise Magazine
Planned Savings Magazine
What Investment?

Leaflets

The Inland Revenue publishes a comprehensive range of explanatory leaflets on a
wide variety of topics. These are generally written in clear, concise language and
are available free from your local tax office or the Inland Revenue Publications
Department.

   Helpful free leaflets are also produced by the Stock Exchange, the Unit Trust
Association and the Association of Investment Trust Companies (see Useful
Addresses, p. 265).

Useful Addresses

Wills & Probate

Capital Taxes Office (CTO)
Minford House
Rockley Road
London W14 0DF
Tel: 071–603 4622

Department of Social Security
(Consult local telephone directory
for nearest office)

**National Association of Funeral
Directors**
618 Warwick Road
Solihull
West Midlands B91 1AA
Tel: 021–711 1343

National Association of Widows
54–57 Allison Street
Digbeth
Birmingham B5 5TH
Tel: 021–643 8348

**Probate Personal Application
Department**
Principal Registry of the Family Division
2nd Floor
Somerset House
Strand
London WC2R 1LP
Tel: 071–936 6000

Tax

Inland Revenue
Somerset House
Strand
London WC2R 1LB
Tel: 071–438 6622

Public Enquiry Room
Inland Revenue
West Wing
Somerset House
Strand
London WC2R 1LB
Tel: 071–438 6420

Publications Department
New Wing
Somerset House
London WC2T 1LB
Tel: 071–438 6692

Investments

**Association of Futures Brokers
and Dealers (AFBD)**
Fifth Floor
Sixth Section
Plantation House
5–8 Mincing Lane
London EC3M 3DX
Tel: 071–626 9763

**Association of Investment Trust
Companies**
Park House
16 Finsbury Circus
London EC2M 7JJ
Tel: 071–588 5347

Building Societies Association
3 Savile Row
London W1X 1AF
Tel: 071–437 0655

Ethical Investment Research Service
504 Bondway Business Centre
71 Bondway
London SW8 1SQ
Tel: 071–735 1351

Department of National Savings
Charles House
375 Kensington High Street
London W14 8SD
Tel: 071–605 9461

**Department of National Savings
Bonds & Stock Office**
Marton
Backpool FY3 9YP
Tel: (0253) 66151

**Department of National Savings
National Savings Bank**
Boydstone Road
Glasgow GS8 1SB
Tel: 041–649 4555

**Financial Intermediaries Managers &
Brokers Regulatory Association
(FIMBRA)**
Hertsmere House
Hertsmere Road
London E14 4AB
Tel: 071–538 8860

**Investment Management Regulatory
Organization (IMRO)**
Broadwalk House
5 Appold Centre
London EC2A 2LL
Tel: 071–628 6022

**Independent Financial Advisers
Promotions (IFAP)**
28 Greville Street
London EC1N 8SU
Tel: 071–831 4027

**Independent Schools Information
Service**
56 Buckingham Gate
London SW1E 6AG
Tel: 071–222 7274

**Life Assurance & Units Trust Regulatory
Organization (LAUTRO)**
Centre Point
103 New Oxford Street
London WC1A 1QH
Tel: 071–379 0444

National Federation of Independent
Financial Advisers (NFIFA)
Merlin House
Lancaster Road
High Wycombe
Bucks HP12 3XX
Tel: (0494) 473018

Registrar of Friendly Societies
15 Great Marlborough Street
London W1V 2AX
Tel: 071–437 9992

Securities & Futures Authority (SFA)
Complaints Bureau
Stock Exchange Buildings
Old Broad Street
London EC2N 1EQ
Tel: 071–256 9000

Securities & Investments Board (SIB)
Gavrelle House
12–14 Bunhill Row
London EC1Y 8RA
Tel: 071–638 1240 or
929 3652 (Central Register)

The Stock Exchange
Public Relations Department
Old Broad Street
London EC2N 1HP
Tel: 071–588 2355

Unit Trust Association (UTA)
65 Kingsway
London WC2B 6TD
Tel: 071–831 0898

Insurance & Pensions

Association of British Insurers (ABI)
Aldermary House
10–15 Queen Street
London EC4N 1TT
Tel: 071–248 4477

British Insurance and Investment
Brokers Association (BIIBA)
BIIBA House
14 Bevis Marks
London EC3A 7NT
Tel: 071–623 9043

Chartered Insurance Institute (CII)
20 Aldermanbury
London EC2V 7HY
Tel: 071–606 3835

The Insurance Ombudsman Bureau
City Gate One
135 Park Street
London SE1 9EA
tel: 071–928 4488

Life Insurance Association
Citadel House
Station Approach
Chorleywood
Rickmansworth
Herts WD3 5PF
Tel: (09278) 5333

National Association of Pension Funds
12–18 Grosvenor Gardens
London SW1W 0DH
Tel: 071–730 0585

Occupational Pensions Board/
Superannuation Funds Office
Lynwood Road
Thames Ditton
Surrey KT7 0DP
Tel: 081–398 4242

Pensions Management Institute (PMI)
PMI House
124 Middlesex Street
London E1 7HY
Tel: 071–247 1452

Society of Pension Consultants
Ludgate House
Ludgate Circus
London EC4A 2AB
Tel: 071–353 1688/9

Insurance Policy Specialists (selling and buying)

Beale Dobie (0621) 851133
Foster & Cransfield 071–608 1941
Policy Network 071–938 3626
Policy Plus 0225–753643
Policy Portfolio 081–203 7221

Miscellaneous

The Charities Aid Foundation (CAF)
48 Pembury Road
Tonbridge
Kent
Tel: (0732) 771333

The Institute of Chartered Accountants
PO Box 433
Chartered Accountant's Hall
Moorgate Place
London EC2P 2PJ
Tel: 071–628 7060

Citizens Advice Bureaux
(see local telephone directory for
nearest office)

The Law Society
The Law Society's Hall
113 Chancery Lane
London WC2A 1PL
Tel: 071–242 1222

Ombudsmen

Banking Ombudsman:
Laurence Shurman
Citadel House
5/11 Fetter Lane
London EC4A 1BR
Tel: 071–583 1395
Complaints about: Forged cheques,
charges and interest, cash-dispensing
machines

Insurance (and Unit Trust) Ombudsman:
Dr Julian Farrand
31 Southampton Row
London WC1B 5HJ
Tel: 071–242 8613
Complaints about: Policy terms and
administration of life insurance, motor,
buildings and contents policies. Also
deals with the performance and
administration of Unit Trusts.

Building Societies Ombudsman:
Stephen Edell
35–37 Grosvenor Gardens
London SW1X 7AW
Tel: 071–931 0044
Complaints about: Cash-dispensing
machines, sale of insurance policies.

Investment Referee:
Richard Youard
6 Frederick's Place
London EC2R 8BT
Tel: 071–796 3065
Complaints about: General financial
advice, portfolio management and
administration.

Corporate Estate Agents Ombudsman:
David Quayle
PO Box 1114
Salisbury
Wiltshire SP1 1YQ
Tel: (0722) 333306
Complaints about: Inconvenience,
unfair treatment or maladministration.

Pensions Ombudsman:
Michael Platt
11 Belgrave Road
London SW1 1RB
Tel: 071–834 9144
Complaints about: Administration by
trustees or managers of a Pension
Scheme.

Index

Administrators
  authority and powers 51–52
  oath 44
Agricultural property 130–131
Annuities 107–109, 138–139
Assent document 46
Assets
  interest under a trust 41
  joint ownership 42
  outside the estate 41
  passing to exempt beneficiaries 41–42
  subject to special valuation rules 42, 50
  winding up an estate 40–43
  see also **Property**
Bank accounts 99
Banks
  Bank Deposit Protection Fund 215
  charges for winding up an estate 55–56
  executors 8
  share-dealing service 204
Bed and breakfast 94
Broker bonds 134
Budgets
  personal 66–67
Building Societies
  Investor Protection Fund 215
  share-dealing service 204
Building Society accounts 99
Business Expansion Schemes (BES) 122–124
  possible changes under a Labour government 256
Business expenses
  tax relief 79
Capital
  definition 73
Capital bonds 114–115
Capital Conversion Plans 164–165
Capital Gains Tax (CGT)
  annual exemption 86
  calculation of the gain 84
  exemptions and reliefs 82–83, 86–87
  gains arising through death 87
  gifts 184, 185, 186
  indexation allowance 85
  liability 83–84
  losses 84
  non-residents 83
  on an inherited house 87–89
  part disposals 85
  rates 83
  rebasing to 31 March 1982 84
  tax-saving tips 94–95
Capital Preservation Plans 165–166
Case studies
  inheritance of £50,000 for childless young couple with mortgage 227–229
  inheritance of £60,000 by a pensioner needing more income 249–251
  inheritance of £80,000 for 35-year-old bachelor 225–226
  inheritance of estate worth £130,000 for a couple in their sixties with grown-up children 244–247
  inheritance of house and £35,000-worth of assets from husband's estate by a 74-year-old widow requiring income 251–253
  inheritance of house and assets worth £200,000 for married son with teenage children 233–235
  inheritance of parents' estates worth £860,000 for a middle-aged couple with grown-up children 238–243
  inheritance of shares and £100,000 for married couple with two young children 230–232
  legacy of £500 to a young child 219
  legacy of £2,000 to grandchildren 220–221
  legacy of £25,000 for a 21-year-old single woman 224
  legacy of £50,000 to married daughter with teenage children 232–233
  legacy of £100,000 in trust for a young child 221–223

Cash unit trusts 101–102
Channel Islands
  investor protection 216
Charities
  Deeds of Covenant 181, 183
  gifts 178–182
  taxation 78–79, 180, 181, 183
  trusts 181–182
Charities Aid Foundation 11, 179–180, 181
  Charitable Account Scheme 179, 181
Children
  appointing guardians 8–9
  investments for 189–193, 218–219
  see also **Case studies**
  tax consequences of gifts from parents
  183, 187
Children's Bonus Bonds 107, 191
Clearance Certificate 51
Codicils 17
Collectibles 127–128
Commissions
  investments 211–213
Commodities 129
Compensation
  investors 215–216
Complaints procedure
  financial advisers 213–214
Compound Annual Return (CAR) 74
Compound interest 74
Convertible unsecured loan stocks 114–115
Coroner 35
Costs
  funerals 36–37
  trusts 200–201
  Wills 15
  winding up an estate 55–56
Currency funds 168–169
Current accounts 217–218
Dealing in shares 113, 203–204
Death
  notification 35
  registration 35, 36
Death certificate 36
Debts
  paying off personal 68
Deeds of Covenant 181, 183
Deeds of Variation 13–14, 47, 52–53, 185
  formalities 53
  intestacy 52–53
Dependents
  claims by 12–13, 52
  definition 12
Discretionary trusts 197–198, 199–200
Endowment policies 135–136, 155
Enterprise zones 125–126
Equities 71–72, 109–115
Estate accounts
  sample 59–61

Ethics
  and investments 97
Europe
  Single European Market 1992 254
Executors
  authority 38–39
  bank 8
  choosing 6–8
  duties 6
  Form of Renunciation 38
  oath 44
Family home 45–47
  gift from parents to children 187
  in the sole name of the deceased 46–47
  joint ownership 45–46
  joint tenants 45–46
  tenants in common 45–46
  valuation 45
Fees
  investment advisers 211–213
Financial Services Act (FSA) 205–206
  Investors Compensation Scheme 216
Flexible Trusts 197
Foreign currency accounts 102
Foreign property 149–152
Friendly Society Bonds 137–138, 192
Funerals 36
  costs 36–37
Futures 129
  Managed Futures Fund 129
Gift and Loan Scheme 166
Gift-aid 79, 181
Gifts 178
  CGT 184, 185, 186
  IHT 184–185, 186
  income tax 183, 185, 187
  protecting 188
  to charity 178–182
  to one's own children 183, 187
Gilts 103–104, 191
Grandparents
  opportunities for transferring assets 243
Grant of Probate 39, 40
  issuing 44
Grant of Representation 38, 39, 40, 44
  intestacy 51–52
  obtaining 43–45
Guaranteed bonds 104–105
Guardians
  for the children 8–9
Health insurance 157–158
Holiday insurance 159
Holiday property bond 151–152
Home Income Plans 175–177
The home see **Family home**
IHT
  avoiding by using a reversion 53–54
  chargeable transfers 23–24

due date of liability 25
exempt gifts 22, 184
gifts 184–185, 186
gifts with a reservation of benefit
(GROBs) 24–25, 187
liability for payment 42
lifetime gifts 22–25
payment 44, 49–50
potentially exempt transfers (PETs) 22–
23, 184–185
rate 21
threshold 21
transfers on death 25–31
valuation rules 25, 42, 50
Income
definition 73
Income tax
allowances 77–78
gifts 183, 185, 187
joint income 81
married women and separate taxation
79–81
method of collection 81
rates 76–79
reliefs 78–79
repayment of tax and non-taxpayers 81–
82
tax-saving tips 92–94
Inflation
and investments 69–72
Inheritance
deciding who should inherit what 9–11
Inheritance tax see IHT
Inland Revenue account 43–44
Inquest 35
Insurance
investments 131–137
legal expenses 159
maintenance protection 159
one-off risks 159
pets 159
possessions 158
third party 159
travel and holiday 159
see also **Health insurance; Life
insurance**
Insurance companies
Policy Holders Protection Board 215
Intestacy 4–6, 51–52
Deeds of Variation 52–53
distribution of the estate 51–52
Investment advisers 205–216, 256–257
choosing 210–211
complaints against 213–214
fees 211–213
independent financial advisers (IFAs)
207–208
services 209

tied agents 206–207
types 206, 208–209
Investment portfolios
children 218–223
married couple with older children 232–
235
married couple with young children 229–
232
married couple without children 226–229
persons in their fifties 235–243
single people 223–226
see also **Case studies**
Investment trusts 118–120
Investments
agricultural property 130–131
and ethics 97
and inflation 69–72
broker bonds 134
cash-based 71, 99–103
collectibles 127–128
commissions 211–213
deposit 99–103
endowment policies 135–136, 155
equities 71–72, 109–115
fixed interest and guaranteed 103–109
for children 189–193
foreign property 149–152
Friendly Society Bonds 137–138, 192
gross interest 91
guaranteed 70
insurance-based 131–137
lump sum 140–142
net interest 91–92
offshore 167–169
possible changes under a Labour
government 255–256
professional advice 205–216
property 124–125, 147–152
qualifying life policy 135–136
regular payment 140–142
regular premium insurance policies 135–
136
return 73–74
risk/reward ratio 72–73
second-hand policies 136–137
single-premium bonds 132–134
tax treatment 82
tax-effective 89–91
tax-free 92
variable 70
woodlands 130–131
Investor protection 205–206
compensation for loss 215–216
complaints procedure 213–214
Investors Chronicle 203
Isle of Man
compensation for loss of investments
215

Letters of Administration 39, 40
  issuing 44
Liabilities
  payment 49–51
  winding up an estate 41–43
Life insurance 153–157
  protective 153–155
  types of policies 155–157
Lloyds
  becoming a 'Name' 142–143
Loans
  interest-free 189
London Gazette 41
Married women
  separate taxation 79–81
Medical insurance premiums
  tax relief for persons over 60 years 79
MIRAS (Mortgage Interest Relief at Source) 78
Mortgage
  pros and cons of paying off 68–69
National Savings Bank
  ordinary and investment accounts 100
National Savings Capital Bonds 106, 191
National Savings Certificates (NSC) 105–106, 191
National Savings Income Bonds 106–107, 191
National Savings Yearly Plan 106, 190
Nominees 188
Oaths
  executors and administrators 44
Offshore investments 167–169
Offshore sterling accounts 102–103
Offshore trusts 169
Options 129
Ordinary shares
  dealing service 113, 204
  investment 71–72, 112–114
  whether to keep or sell inherited shares 114
Penny Share Guide 203
Pensions 139–140
  additional contributions to an existing Occupational Pension Scheme 172–173
  Basic State Pension Scheme 170
  Personal Pension Plans (PPPs) 173–174
  possible changes under a Labour government 255
  private schemes 171–172
  self-employed 173–174
  State Earnings-Related Pension Scheme (SERPS) 171
  tax relief on contributions 79
Personal Equity Plans (PEPs) 120–122, 175
  possible changes under a Labour government 256
Personal Representatives (PRs) 39

Post-mortem 35
Power of Appropriation 46
Power of Attorney 30–31
Preference shares 114–115
Premium Bonds 107
Probate Registry 39
  lodging papers 44
Promissory note 189
Property
  investment 124–125, 147–152
  investment in foreign 149–152
  joint ownership 40
  taxation 147–148
  time-sharing 149–150
  see *also* **Assets**
Publicity
  Wills 44–45
Recognized professional bodies 205
Rees-Mogg, William 96
Retirement
  planning 170–177
  post-retirement revision of personal balance sheet 247–248
  see *also* **Pensions**
Reversioner 53–54
Risk
  investments 72–73
School fees plans 161–164
  possible changes under a Labour government 255–256
Securities and Investments Board (SIB) 205
Self-employed
  pensions 173–174
Self-regulatory organizations 205
Settlors 194
Shares in a family company
  valuation for IHT purposes 50
Sharp (Albert E) 204
Single European Market 1992 254
Solicitors
  charges for winding up an estate 55–56
Stockbrokers
  services 203–204
TAURUS 113, 204
Taxation
  charities 78–79, 180, 181, 183
  investments 82
  possible changes under a Labour government 255
Templeton, John 96
TESSAs (Tax-Exempt Special Savings Accounts) 100–101, 191
Time
  winding up an estate 54–55
Time-shares 150–151
Travel insurance 159
Trustees 194–195
  choosing 6–8

duties 6
professional 7–8
Trusts 25, 194–201
Accumulation and Maintenance (A & M)
198, 199–200
advantages of using 195–196
charitable 181–182
costs 200–201
discretionary 197–198, 199–200
Flexible 197
interest in possession 196–197, 198–199
no interest in possession 197
offshore 169
protecting a gift 188
taxation 198–200
using to save tax 195–196
UCITS 254
Undertakers 36
Unit trusts 115–118

purchasing 203
Valuation
family home 45
Wills
codicils 17
costs 15
Deeds of Variation 13–14, 47, 52–53,
185
formalities of executing 14–15
keeping it up to date 17
preparation for making 16–17
publicity 44–45
reasons for making 3–4
signatures 14
specimen 17–19
witnesses 14
wording 15
see *also* **Intestacy**
Woodlands 130–131